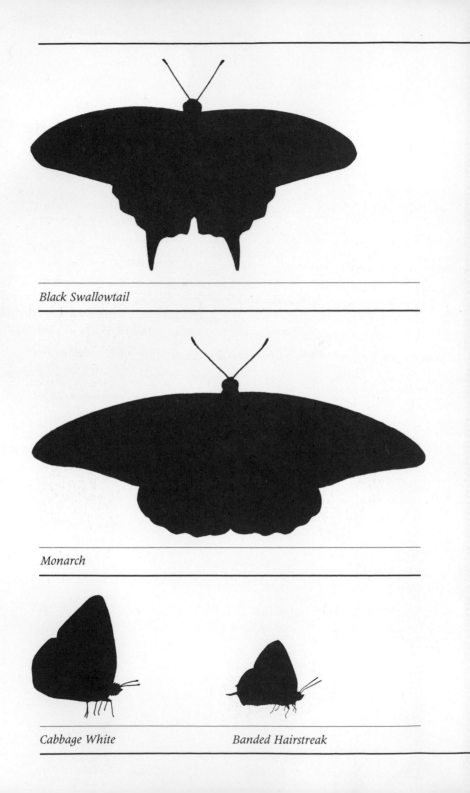

Black Swallowtail

Monarch

Cabbage White

Banded Hairstreak

Eastern Tailed Blue

Northern Metalmark

American Snout

Pearl Crescent

American Lady

Little Wood Satyr

Wild Indigo Duskywing

Hobomok Skipper

Oxford University Press

Oxford   New York   Toronto
Delhi   Bombay   Calcutta   Madras   Karachi
Kuala Lumpur   Singapore   Hong Kong   Tokyo
Nairobi   Dar es Salaam   Cape Town
Melbourne   Auckland   Madrid

and associated companies in
Berlin   Ibadan

Copyright © 1993 by Jeffrey Glassberg

Published by Oxford University Press, Inc.,
200 Madison Avenue, New York, New York 10016

Library of Congress Cataloging-in-Publication Data
Glassberg, Jeffrey.
Butterflies through binoculars : a field guide to butterflies
in the Boston-New York-Washington region / by Jeffrey Glassberg.
p. cm.   Includes bibliographical references and index.
ISBN 0-19-507982-5
ISBN 0-19-507983-3 pbk
1. Butterflies—Northeastern States.
2. Butterflies—Northeastern States—Identification.
3. Butterfly watching—Northeastern States.
I. Title.   QL551.N65G58   1993
595.78'9'0974—dc20   92-33087

9 8 7 6 5 4 3 2

Printed in Korea

Butterflies through Binoculars

*A Field
and Finding Guide
to Butterflies
in the
Boston
New York
Washington
Region*

Jeffrey Glassberg

Butterflies
through
Binoculars

New York
Oxford

OXFORD UNIVERSITY PRESS

1993

Foreword

A lifetime of natural history and perhaps a professional scientific career as well can begin with the tracking of butterflies. A case in point: when I was nine years old I hunted these insects in Rock Creek Park, a short walk from our apartment in the District of Columbia. Still inscribed vividly in my memory from half a century ago are the territorial aerobatics of red admirals, the fleeting apparition of a mourning cloak along a springtime trail, and an unidentifiable swallowtail feeding on mimosa blossoms, tantalizingly out of reach. I confess to an occasional faint Nabokovian desire to shuck it all and wander from place to place in search of ever rarer and more beautiful butterflies. On recent trips to New Hampshire I ignored ants (my favored group) for a while and started a checklist of butterfly species, just for the private pleasure of it, to re-acquire a sense of timeless languor. I believe I must share this desire with others: to be free in a world without destruction or pollution, an aurelian again!

But not to kill and pin specimens. Most of those who search for butterflies in settled areas have matured to the level of birders. The game now is to find, identify, enjoy—and leave alone. Yet anyone who has tried to understand these insects netless and with binoculars or unaided vision knows how daunting many species can be. They show you an ambiguous wing band here or row of spots there and are gone, while you fumble with your field guide, struggling to get to the right genus in order to begin the process of identification. And then you must thumb through a flock of species, most of which are not found in that habitat or even that part of the state. Before you are half done your butterfly has long vanished and another kind has come into view. What is needed in addition to comprehensive books is a user-friendly guide that focuses on the most accessible localities, narrows the species list to a likely few, tells you how to identify them with the kind of key characters living butterflies are most likely to display, and offers the basic natural history of each species in turn.

This is what Jeffrey Glassberg has provided in his welcome new field guide. His work might have been entitled *The Butterflies of Bosnywash: A People's Natural History*. Bosnywash (Boston–New York–Washington) is where by far the heaviest concentration of people in the eastern United States live. It is the zone of greatest environmental damage, where appreciation and protection of nature are most needed. Glassberg details some of the best places to visit, tells the reader what to expect and when, and presents the species as they can be expected to appear on first encounter.

Yet there is nothing cut and dried about this account. Butterfly biology is in an early stage of exploration. A great deal needs to be learned about the distribution and natural history of even the most common species. In some parts of the world, especially the tropics, large numbers of new species remain to be discovered. Like all experienced entomologists, Glassberg treats his subject as an open door. Walk through it and begin what can be a lifetime adventure.

Edward O. Wilson

Preface

This book and a pair of binoculars are all that you need to identify butterflies with reasonable accuracy in the northeastern United States. The idea is not novel, but the book is. It is the first one that relies totally on field-marks to distinguish species, including the difficult skippers, which are a challenge to amateur and professional alike. The field-marks have been tested and improved upon for the last decade by Glassberg and his colleagues in the New York City Butterfly Club.

More than half a century ago, the first field guides to birds—based on the idea that species could be recognized in the field using binoculars—revolutionized the way that we interact with nature. As a result, bird-watching is now a quality recreation for thousands upon thousands of people throughout the world.

I anticipate a similar explosion of interest in butterflies. For those of you who are birders, butterfly-watching is a natural extension of what you already do. For butterfly collectors who are bored catching the same species again and again, it is now possible to view butterflies in a new light. And for those harried by the noise and commotion in the world of people, consider a walk through fields and woods. There is much to be learned and enjoyed, and this book and a pair of binoculars are the keys that unlock the world of butterflies.

Robert Robbins

Acknowledgments

Not surprisingly, many people helped in the transformation of this book from its rudimentary beginnings to its present incarnation. Without the active encouragement and support of my wife, Jane Vicroy Scott, I would not have embarked on this project at all. Guy Tudor convinced me to expand the book, originally conceived as a guide to the butterflies of the New York area, to its present scope. In addition to the many specific contributions listed below, Bob Robbins has provided a semi-continuous stream of encouragement and companionship, both in this country and throughout the neotropics, since we attended first grade together almost forty years ago.

Many people contributed butterfly records and information pertaining to their areas. These include Robert Abrams, Stan Bolton, Brian Cassie, Tom Dodd, Chris Leahy, Paul Miliotis, Robert Pease, Robert Robbins, Dale Schweitzer, Richard Walton, and William D. Winter for MA; Victor DeMasi, Larry Gall, Dave Norris, and Dale Schweitzer for CT; Chris Adams, Jim Dowdell, Melville Osborne, Dale Schweitzer, Pat Sutton, and Ben Ziegler for NJ; Jane Ruffin, Dale Schweitzer, and David Wright for PA; E. N. Woodbury for DE; William A. Andersen, Nathan Erwin, John Fales, David Flame, W. R. Grooms, Philip Kean, Harry Pavulaan, Robert Robbins, and Richard H. Smith for MD and the Washington D.C. area.

I owe a special debt of gratitude to the members of the New York City Butterfly Club who, over the past eight years, have amassed what is probably the largest compiled data base in North America relating to butterfly species occurrences, abundance, and fluctuation over a large area. Providing especially plentiful and wide-ranging reports were Rich Kelly, Don Riepe, Guy Tudor, Nick Wagerik, and Steve Walter. Also supplying many reports were Jim Ash, Skip Blanchard, Rick Cech, Mike Gochfeld, Mary Hake, Jeff Ingraham, John Lawrenson, Peter Post, John Yrizarry, Harry Zirlin, and John Zuzworsky. Thanks to the patient and knowledgeable efforts of NYC Butterfly Club member Steve Kinyon and my son, Matt Scott, we were able to convert the hand-drawn phenograms into computer print-outs.

Dale Schweitzer and Jamie Cromartie kindly directed me to a NJ colony of the Rare Skipper while Dave Norris escorted me to a Fairfield Co., CT, colony of the Northern Metalmark. Paul Miliotis and Larry Gall accompanied me on field trips to the Blue Hills Reservation, MA, and to North Branford, CT (where there is a colony of West Virginia Whites), respectively. Harry Zirlin directed me to the colony of Common Roadside Skippers in Nottingham County Park, Chester Co., PA. R. Lederhouse of Michigan State University provided me with information regarding the Tiger Swallowtails. I am grateful to all of them.

Many museum curators allowed me to examine butterfly specimens under their care. I thank Fred Rindge, American Museum of Natural History, NY; David Furth, Museum of Comparative Zoology, Harvard University, Cambridge, MA; Jim Liebherr, Cornell University Collection, Ithaca, NY; Robert Robbins and John Burns, United States National Museum, Smithsonian Institution, Washington, D.C.; Larry Gall and Ray Pupatus, Peabody Museum, Yale University, New Haven, CT.

I believe that the inclusion of the Locality Reports in Appendix A adds to the value of this book. I thank Bob Robbins, Harry Pavulaan, Larry Gall, Don Riepe, Guy Tudor, David Wright, Pat Sutton, Paul Opler, Philip Kean, and Richard H. Smith for generously taking the time to share with me, and thus the reader, their knowledge of these exciting localities.

The following individuals graciously provided their own photographs to plug the holes in my own photographic collection: Chris Adams, Robert Dana, Harry Darrow, Peter Post, and Don Riepe.

E. O. Wilson and Robert Robbins generously took the time from their busy schedules to write the Foreword and Preface. I thank them both.

Following the completion of a first draft of this manuscript, several individuals took the considerable time and effort to read through it and make many corrections and helpful suggestions. Brian Cassie, Larry Gall, Bob Robbins, Dale Schweitzer, Jane V. Scott, Guy Tudor, and Dave Winter, all immeasurably improved the manuscript. Dale Schweitzer, Guy Tudor, and Dave Winter did a particularly thorough, line-by-line, reading of the entire manuscript while Bob Robbins gave close attention to the introductory sections and the species accounts of the Lycaenidae. At this point most authors state that "of course I am responsible for any errors that remain." I would like to take a different approach. If you find something you find objectionable in this book, please randomly choose one of the above reviewers and assign the responsibility for the error to them.

Contents

Butterflies
through
Binoculars

Introduction

If you enjoy flowers, sunshine, and warmth, then you'll probably enjoy butterflying (actively searching for butterflies in order to observe and identify them). Throughout history, human beings have been drawn to and fascinated by butterflies. Now, using the latest technological advances in binoculars and cameras, we can enjoy these beautiful animals in the wild even more vividly than was possible in the past. High-power, very short focal-distance binoculars enable one to observe butterflies greatly magnified, enhancing one's enjoyment of their detailed, jewel-like beauty and significantly facilitating their identification. Auto-focus cameras now allow even the photographically inept (like me) to take spectacular photographs that can be shared with other enthusiasts.

Besides being just plain fun, butterflying can be rewarding in many ways. It can serve as a stimulus to be outdoors, engaged in a healthy physical activity. It can be a challenging and gratifying experience as one learns how to identify butterflies, especially skippers. Your knowledge of the butterflies of your area may make a significant contribution to science, since so much remains to be learned about these fascinating insects. Lastly, butterflying allows one and one's fellow enthusiasts to monitor the local environment. Knowledge of the stability or decline of local butterfly populations can be an important tool in environmental protection. Because butterflies are very sensitive indicators of the health of even small patches of land, they can serve an especially important role in urban and suburban areas where land-use patterns have already resulted in too much habitat fragmentation to support many larger animals.

The purpose of this book is to enable you to find and identify butterflies in the area from Boston to Washington, D.C. The area covered by this guide is shown in Figure 1. Many interesting topics related to butterfly study are either not included or are treated in a cursory fashion. If you are interested in learning more about butterfly natural history, systematics, ecology, or gardening, please refer to the bibliography where many fine books covering these and other subjects are listed.

How to Find Butterflies

Most of our butterflies prefer open areas with native plants. Large areas of manicured lawns are essentially biological deserts. Some of the best types of habitats are wet meadows and brushy fields. The boundary between two types of habitats generally will support a more diverse butterfly population than either habitat by itself. Thus, butterflying an open meadow adjacent to a woodland will be more productive than searching either in a woodland or in a meadow distant from a woodland. If you live near one of the Butterfly Localities covered in Appendix A, that locality would be a good place to see a large selection of the butterflies found in your area. Other spots can be found by checking your local parks and searching for abandoned fields, natural barrens (areas that support an impoverished, but specialized, flora due to the infertile soil), and openings such as rock outcrops or burn scars in dry forest. Look for different types of habitats. Most of the species you find in a pine barrens will be different from ones found in the openings of rich woodlands. One of the easiest ways to find a productive area is to look for power-line right-of-ways. Because these areas are periodically cut back by the utility company and usually traverse a wide variety of natural areas, they are often excellent places to observe butterflies. Additionally, they are usually very accessible and often easy to butterfly. Power-line cuts can be found by checking maps (topographic and other maps often indicate power lines) or by searching your area more or less at random. As you become more familiar with butterflies, you will learn to recognize potentially rewarding habitats for many of the species in your area.

Remember that most butterflies avidly visit flowers to obtain nectar. Examining a good stand of a favorite nectar source should enable one to see many of the butterflies then flying in that area. Finding a mixed wet/dry meadow with large patches of dogbane and milkweeds adjacent to a rich woodland lets you preview your space in heaven. A list of especially good nectar sources is given on page 11. While some cloud cover may be tolerated, especially when it is hot, butterflies are likely to be most active when the sun is shining. To see all the species in your area you will have to be in the field periodically throughout the warmer months. The Elfins only fly in the early spring and Leonard's Skipper only flies in late August and September. Because behavioral patterns differ among species, you will find the most butterflies by searching at different times of day. Some species, like the Northern Pearly Eye, are easiest to find late in the day. Another suggested way to discover some uncommon species is to visit open hilltops with steep slopes. Many species of butterflies congregate on such hilltops, presumably as a mechanism to concentrate low-density populations for mating.

Binoculars

You need very little equipment to identify butterflies on the wing. A good pair of binoculars is extremely useful. This point was driven home to me while I was birding in Africa. My driver knew a fair amount about local birds, but he was amazed by my ability to identify the birds that we saw. Finally, he borrowed my binoculars. A big smile spread across his face. "It's easy to identify birds when they look like the pictures in the book," he said. Butterflies are also easy to identify when they "look like the pictures in the book."

A critical feature determining whether a particular pair of binoculars is suitable for butterflying is their minimum focal distance. Many members of the New York City Butterfly Club use the Minolta "Pocket" binoculars. These focus down to a distance of less than 6 feet. You should try to find binoculars with the closest focusing possible; otherwise you will be continually backing up to view the butterflies, in part defeating the reason for using binoculars in the first place. A minimum focal distance of greater than about 12 feet becomes unacceptable. Because the minimal focal distance will often vary slightly among different binoculars of the same model, it is worthwhile to check a whole series for this feature.

Other factors to consider in buying a pair of binoculars are power, size, weight, field of view, and ease of focusing. Two numbers (for example, 8 x 40) describe some other basic features of binoculars. The first number is the "power." Eight-power binoculars will make an object 80 feet away appear as large as if it were 10 feet away. The second number is the diameter of the objective lens. The larger the number the brighter the image will be.

I use 10x pocket binoculars but many others prefer using 7x or 8x binoculars. The choice is one of personal preference.

How to Identify Butterflies

If you are just beginning to butterfly, the first step is to learn to recognize the seven families of butterflies and skippers found in our area. This shouldn't be too difficult because, in general, butterflies belonging to these different families have different wing shapes, different sizes, different colors, and different behaviors. Silhouettes of typical species in each of the seven families are shown on the endpapers. Refer to the short discussion of each butterfly family directly preceding the species accounts of that family. Once you know what family the butterfly belongs to, go to the appropriate plate(s) and see if you recognize the butterfly that you have found. Many species, such as the Zebra Swallowtail, are so distinctive that you will probably immediately recognize the illustration. If you are looking at a "black" swallowtail, you will see that there are four possible species. Look at the plate and read the notes on the facing page. You will see that most species can be identified by observing certain "field marks" that distinguish that species from similar species. A quick measure of the relative abundance of the species in the Boston, New York, Philadelphia, and Washington areas is also given. If you are in the Boston area, you will note that a Pipevine Swallowtail is rare. If you have time, turn to the species account in the text where more detailed information is given regarding identification, flight times, and so on. If you are northwest of Boston in May, you are not likely to be looking at a Pipevine Swallowtail.

Remember that the appearance of a species of butterfly can vary greatly from individual to individual and that the appearance of the same individual can vary with the quality and quantity of light. Often when a species undergoes a population explosion the range of variation increases even more. Additionally, the appearance of the same individual butterfly will change over time. When it first emerges from its chrysalis it will be very bright and in pristine condition. Often its wings will have a beautiful sheen. As the adult butterfly ages, scales will be lost and wings will become frayed and torn. Its color will fade. Identifying the last Northern Broken Dash of the season can be a real challenge! Sometimes identifying an individual butterfly is too great a challenge for anyone and it should be left as "unidentified." This might be because the butterfly was too worn, not seen well enough, or was too easy to confuse with similar species. As you gain experience, you will begin to identify an ever greater percentage of the butterflies you encounter.

Photography

It is relatively easy to obtain good photographs of butterflies and, once obtained, these photographs have great value. They allow one to share one's sightings with others. Good photographs enable you to identify butterflies whose identity was uncertain in the field. They can be an aid to observing field marks for future identifications. They can serve as documentation for the presence, at that location and date, of the species photographed. Lastly, they can serve to assuage the primitive urge to collect things.

Although I provide some tips on butterfly photography, if you are seriously interested in the technical side of photography you will need to consult another source—my technical expertise does not extend much beyond the knowledge that an f stop differs from a bus stop. One can achieve some usable photographs of butterflies using any good 35-mm single-lens reflex camera, but for best results you need a macro lens and a flash. A macro lens allows you to approach the butterfly very closely and obtain photographs where the image will be life size. While a 50-mm macro lens will work, a 100- or 105-mm macro is much more satisfactory (although much more expensive). Although some photographs can be taken with available sunlight, a flash confers much greater flexibility, depth of field, and more frequent good results. Many photographers use elaborate flash equipment and get excellent results. I use a ring flash, which mounts directly around the macro lens of the camera. With a 35-mm auto-focusing camera outfitted with a 100-mm macro lens and a ring flash, you can take very good photographs of a large percentage of the butterflies that you will see.

After you have the proper photographic equipment, the keys to butterfly photography are patience and the ability to contort oneself into various poses without fear of appearing ludicrous. It is usually best to approach a butterfly from the side rather than overhead. This often necessitates bending very low or crawling. When approaching a butterfly two different desires are in tension. On the one hand, the slower one moves, the less likely one is startle the butterfly into flight. On the other hand, the slower one moves, the more likely it is that the butterfly will have flown of its own accord before you have obtained a photograph. The optimal speed for moving toward a butterfly will vary from species to species, and within a species depending on such factors as the activity the butterfly is engaged in, the temperature, and an individual butterfly's propensities. Cool weather tends to make butterflies move more slowly. This makes easier photographing the butterflies you find but may render it more difficult to find the butterflies in the first place. Many times you will be able to take an excellent photograph of an individual on the first try. Sometimes you will need to try twenty or thirty times before you finally succeed.

You will greatly enhance your photographs' value if you label them with the exact dates and localities where the pictures were taken. If photographs are of the same individual butterfly, this should be indicated. It is especially important to cross-reference photographs of the upper and lower wing surfaces for identification purposes. To do this, you will need a log in which you record these data at the time you take the photographs.

Checklists

As you spend more time in the field, you might like to keep lists of the species you see and where you see them. This will help you to remember which butterflies are at which localities and to communicate this information to others. You might also want to keep a "life-list," a list of all the species of butterflies you have seen. For your convenience, a checklist of the butterflies occurring in our region is provided as Appendix D.

What Is a Butterfly?

Butterflies are a group of evolutionarily related animals. They are grouped as part of the class Insecta, and together with the moths constitute the order Lepidoptera. This word derives from the Greek words for scale (=lepid) and wing (=ptera). True butterflies (superfamily Papilionoidea) and skippers (superfamily Hesperioidea) are usually considered together as "butterflies," and separately from moths. It is generally easy to distinguish butterflies and moths.

Almost all our butterflies are active exclusively during the day while the great majority of moths are active only at night. Some moths are active during the day, but these can usually be identified by their flight which is characteristically stiff and very erratic. When seen well, our butterflies and moths almost always can be distinguished by the shape of their antennae. Butterflies and skippers have a club (a swelling) at the end of their antennae while almost all moths do not (see Fig. 2).

Butterfly Lives

Adult female butterflies lay eggs. These eggs are almost always laid on the plant that the newly hatched caterpillar (larva) will eat. The butterfly usually recognizes the right plant by a combination of sight and smell. Butterflies have a very acute sense of smell. They have chemoreceptors (cells that respond to "smells") both on their antennae and the bottom ends of their legs. The larvae of many species of butterflies are capable of growing successfully on only one type of plant. Some species prefer to eat only a special part of the one plant species, such as the flower or tender new growth. Other butterflies are more catholic in their taste and can grow on many species of plants, sometimes on species from many unrelated plant families. As the larva gets larger it begins to outgrow its skin. Eventually the larva moults and the old skin is split off and replaced by a new larger skin. This will happen a number of times before the larva is full grown. Once the larva is full grown it undergoes a remarkable change. The larva now takes the form of a chrysalis, protected by a hard outer covering and seemingly inert. During this stage the larval structures are destroyed and reorganized and the structures of the adult butterfly are formed in their place. Eventually, the chrysalis splits open and the adult butterfly emerges. Its wings unfurl as fluid pumps through the wing veins. After the sun has warmed and dried the insect, the butterfly flies off.

Life as an adult butterfly is often brief. Most butterflies live for only one to two weeks as an adult while it is believed that some of the smaller species only live for a few days as an adult. Some of the larger nymphalids that overwinter as adults (e.g., Mourning Cloak, Monarch) are capable of living for eight or nine months. While some of our nymphalids overwinter as adults, the vast majority of our butterflies overwinter either as eggs, larvae, or pupae. Some species can overwinter in any of these stages but most are restricted to overwintering in one stage.

Butterfly Gardening

If you have a garden, even a small one, the chances are good that you can enjoy butterflies right at home. Many common garden flowers, such as zinnias and marigolds, are attractive to butterflies. If you plant special plants such as Butterfly Bush *(Buddleia)* and Orange Milkweed *(Asclepias tuberosa)* you will attract many of the butterflies in your neighborhood to your garden while these plants are in bloom. Of course, which species of butterflies you attract will depend on which species are present in your vicinity. If you live very close to woodlands and meadows, you will attract many more species than if you live in a suburban development. But even flower gardens in Manhattan, e.g., Riverside Garden, can attract a significant number of species, including late-season southern immigrants. Species that are commonly seen in many of the gardens in our region are listed below. If you have a large enough garden, you might want to consider planting the larval foodplants of butterflies to attract and possibly establish a population where none existed before. For example, just a few Hackberry Trees can support a small population of Hackberry Emperors or Tawny Emperors. Thorough discussions of butterfly gardening can be found in the Xerces Society/Smithsonian Institution book *Butterfly Gardening.*

Butterflies Most Likely to Be Seen in Gardens

Pipevine Swallowtail

Black Swallowtail

Eastern Tiger Swallowtail

Cabbage White

Clouded Sulphur

Orange Sulphur

Gray Hairstreak

Summer Azure

Eastern Tailed Blue

Great Spangled Fritillary

Pearl Crescent

Question Mark

Mourning Cloak

American Lady

Red Admiral

Little Wood Satyr

Monarch

Silver-spotted Skipper

Common Sootywing

Fiery Skipper

Peck's Skipper

Tawny-edged Skipper

Sachem

Zabulon Skipper

Some Important Nectar Sources

SPRING

Common Cinquefoil *(Potentilla simplex)*
Dandelion *(Taraxacum officinale)*
Wild Geranium *(Geranium maculatum)*
Blueberries *(Vaccinium)*
Red Clover *(Trifolium pratense)*
Blue Flag *(Iris versicolor)*

SUMMER

Dogbanes *(Apocynum androsaemifolium & A. medium)*
Common Milkweed *(Asclepias syriaca)*
Swamp Milkweed *(Asclepias incarnata)*
New Jersey Tea *(Ceanothus americanus)*
Stag-horn Sumac *(Rhus typhina)*
Pepperbush *(Clethra alnifolia)*
Privet *(Ligustrum vulgare)*

LATE SUMMER/FALL

Mountain Mints *(Pycnanthemum)*
Asters *(Aster)*
Thistles *(Cirsium)*
Goldenrods *(Solidago)*
Purple Loosestrife *(Lythrum salicaria)*
Blazing-stars *(Liatris)*

Migration

When people think of migrations, they usually think of bird migrations. Surprisingly, there is more movement of butterflies into and out of our region than most people suspect. We can class the movements of butterflies into three types.

1. *Normal dispersal of resident butterflies.* Although many butterflies remain very close to the foodplant on which they were born,

some percentage of the population will disperse with the hope (ours) of finding suitable new habitat. Thus it is always possible to find an individual butterfly out of the "correct" habitat for its species.

2. *Dispersal movement northward by nonresident species.* Depending on the severity of the winter, many essentially southern species do not survive year-round in our region. Our region is either repopulated by an influx of dispersing individuals from the south or our decimated local population is replenished by these individuals. The extent of the northward invasion of these species is extremely variable from year to year. Searching for rare southern species that are pushing northward in the late summer provides the butterflier with exciting field trips from late August into October, a season when most local species are waning. Because many of these southern species are multiple-brooded and essentially continue to fly until a hard frost, in exceptional years they may outnumber local species late in September. Examples of this type of species are Common Checkered Skipper, Clouded Skipper, Fiery Skipper, Sachem, Cloudless Sulphur, Sleepy Orange, Little Yellow, and Painted Lady.

3. *Directional movement southward in the fall followed by directional movement northward in the spring.* Although not really noted by previous authors, this classic migration pattern is followed by many of our larger Nymphalids. Migrating nymphalids are seen each year and, given the right weather conditions and year, great numbers of these butterflies mass along our coasts, streaming southward in the fall. On September 25, 1981, I observed approximately 6000 Monarchs, 4000 Red Admirals, 4000 Question Marks, and 2000 Mourning Cloaks moving south through a 10-foot wide path adjacent to the beach at Riis Park, Brooklyn, NY. Although that particular migration was exceptional, every fall sees congregations of these butterflies heading south. The exact nature of these migrations is still not well understood. With many of these species we are not sure where they spend the winter. The migration northward is usually not as marked but early spring brings an influx of Question Marks, American Ladies, and Red Admirals to the beaches. Of course, the migration of the Monarch is the most famous butterfly migration. Millions of Monarchs, from much of North America, fly south in the fall, eventually spending the winter in roosts in the mountains of central Mexico. Many of the Pacific Coast Monarchs congregate in spectacular roosts in the vicinity of Pacific Grove, California to spend the winter. Our Atlantic coast Monarchs migrate south and most of them probably spend the winter in Mexico but this is not yet proven.

Because so little is known about the migratory movements of butterflies, this is an area where the observations of amateurs can be of real value. Observation can be submitted to one of the appropriate groups listed in Appendix E.

Conservation

Many species of butterflies are rapidly losing ground in their battle for existence. Regal Fritillaries, Silver-bordered Fritillaries, and Bronze Coppers, all of which were common throughout our region as recently as fifteen years ago, are now either rare or extirpated from many or most areas. Other species that were always local have also significantly declined. These include Mottled Duskywing, Columbine Duskywing, Grizzled Skipper, Arogos Skipper, Checkered White, West Virginia White, Frosted Elfin, Hessel's Hairstreak, and Mitchell's Satyr. Of the approximately 130 species of butterflies recorded from the New York City area, 32 are listed on the "Endangered and Threatened Butterflies" list of the New York City Butterfly Club. Nine of these species have not been recorded in the New York City area for the last ten years.

The most important factor contributing to the decline of butterfly populations is habitat loss. As humans increase in number and radiate out from urban areas in ever greater density, natural areas are converted into suburban housing lots, golf courses, and parks with large swaths of non-native grasses. Since it is often easier to develop "open" areas with few trees and since most butterflies are in relatively open habitats, butterfly habitats are often especially vulnerable to development. Because important habitats for butterflies are often distinct from those in which rare birds or mammals might be found, a specific focus on the acquisition of special habitats for butterflies is required. The loss of butterfly species from urban and suburban areas is especially unfortunate because it is so easily preventable. Because most butterfly populations do not need very large expanses of habitat, preservation of most species is feasible by creating an interconnecting network of small protected habitat units along with a few larger units.

A second factor reducing butterfly populations is pollution of the environment, especially pollution with pesticides. The past use of DDT greatly reduced many of our native butterfly populations. Although DDT is now banned, the use of other pesticides is widespread. These pesticides are employed especially for mass sprayings against gypsy moth infestations and for agricultural use but also by private homeowners. In most cases, the harm caused by these pesticides outweighs any possible usefulness.

A third activity capable of having a significant negative effect on butterfly populations is the continued killing of rare and local butterfly species by collectors. A particularly tragic case is Mitchell's Satyr. Originally found in a limited number of fens in northern NJ, this butterfly is now almost certainly gone from the northeastern United States, extirpated by relentless collection pressure. One major colony was wiped out almost singlehandedly in the late 1970s by an individual who returned to the fen daily during successive seasons and each day killed every Mitchell's Satyr he saw.

Some people might ask: Why save butterfly species? Are they of any value? An extensive consideration of this question is obviously outside the scope of this book but I would like to put forward a few short answers (see "Why Preserve Natural Variety?" by B. G. Norton for a recent comprehensive discussion). Each species, being unique, may possess unique properties useful to humans that will be irretrievably lost should it become extinct. The recent discovery of a potent anti-cancer drug, taxol, in a species of yew that had been considered a "trash species" highlights this possibility. Because ecological systems are interrelated in complicated ways, the removal of a single species can have a much greater adverse effect than might have been anticipated. In many cases, the extinction of but a single species will result in the removal of a number of other species that are, in some way, dependant on the first species. Often, the fact that a species of butterfly is close to extinction can be seen as a symptom that an entire unique habitat is about to be destroyed. The collapse of many of the earth's ecosystems may result in a world hostile, at best, to humans.

In addition to these and other such "practical" arguments for the preservation of butterflies, there are clearly aesthetic and moral reasons to insist that butterflies survive. Only recently have human beings seen peoples from other "tribes" as similar to themselves and thus "real human beings" worthy of protection. As people become ever more conscious of their environment, they may come to see that all biological entities have intrinsic value and are worthy of protection. Many years ago, the Greeks equated butterflies with the souls of people, using the Greek word "psyche" for both. One does not have to believe in Greek mythology to know that in a world without butterflies, the souls of all people would be greatly diminished.

Species Accounts

Introduction

The accounts of the species occurring in our area are organized as follows.

NAME   The situation regarding the English names of American butterflies has been rather a mess. There are two major, related reasons for this confusion. First, no central authoritative body has put its official imprimatur on a set of chosen names. Second, until very recently, English names have rarely been used by people interested in butterflies. This has led to the coining of a confusing plethora of largely unused English names. A recent publication, *The Common Names of North American Butterflies* by Jacqueline Miller, presents a fairly exhaustive compilation of English names used for American butterflies. In July 1992, using this publication as a starting point, The English Names Committee of the North American Butterfly Association adopted an official English Names Checklist covering the species in our region. In all cases I have used the name chosen by this committee. Where a major, currently in-print field guide has used an English name different from the one used here, that name is also included in the index.

Unfortunately, scientific names can also cause confusion. The first part of the two-part scientific name is the genus name and represents a grouping of closely related species. Authors sometimes disagree about genus names. For example, I place many hairstreaks in the genus *Callophrys* while some other authors split this genus, placing some species in *Mitoura,* some in *Incisalia,* and so on.

The second part of the scientific name is the species name. Amazingly, the potential for confusion abounds here as well. One obvious possibility is that some authors will consider two populations to be different species while another author might lump them into one species. This is unavoidable. Another, altogether avoidable, possibility is that an author will change the species name to agree with the gender of the genus name. At this point the reader might well scratch his or her head and give up, but I will push on. Because scientific names are considered to be Latin or Greek, the words have gender, that is, feminine, masculine, or neuter. Technically, the rules of the International Code of Zoological Names dictate that the gender of the species name must agree with the gender of the genus name. Following the rule means that each time a species is placed in a different genus its specific name may also have to be changed. In practice, many authors have not complied with this rule, for good reason. An example of the confusion created is the Olive Hairstreak. The scientific name in this book is *Callophrys gryneus,* while in another recent guide (Opler, 1992) the name is *Mitoura grynea.* A reader might be excused for questioning whether the two names refer to the same species. With the rapid growth of information retrieval by computer there is an ever more compelling reason to refrain from following a rule that only a pedant could love.

SIZE   The size of different individuals of the same species of butterfly can vary dramatically. Females tend to be larger than males, often significantly so, and different broods may have different average sizes. Many species occasionally produce "runt" individuals whose size may be much less than the average size. In the following accounts size is related to a set of species that will serve as "size standards." These species are generally common and widespread, and thus you should rapidly become familiar with them. The size of the "size standard" species themselves is given in Table 1 and in the species account for these species. Because different groups of butterflies and skippers typically are seen with their wings in different positions, I have chosen to use the length of the front margin of the forewing (FW), which should be visible in all cases, as the measure of size. The size given is the average size in inches. Symbols used in this section are (=), meaning that the size of the species being discussed is equal to the "size standard" species, (<) meaning that the size of the species being discussed is less than the "size standard" species, (<<) meaning much less than, (>) meaning greater than, (>>) meaning much greater than, (≤) meaning less than or equal to, and (≥) meaning greater than or equal to.

SIMILAR SPECIES   This section lists species that might be confused with the species being discussed.

IDENTIFICATION   A discussion of how to distinguish this species from others, especially from those listed under similar species. Generally, if a species is significantly more common than a similar species, a **discussion of how to separate them will appear only under the species account of the less common species.**
   Figure 2 illustrates a set of imaginary butterfly wings and shows how the different parts of the wing are described. When describing the wings, "above" refers to the upper (dorsal) wing surfaces while "below" refers to the lower (ventral) wing surfaces.

TABLE 1 Sizes of "Size Standard" Species

Size Standard	Size (length of the FW in inches)
Black Swallowtail	1 13/16
Eastern Tiger Swallowtail	2 3/16
Cabbage White	15/16
Eastern Tailed Blue	8/16
Banded Hairstreak	10/16
Pearl Crescent	11/16
American Lady	1 2/16
Mourning Cloak	1 10/16
Great Spangled Fritillary	1 11/16
Little Wood Satyr	13/16
Common Wood Nymph	1 4/16
Monarch	2
Common Sootywing	9/16
Wild Indigo Duskywing	11/16
Northern Cloudywing	12/16
Silver-spotted Skipper	1 2/16
Least Skipper	8/16
Tawny-edged Skipper	9/16
Hobomok/Zabulon Skipper	10/16

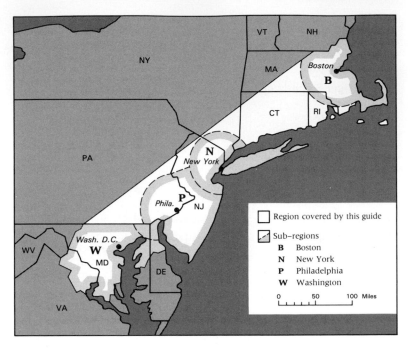

Figure 1.   Map of the Region Covered

Figure 2.   Butterfly Wing Areas and Body Parts

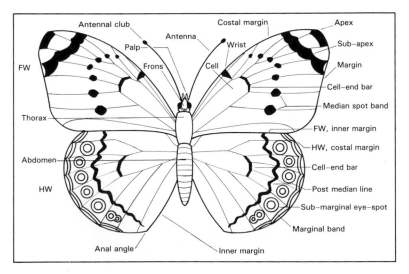

HABITAT   This section describes the types of areas where this butterfly might normally be found.

RANGE   The portion of our region where this butterfly is found is given and reflects the current status of the species in our region. This "within region" range is based on a combination of the author's personal experience, that of the field observers listed in the acknowledgments, and some published reports in the Season Summary of the Lepidopterists' Society. The range of many species is given as "north" (or "south") to about the Fall Line. The Fall Line begins at the Palisades, near the mouth of the Hudson River, and runs southwest through central NJ and Philadelphia and through the northwestern Washington, D.C., area. It is the region where many rivers have falls or rapids and separates the coastal plain from the piedmont. Also given is a brief summary of the entire range of the species. This "outside the region" range is based largely on data published in *Butterflies of North America* by J. Scott, and *Butterflies East of the Great Plains* by P. Opler. It is included to give the reader a general picture of how the range in our region fits into the total range of the species and is not intended to be a detailed range description.

SPECIFIC LOCALITIES   When a species is rare and/or local in one of the subregions, I have sometimes listed a particular site in the subregion where you might expect to see that species. If the locality is listed in Appendix A, the complete address is given there. In general, I have tried to mention localities that are easily accessible to the public. For some rare species, localities are not given because they are private and/or because of the substantial danger of butterfly collectors destroying the localized colonies.

FLIGHT PERIOD AND ABUNDANCE   The flight period and abundance for each species are given for four subregions, the Boston area, the New York area, the Philadelphia area, and the Washington area. The extent of these subregions is defined on page 21 under abbreviations. Note that the Boston and New York areas do not overlap. Users in much of Connecticut will need to interpolate the flight period and abundance data from those two areas.

I try to give information that will allow you to know when to search for a particular species and how likely you might be to find it. **I cannot emphasize enough that this section is intended as a rough guide.** Butterfly abundance can, and usually does, vary dramatically from year to year and within each of the subregions. One of the pleasures of butterflying is that each year is certain to bring its quota of surprises. To give one of many possible examples, the following is the number of Mourning Cloaks seen on the Northern Westchester, NY Xerces Society 4th of July Butterfly Count for the years 1984–1991: 0, 0, 1, 5, 27, 300, 22, 2. Flight dates can also vary tremendously. The winter of 1990–91 was very warm and the spring of 1991 was torrid. As a result, all through our region, species emerged two to three weeks earlier than normal. If global warming is a reality, these early dates may become the norm.

Because each subregion is rather large, butterflies in the southern portions of the subregion may emerge a week before those in the northern portions. For the New York subregion, additional information is provided. Comparable data from other subregions were not available and in most cases do not exist. Perhaps future editions of this guide can include such data.

For the New York subregion, detailed phenograms for five years are provided in Appendix C. These give the actual abundance for each species during five-day blocks throughout each of those years. The three bar widths correspond to uncommon, common, and abundant. This should give you both a good idea as to the best time of year to search for a species as well as the type of year-to-year variation you might encounter. Also given is the maximum number of individuals of that species observed at one time at one locality. If a species has multiple broods, the maximum for each brood is usually given. The phenograms and maxima are compiled from records of all New York area observers known to the author over the past eight years.

MAJOR FOODPLANT   Listed as an aid to finding the adult butterflies are the major plant(s), or group of plants that are eaten by the larvae in our area. For many uncommon butterflies the easiest way to locate colonies is to search for sites where the foodplant is common.

COMMENTS   Here I include remarks of an unpredictable nature. You will occasionally come across phrases such as "heart-stopping beauty." You may either accept these at face value or view them as having been written with an ironic sense of detachment, laced with a nostalgia for an imagined simpler time.

Abbreviations

A   abundant, likely to encounter more than 20 individuals per field trip to the right locality at the right time.

B   roughly a 50-mile radius circle with Boston at its center but including all of Cape Cod and excluding NH, ME, and areas west of the regional limits of this book.

C   common, likely to encounter between 4 and 20 individuals per field trip to the right locality at the right time.

FW   Forewing.

H   historically present but may no longer occur.

HW   hindwing.

L   local (not widespread, usually occurring in localized colonies).

N   roughly a 50-mile circle with Manhattan at its center but also including all of Long Island and Monmouth Co., NJ.

P   roughly a 50-mile circle with Philadelphia at its center, including Hunterdon and Mercer Cos., NJ, southern NJ, Cecil Co., MD, and New Castle Co., DE.

R   rare, rarely seen even at the right place at the right time.

S   stray, not part of the region's normal fauna and not seen most years.

U   uncommon, likely to see 0 to 3 individuals per field trip to the right place at the right time.

W   Washington, D.C., Kent, Queen Anne's, Harford, Baltimore, Carroll, Frederick, Howard, Montgomery, Anne Arundel, Prince Georges and Charles Cos., MD, and Prince William, Fairfax and Loudoun Cos., VA.

X   not normally found in this subregion.

♂   Male

♀   Female

Species Accounts

Swallowtails *(Papilionidae)*

The swallowtails are our largest butterflies. Their long tails and often slow, hovering flight make them among our most graceful.

Pipevine Swallowtail *(Battus philenor)* Plate 1

SIZE = Black Swallowtail.

SIMILAR SPECIES Spicebush Swallowtail, Black Swallowtail.

IDENTIFICATION A very dark swallowtail above with strongly iridescent blue HW. Below, note the large **single** orange spot-band on **iridescent blue**. Spicebush and Black Swallowtails have blue that is not iridescent and **two** orange spot-bands.

HABITAT Wide ranging, this swallowtail could be encountered almost anywhere, but is found primarily in open situations near woodlands, including gardens and beach areas.

RANGE Entire region, progressively rarer farther north. Also south to Florida and west to California.

SPECIFIC LOCALITIES In the NY area, a sizable population inhabits the base of the Palisades (where *Aristolochia* grows) and individuals can often be seen nectaring at the private Greenbrook Sanctuary in Englewood, NJ.

FLIGHT PERIOD & ABUNDANCE **B:** R, immigrant to southeastern MA, July. **N:** R-LC, late May–Sept., most frequent late July. Maximum 29, 7/19/87 Jamaica Bay Wildlife Refuge, NY. **P:** C, but rare southern NJ, late April– early June, July, early Aug.–Sept. **W:** C, late April–late July, mid Aug.–late Oct. Most common June–July, Aug.–Sept.

MAJOR FOODPLANT *Aristolochia* including ornamental vines and the native hosts *A. durior* and *A. serpentaria*.

Zebra Swallowtail *(Eurytides marcellus)* Plate 1

SIZE ≤ Black Swallowtail.

SIMILAR SPECIES None.

IDENTIFICATION   The aptly named Zebra Swallowtail can be confused with none of our other butterflies. The black-striped white triangular wings with graceful tails are distinctive. Also note the bright red median HW stripe below.

HABITAT   Open brushy fields and woodlands, especially along watercourses.

RANGE   North to around Philadelphia and (as a stray) NJ. Also south to Florida and west to Texas.

SPECIFIC LOCALITIES   Elk Neck State Park, Cecil Co., MD; Great Falls National Park, MD; McKee-Beshers Wildlife Management Area, MD; Mattawoman Natural Environment Area, MD.

FLIGHT PERIOD & ABUNDANCE   **B:** X.   **N:** X.   **P:** LR, but LC Cecil Co., MD, late April–early May, early June–frost.   **W:** LC, along the Potomac River and the shore of Chesapeake Bay, otherwise U, late March–late May, early June–frost.

MAJOR FOODPLANT   Papaw *(Asimina triloba)*.

COMMENTS   Spring individuals are smaller with narrower black bands than summer individuals.

Black Swallowtail *(Papilio polyxenes)* Plate 2

SIZE   1 13/16 in.

SIMILAR SPECIES   Spicebush Swallowtail, Pipevine Swallowtail, Eastern Tiger Swallowtail (black form female).

IDENTIFICATION   There are four species of "black" swallowtails in our area: The Black Swallowtail, Spicebush Swallowtail, Pipevine Swallowtail, and the black form of the female Eastern Tiger Swallowtail. Below, the Black and Spicebush Swallowtails have two rows of orange spots, the Pipevine and black female Eastern Tiger Swallowtails, only one. Below, the yellow orange HW cell spot or the FW subapical yellow spot distinguish this species from all others.

　　Above, males, with their bright yellow median bands across both wings are obvious. Some females can appear surprisingly similar to some female Spicebush Swallowtails but can be separated from this and other species by the presence of a yellow FW subapical spot. The Black Swallowtail usually has a less powerful flight than the Spicebush Swallowtail.

HABITAT   A swallowtail of open areas, especially of disturbed habitats; fields, meadows, tidal marshes, and suburban lawns.

RANGE   Entire region. Also southern Canada west to the Rocky Mountains and south to northern South America.

FLIGHT PERIOD & ABUNDANCE   **B:** C, early May–Oct.   **N:** C, Late April–Sept. Maximum 93, 7/19/87 Jamaica Bay Wildlife Refuge, NY.   **P:** C, mid April–Oct.   **W:** C, early May–early Oct.

MAJOR FOODPLANT   Parsley, carrot (wild or not), and other Umbellifera.

COMMENTS   The beautiful Black Swallowtail has adapted well to suburban and urban environments. Sometimes, eggs are laid even on parsley growing on the terraces of Manhattan's high-rise apartments. Early spring males can be quite small. Males gravitate to open hilltops. This swallowtail is quite fond of clovers as nectar sources and tends to stay closer to the ground than our other swallowtails.

Giant Swallowtail *(Papilio cresphontes)* Plate 3

SIZE   ≥ Eastern Tiger Swallowtail.

SIMILAR SPECIES   None.

IDENTIFICATION   At a distance, note the contrast between the dark wings above and the pale wings below. Above, the wings are dark brown (almost black) with prominent yellow bands. Note the x's these bands form near the apices of the FW's and the yellow spot in the HW tails. Below, note the striking cream-colored body and cream-colored wings with HW blue median spot-band.

HABITAT   Open woodlands and fields, gardens, and hillsides near woodlands. Northward found chiefly in the limestone belt where prickly ash occurs.

RANGE   North to around Philadelphia, straying north rarely and erratically but sometimes forming small colonies. Also west to the Rocky Mountains and south through South America.

SPECIFIC LOCALITIES   McKee-Beshers WMA, MD.

FLIGHT PERIOD & ABUNDANCE: **B:** X.   **N:** R, one seen in Sussex Co., NJ, in 1984 and another on Long Island, NY, in 1990. Perhaps resident in northwestern NJ.   **P:** LR, late May–June, Aug.–Sept.   **W:** U, early May–late June, mid July–late Sept.

MAJOR FOODPLANT   Prickly Ash *(Xanthoxylum americanum)* and Hop Tree *(Ptelia trifoliata).*

COMMENTS   Formerly found farther north. A colony existed in the 1950s in Dutchess Co., NY. There are recent reports of a colony in the Meriden, CT, area.

Eastern Tiger Swallowtail *(Papilio glaucus)* Plates 1, 3

SIZE   2 3/16 in.

SIMILAR SPECIES   None.

IDENTIFICATION   This boldly colored swallowtail is one of our most spectacular butterflies. The bright yellow wings with black stripes make this usually very large swallowtail immediately identifiable. The females are dimorphic with some having black wings. The percentage of black-form females increases as one moves southward. Below, these are easy to differentiate from other "black" swallowtails because they lack the HW median orange spot-band of the Black and Spicebush Swallowtails and the iridescent blue of the Pipevine Swallowtail. They also usually retain a "shadow" of the "tiger" pattern.

The Canadian Tiger Swallowtail *(Papilio glaucus canadensis),* heretofore treated as a subspecies of the Tiger Swallowtail, is probably a separate species (Hagen et al. 1992). It is a small, single-brooded spring tiger swallowtail (generally flying in late May rather than April) without black form females. Below, note the nearly continuous submarginal yellow band. Eastern Tiger Swallowtail has this band broken into spots. Also below, try to note the width of the black band along the bottom wing margin. Canadian Tiger Swallowtail has this band greater than half the width of space from the wing margin to the first vein. Eastern Tiger Swallowtail has this band narrower than half the width. The pure form of the essentially northern Canadian Tiger Swallowtail probably does not occur in our region at all but there seems to be a blend zone between these two populations extending over much of the area between Boston and NY (similar to the White Admiral/Red-spotted Purple blend zone).

HABITAT Deciduous woodlands, especially woodland edges and wooded watercourses. Often seen soaring high among the trees in suburban yards.

RANGE Entire region. Also north to Canada and west to Alaska and Texas.

FLIGHT PERIOD & ABUNDANCE **B:** C, late April–early July, mid July–late Aug. **N:** C, late April–late June, early July–mid Sept. Maximum 34, 7/28/88 Chappaqua RR Station, NY. **P:** C, April–July, July–Sept. **W:** C, April–July, July–Sept.

MAJOR FOODPLANT Wild Black Cherry *(Prunus serotina)* and Tulip Tree *(Liriodendron tulipifera)*. Aspen and birch for the Canadian Tiger Swallowtail.

COMMENTS Inordinately fond of aromatic Oriental Lilies *(Lilium rubrum)*. The Tiger Swallowtails and the lilies are each wonderful by themselves. Together, they induce a state of bliss.

Spicebush Swallowtail *(Papilio troilus)* Plate 2

SIZE ≥ Black Swallowtail.

SIMILAR SPECIES Black Swallowtail, Pipevine Swallowtail, black-form female Eastern Tiger Swallowtail.

IDENTIFICATION Below, note two orange spot-bands (marginal and post-median) on the HW and the absence of a yellow spot in the HW cell. Pipevine and black-form female Eastern Tiger Swallowtails have only one orange spotband while Black Swallowtail has a yellow spot in the cell.

Above, males with greenish cast on the HW are distinctive. Distinguish females from female Black Swallowtail by the absence of a yellow FW subapical spot. Its flight tends to be faster and more direct than the Black Swallowtail. Females also have orange costal spots and orange anal spots without black pupils. These are distinguishing marks but are often not visible in the field.

HABITAT Open woodlands and their borders. Confined more closely to woodlands than our other swallowtails.

RANGE Entire region. Also north to southern Maine, west to the Mississippi, and south to Florida and Texas.

FLIGHT PERIOD & ABUNDANCE **B:** U-C early May–mid July, early Aug.–mid Sept. **N:** U-C, late April–mid June, late June–mid Sept. Max. 34, 8/1/87 Pound Ridge Reservation, NY. **P:** C, late April–June, July–Sept. **W:** C, late April–June, July–early Oct.

MAJOR FOODPLANT Sassafras *(Sassafras albidum)* and Spicebush *(Lindera benzoin)*.

Palamedes Swallowtail *(Papilio palamedes)* Plate 3

SIZE = Eastern Tiger Swallowtail.

SIMILAR SPECIES Black Swallowtail, Giant Swallowtail.

IDENTIFICATION Below, note the **yellow stripe along the base of the wings.**

Above, note the **wide yellow HW post-median band.** Black Swallowtail is smaller and blacker without the yellow stripe below and above with a yellow HW post-median band that is narrower and broken into discrete spots. In flight the yellow "flash" on the HWs distinguishes the Palamedes from the Giant Swallowtail.

HABITAT   Southern swamps.

RANGE   Southeastern U.S. south to Mexico. Rarely ranges north into our area.

FLIGHT PERIOD & ABUNDANCE   **B:** X.   **N:** X.   **P:** S.   **W:** S.

MAJOR FOODPLANT   Red Bay *(Persea borbonica).*

Pierids or Whites and Yellows *(Pieridae)*

Pierids are medium-sized white and yellow butterflies. Their fairly rapid and low flight, usually with only short stops for nectar, makes them obvious objects as they nervously flit about open fields. They often will not sit still to allow you a leisurely study of their appearance. So ubiquitous are they that many people believe that the word "butterfly" derives from a common European yellow. Unlike most of our other butterflies that tend to have definite broods and appear only at specific times of the year, many of the whites and yellows are continuously brooded and thus fly essentially all season long.

Checkered White *(Pontia protodice)* Plate 5

SIZE   = Cabbage White.

SIMILAR SPECIES   Cabbage White, Falcate Orangetip.

IDENTIFICATION   When well seen, the extensive black or dark brown wing markings are distinctive. Females have significantly more extensive markings than males. In flight, this species is similar to the Cabbage White but the white ground color appears chalky with a slight bluish tinge. Its flight tends to use deeper wingbeats and to be more direct than the swerving flight of the Cabbage White.

HABITAT   Disturbed open areas, especially beach areas and railroad tracks along the coast.

RANGE   North to the New York area. Also west to Washington State and California and south to Mexico.

SPECIFIC LOCALITIES   Jamaica Bay Unit of Gateway National Recreation Area, NY.

FLIGHT PERIOD & ABUNDANCE   **B:** S, not recorded in recent years.   **N:** R-LC, very variable immigrant, July–Sept. Max 21, 9/7/86 Jamaica Bay Wildlife Refuge, NY.   **P:** LC, variable, R, southern NJ. May–mid June, July, late Aug.–Oct.   **W:** LU, April–early June, late June–late Aug, late Aug.–frost.

MAJOR FOODPLANT   Crucifers, especially Peppergrass *(Lepidium).*

COMMENTS   The Checkered White has been described as "formerly much more abundant" by about every author for the past 100 years! It seems likely that this primarily southern and midwestern butterfly never has been very common in our region except for sporadic outbreaks.

West Virginia White *(Pieris virginiensis)* Plate 4

SIZE   ≤ Cabbage White.

SIMILAR SPECIES   Cabbage White.

IDENTIFICATION   Below, note the wing veins edged in gray. Above, it is immaculate white but early spring Cabbage Whites often have reduced black spots above and are sometimes immaculate. Check below. In flight, the West Virginia White appears grayer than the Cabbage White with a weaker flight that keeps closer to the ground. But, check below.

HABITAT   Rich transition-zone deciduous woodlands with good stands of the foodplant (this is usually near streams).

RANGE   Springfield, MA, area south through western CT and southeastern NY to northern NJ. Also north to southern Vermont, west to Wisconsin, and south through the Appalachian Mountains.

SPECIFIC LOCALITIES   Steep Rock Reservation, CT; Catoctin Mountain Park, MD.

FLIGHT PERIOD & ABUNDANCE   **B:** X, but U, Springfield area, early May–early June.   **N:** LR, no active local colonies known. LR in CT, mid April–early May.   **P:** X.   **W:** LR, in Frederick Co., MD.

MAJOR FOODPLANT   Toothworts *(Dentaria diphylla* and *D. laciniata).*

COMMENTS   On sunny, but cool spring days the West Virginia White will bask in the sun. Holding their wings at an angle, their white surfaces act as sun reflectors directing the warming rays of sun to their black, and thus light-absorbing, bodies. This species seems to have declined recently, at least in the New York area. Now absent from many seemingly appropriate localities where its foodplant is present.

Cabbage White *(Pieris rapae)* Plates 4 & 5

SIZE   15/16 in.

SIMILAR SPECIES   Clouded Sulphur (white female).

IDENTIFICATION   This common to abundant European introduction is an often high flying White with a fairly strong but erratic (swerving) flight. Seen well, the Cabbage White has either 1 (male) or 2 (female) black spots and a dark subapex on the FW but early spring individuals sometimes have these markings greatly diminished. Below, there is usually a strong yellowish cast to the HW.

HABITAT   Any type of open or lightly wooded terrain, especially gardens, roadsides, and agricultural lands. Also present in urban areas.

RANGE   Entire region. Also north to Maine, south to Florida, and west to California.

SPECIFIC LOCALITIES   Widespread.

FLIGHT PERIOD & ABUNDANCE   **B:** A, late March–hard frost.   **N:** A, late March–hard frost. Max. 707, 7/19/87 Jamaica Bay Wildlife Refuge, NY.   **P:** A, early March–hard frost.   **W:** A, early March–hard frost.

MAJOR FOODPLANT   Crucifers.

COMMENTS   Probably our most ubiquitous butterfly. The Cabbage White is one of only two non-native butterfly species now found in our area. In the middle of summer the vision of hundreds of these Whites dancing around the blooming Purple Loosestrife plants (another introduced species that is generally considered a pest) creates the impression that one has been transported into a Walt Disney movie.

Falcate Orangetip *(Anthocharis midea)* Plate 4

SIZE   < Cabbage White.

SIMILAR SPECIES   Checkered White.

IDENTIFICATION   This is a small, early spring White. Males, with their bright orange wing-tips contrasting with otherwise white wings gladden the heart and are unmistakable. Females have blunt (falcate) FWs and are heavily marbled below, unlike any of our other Whites. Its flight is fairly weak and very close to the ground, rarely rising more than a couple of feet high.

HABITAT   Open woodlands with small crucifers. North of NYC this is usually a steep, south-facing wooded but rocky slope. More general to the south of NYC, especially in pine barrens and sandy woods.

RANGE   Northern CT south through our region. Also, south to Georgia and west to Texas.

SPECIFIC LOCALITIES   West Rock, CT; Hook Mtn. summit, NY; Great Falls National Park, MD.

FLIGHT PERIOD & ABUNDANCE   **B:** X, but small colonies approach the Springfield area in northern CT. **N:** LC, mid April–mid May. Max. 50, 5/27/86 Hook Mtn., Rockland Co., NY. **P:** LC, early April–early May. **W:** LC, late March–mid May.

MAJOR FOODPLANT   Crucifers, mainly Rock Cresses *(Arabis).*

COMMENTS   Females appear a week or so later than the males.

Clouded Sulphur *(Colias philodice)* Plates 5 & 6

SIZE   = Cabbage White.

SIMILAR SPECIES   Orange Sulphur, Cabbage White.

IDENTIFICATION   A strong-flying, medium-sized sulphur of open fields. Since the sulphurs almost always land with their wings closed, it is difficult to get a good view of their upper wing surfaces. Above, clear lemon-yellow with **no** orange patches. Both sexes have black FW borders above but females have yellow spots within the border. Orange Sulphur has at least some orange above. Some females of the Clouded and Orange Sulphurs lack the yellow and/or orange pigments and are off-white with the usual black pattern. They can be distinguished from Cabbage Whites by their lower to the ground, less swerving flight patterns, their off-white appearance, and their black markings. Although Clouded Sulphur females generally have a narrower black FW border than Orange Sulphur females, distinguishing the albino females in the field may not be possible. Because both are so common this isn't a major concern of many people.

HABITAT   Open fields, roadsides, suburban areas, etc.

RANGE   Entire region. Also north to Canada, south to the Gulf States and west to California.

FLIGHT PERIOD & ABUNDANCE   **B:** C, April–Nov.   **N:** C-A, April–Nov. Max. 115, 7/15/89 Raritan Canal, NJ.   **P:** A, April–Nov.   **W:** A, April–Nov.

MAJOR FOODPLANT   White Clover *(Trifolium repens)*.

Orange Sulphur *(Colias eurytheme)* Plates 5 & 6

SIZE   = Cabbage White.

SIMILAR SPECIES   Clouded Sulphur.

IDENTIFICATION   A strong flying medium-sized sulphur of open fields. Above with at least some orange (this can be seen in flight). Because this species hybridizes with the Clouded Sulphur, calling *all* individuals with any orange above Orange Sulphurs is only an operational definition. See Clouded Sulphur for a discussion of white females.

HABITAT   Open fields, roadsides, suburban areas, etc.

RANGE   Entire region. Also, north to Canada, south to Florida, and west to California.

FLIGHT PERIOD & ABUNDANCE   **B:** C, April–Nov.   **N:** C-A, April–Nov. Max. 207, 7/15/89 Raritan Canal, NJ.   **P:** A, April–Nov.   **W:** A, April–Nov.

MAJOR FOODPLANT   Alfalfa *(Medicago sativa)* and other Fabaceae.

COMMENTS   Not established in the northeast until around 1930.

Pink-edged Sulphur *(Colias interior)* Plate 40

SIZE   = Cabbage White.

SIMILAR SPECIES   Clouded Sulphur.

IDENTIFICATION   This denizen of northern blueberry barrens is not normally a part of our fauna. Distinguished by the **single HW central spot** (Clouded Sulphur has a doubled HW central spot), the more prominent pink wing edging (although Clouded Sulphurs can have a significant amount of pink), and its generally more delicate, more translucent appearance.

HABITAT   Northern barrens.

RANGE   South to Maine and the mountains of New Hampshire, Vermont, and upstate NY and then west across Canada. Isolated populations exist in the Appalachians.

FLIGHT PERIOD & ABUNDANCE   **B:** X. Recorded once from Rockport, MA.   **N:** X.   **P:** X.   **W:** X.

Southern Dogface *(Colias cesonia)* Plate 6

SIZE   > Cabbage White.

SIMILAR SPECIES   Clouded Sulphur.

IDENTIFICATION   A bright yellow sulphur, slightly larger than the Clouded Sulphur with a bold black outline of a dog's head above. Below, note pointed forewings and the outline of dog's head pattern through the FW. The fall form has the HW below suffused with pink.

HABITAT   Dry roadsides and fields, usually near open woodlands.

RANGE   An immigrant from the south into our area. Occasionally (perhaps every few decades) becomes common (as in the Philadelphia area in 1961), but generally very rare and irregular. It is probably most frequent on the Western Shore of MD. Also south through South America.

FLIGHT PERIOD & ABUNDANCE   **B:** X.   **N:** X, but has been recorded from Long Island.   **P:** S, immigrant, not seen for many years at a time.   **W:** S, immigrant, not seen for many years at a time.

MAJOR FOODPLANT   Pea family.

Cloudless Sulphur *(Phoebis sennae)* Plate 6

SIZE   > Common Wood Nymph.

SIMILAR SPECIES   None.

IDENTIFICATION   A very large sulphur. It has a high, directional, sailing flight with characteristic deep, powerful wingbeats. Green-yellow below, males are pale yellow above, females pale yellow to orange.

HABITAT   In our region, open areas, especially beach dunes.

RANGE   A resident of the south, the Cloudless Sulphur appears regularly in late summer and fall in small numbers along the coast, north to at least southeastern MA. Occasionally common north to Long Island and increasingly common farther south. Also, south to Argentina.

FLIGHT PERIOD & ABUNDANCE   **B:** R, irregular and very variable immigrant, mainly in Sept.   **N:** R, irregular and very variable immigrant, mainly in Sept. Max. 15, 9/16/87 Gateway National Recreation Area.   **P:** R-U, regular but very variable immigrant, mainly in Sept.   **W:** R-U, regular but very variable immigrant, mainly in Sept.

MAJOR FOODPLANT   Sennas *(Cassia).*

Barred Yellow *(Eurema daira)* Plate 40

SIZE   << Cabbage White.

SIMILAR SPECIES   Little Yellow.

IDENTIFICATION   Not normally part of our fauna. A very small yellow whose males, in flight, display a black bar along the FW lower margin.

RANGE   Southeastern U.S. south through Mexico to Argentina. Strays north to central VA.

FLIGHT PERIOD & ABUNDANCE   **B:** X.   **N:** X.   **P:** X.   **W:** X. One record.

Little Yellow *(Eurema lisa)* Plate 6

SIZE   < Cabbage White.

SIMILAR SPECIES   Clouded Sulphur.

IDENTIFICATION   A small, very bright yellow with a rapid, low, and straight flight path. Much smaller and brighter yellow than the Clouded Sulphur. If seen landed, note the scattered, smudged dark markings on the HW below and the **black** (not dull pink) antennae.

HABITAT   Disturbed open areas, especially dry sandy grassy fields.

RANGE   An annual immigrant into our area. Much more common along the coast than inland. Also, rarely north to Maine and south to Central America.

SPECIFIC LOCALITIES   Marine Park, NY.

FLIGHT PERIOD & ABUNDANCE   **B:** R, irregular and very variable immigrant, mainly in Sept.   **N:** R-U, regular but variable immigrant, Aug.–Sept. Max. 35, 9/21/91 Marine Park, Brooklyn, NY.   **P:** R-C, mid May–Sept., most numerous in Aug.   **W:** C, mid May–Oct. most numerous south of Washington, D.C., in early Sept.

MAJOR FOODPLANT   Sennas *(Cassia).*

Sleepy Orange *(Eurema nicippe)* Plate 6

SIZE   = Cabbage White.

SIMILAR SPECIES   Orange Sulphur.

IDENTIFICATION   Like the Orange Sulphur, this butterfly is bright orange above with black borders but it flies closer to the ground than the Orange Sulphur with weaker wingbeats. Seen well, note the black antennae (Orange Sulphur-dull pink) and the characteristic diagonal brown markings on the HW below. This species is dimorphic and the HW ground color below can be either yellow or a dull reddish color. Both forms have been seen in our area.

HABITAT   Wet meadows, open fields, roadsides.

RANGE   A permanent resident north to about North Carolina, the Sleepy Orange invades our region to a variable extent each summer. Accidental north to northeastern MA.

SPECIFIC LOCALITIES   Mattawoman Natural Environment Area, MD.

FLIGHT PERIOD & ABUNDANCE   **B:** X.   **N:** S, not recorded for many years at a time.   **P:** R, irregular immigrant, late May–Oct., most likely in Aug.   **W:** R-U, late May–Sept., maximum in July.

MAJOR FOODPLANT   Sennas *(Cassia).*

The Lycaenids or Gossamer Wings *(Lycaenidae)*

This is a very large worldwide family of butterflies consisting, in our area, of the Coppers, the Hairstreaks, the Blues, and the Harvester. Most species are quite small, although a few tropical hairstreaks are larger than an American Lady. Many lycaenid species are myrmecophilous (ant-loving). The larvae secrete a "honey-dew" from special glands that attract certain species of ants. These ants then "tend" the larvae helping to protect them from predator species. The larvae of many lycaenid species (including some of ours) feed on flower parts.

Harvesters

Harvester *(Feniseca tarquinius)* Plate 7

SIZE   = Banded Hairstreak.

SIMILAR SPECIES   American Copper.

IDENTIFICATION   A medium-sized Lycaenid, bright orange above with bold black markings. Below, note the orange disc of the FW and the dull reddish-brown HW with **delicate white markings.** Unlike the American Copper, this butterfly is often seen on tree leaves.

HABITAT   Woodlands, especially near watercourses or wet areas with alders.

RANGE   Entire region. Also north to Canada, south to Florida, and west to Texas.

FLIGHT PERIOD & ABUNDANCE   **B:** LU, erratic, late May–Sept.   **N:** LR, May–Sept. Max. 100, 9/5/85 Bronx Zoo, Bronx, NY (usually only solitary individuals.   **P:** R-U, erratic, May–Sept.   **W:** R-C, erratic, April–Oct.

FOOD   Woolly Aphids, usually on alders or beech.

COMMENTS   The Harvester is our only butterfly with carnivorous larvae. The larvae feed on other insects (woolly aphids) rather than on plants. Adults can sometimes be found sunning themselves in woodland glades in the late afternoon. Usually quite rare and a good find, this species occasionally undergoes local population irruptions (especially in late summer).

Coppers

American Copper *(Lycaena phlaeas)* Plate 7

SIZE   = Banded Hairstreak.

SIMILAR SPECIES   Bronze Copper, Harvester.

IDENTIFICATION   A tiny flash of orange announces this whirling dervish. Above, the FWs are lustrous orange with black spots while the HWs are dark brownish-gray with a brownish-orange submarginal band. Below, note the orange FW disc and grayish HW with narrow orange marginal band.

HABITAT   Disturbed open areas, fields, power-line cuts, etc.

RANGE   Entire region. Also, north to Maine, south to Georgia, and west to the midwest.

FLIGHT PERIOD & ABUNDANCE   **B:** A, early May–mid June, early July–mid Aug., late Aug.–early Oct.   **N:** A, late April–mid June, late June–mid Aug., late Aug.–mid Oct. Max. 50, 5/29/89 Bear Mtn., Rockland, NY; 1253 7/6/91 Jamaica Bay Wildlife Refuge, NY; 68, 9/7/86 Floyd Bennet Field, Brooklyn, NY.   **P:** C, mid April–May, late June–July, Aug.–Oct.   **W:** C, mid April–early June, mid June–early Aug., early Aug.–late Aug., early Sept.–Nov.

MAJOR FOODPLANT   Various docks *(Rumex)* including Sheep Sorrel *(Rumex acetosella).*

Bronze Copper *(Lycaena hyllus)* Plate 7

SIZE   ≥ Pearl Crescent.

SIMILAR SPECIES   American Copper.

IDENTIFICATION   A very large, floppy-flying Copper. Although in a picture it closely resembles the American Copper, when encountered in the field there is no doubt of its identity. The logical flip side of this is that if you are in doubt of a butterfly's identity, it is not this species. Above, the males are purple with orange tints, while females have their ground color paler yellowish-orange. Below, note the pale, almost white ground color and the broad marginal orange band.

HABITAT   Low wet meadows/marshes, especially in river flood plains.

RANGE   Entire region. Also north to Maine and west to Utah.

SPECIFIC LOCALITIES   Sudbury River Valley drainage, Sudbury and Concord, MA; Fowl Meadow (just north of Blue Hills Reservation), Norwood, MA; Tinicum Environmental Center, PA; Middle Creek WMA, PA.

FLIGHT PERIOD & ABUNDANCE   B: LU, mid June–mid July, early Aug.–Sept.   **N:** LR, none seen since 1982, in the 1970s at least 8 colonies were known. Since 1982 only known from Sussex Co., NJ. Mid June–late June, late July–Sept.   **P:** LR, late May–mid June, early-mid July, Sept.   **W:** LR, mid May–Oct.

MAJOR FOODPLANT   Water Dock *(Rumex orbiculatus)* and Curled Dock *(R. crispus).*

COMMENTS   This heart-stopping species has declined drastically over the past twenty years. It may be that the Bronze Copper is basically an invasive species that does best in freshly created habitat (newly wet due to flooding, or fresh wet soil exposed by the receding water line of a pond). Man's penchant for stability may be in conflict with this species survival.

Bog Copper *(Lycaena epixanthe)* Plate 7

SIZE   = Eastern Tailed Blue.

SIMILAR SPECIES   None.

IDENTIFICATION   A very small, weak flying, dull copper—limited to acid bogs. It is so inconspicuous that it is easy to miss flying about one's feet. Above purplish (male) or gray (female). Below, ground color very pale off-white in the south, pale yellow in the north, with **no** orange on the FW.

HABITAT   Acid bogs with cranberries.

RANGE   South to southern NJ. Also, north to Canada and west to Minnesota.

SPECIFIC LOCALITIES   Blue Hills Reservation, MA; Lakehurst bog, NJ.

FLIGHT PERIOD & ABUNDANCE   B: LC, late June–late July.   **N:** LU, eastern Long Island, late June–late July, Max. 8, 6/22/89 Quogue, NY.   **P:** LA, mid June–mid July, NJ pine barrens.   **W:** X.

MAJOR FOODPLANT   Cranberries *(Vaccinium macrocarpum).*

COMMENTS   Not usually found in commercial cranberry bogs due to the use of pesticides.

Hairstreaks

The name of these small but intricately patterned butterflies is thought to be derived either from the many lines or streaks that tend to appear on the HW below or from the usual presence of fine, hair-like tails. Eighteen species occur in our region while over 1000 species of hairstreaks inhabit Central and South America. Many species have an "eye-spot" near the anal angle of the HW below that tends to attract the attention of predators to the wrong end of the butterfly. The subterfuge that this is the real eye of the butterfly is usually enhanced by the presence of tails (which can mimic antennae). When the hairstreak lands with its head facing downward and its tails move in the air as it "saws" its HWs back and forth, the effect is complete. Many tropical species have this eye-spot pattern greatly developed and it is not unusual to find individuals who have sacrificed the missing portions of their HWs to birds (see Robbins, 1981).

Great Purple Hairstreak *(Atlides halesus)* Plate 10

SIZE >> Banded Hairstreak.

SIMILAR SPECIES None.

IDENTIFICATION This butterfly is much larger than any of our other hairstreaks. When it flies, one can see the flash from the shining iridescent blue (not purple) scales covering the entire wings above. Below, the FW has an iridescent turquoise patch, while both the FW and the HW have large red spots near their bases. Note the striking orange abdomen.

HABITAT Edges of moist woodlands.

RANGE North into Queen Anne's, Prince George's, and Charles Cos., MD. Also south to Florida, west to California, and south to Guatemala.

FLIGHT PERIOD & ABUNDANCE **B:** X. **N:** X, but one very old record from Brooklyn. **P:** S, reported from southern NJ. **W:** LR, Queen Anne's, Prince George's, and Charles Cos., MD.

MAJOR FOODPLANT Mistletoe *(Phoradendron).*

COMMENTS Our only representative of an impressive group of tropical hairstreaks.

Satyrium Hairstreaks

The seven *Satyrium* hairstreaks in our area are similar. All are basically brown to brownish-gray to gray. Although they have rapid and very erratic flight paths, they are easier to follow than one would think since they often alight not far from where they began! All are most easily found nectaring at milkweeds or dogbane. Like many groups of hairstreaks, male *Satyrium* hairstreaks have scent pads on the FWs above. These pads contain specialized scales through which a pheromone (a specialized type of scent) is released. The pheromone induces females to interact appropriately during courtship rituals.

Coral Hairstreak *(Satyrium titus)* Plate 9

SIZE = Banded Hairstreak.

SIMILAR SPECIES Acadian Hairstreak.

IDENTIFICATION A brown, **tailless** hairstreak. It has a prominent marginal row of red-orange spots but no blue marginal eye-spot. Acadian Hairstreak has a tail, gray ground color and a blue eye-spot.

HABITAT   More a denizen of brushy fields, overgrown orchards, and the like than our other *Satyrium* Hairstreaks.

RANGE   Entire region. Also, north to Maine, west to California, and south to Florida.

FLIGHT PERIOD & ABUNDANCE   B: C, early July–late Aug.   **N:** C, mid June–July. Max. 18, 7/8/89 Pound Ridge Reservation, NY.   **P:** R-C, mid June–mid July.   **W:** R-C, mid-June–mid July.

MAJOR FOODPLANT   Wild Cherry and Wild Plum *(Prunus).*

COMMENTS   Orange Milkweed is a magnet for this butterfly, much more so than for any other hairstreak.

Acadian Hairstreak *(Satyrium acadica)* Plate 9

SIZE   ≥ Banded Hairstreak.

SIMILAR SPECIES   Gray Hairstreak, Edwards' Hairstreak, Coral Hairstreak.

IDENTIFICATION   A tailed, pale gray hairstreak with a **HW post-median band of black spots.** Gray Hairstreak has a post-median **line.** Edwards' and Coral Hairstreaks have brown ground color and Coral Hairstreak also lacks a tail.

HABITAT   Open areas and thickets near streams and marshy places where willows grow.

RANGE   South to the Philadelphia area (but not southern NJ). Also, north to Canada and west to Montana.

SPECIFIC LOCALITIES   Broad Meadow Brook Sanctuary, MA; Pound Ridge Reservation, NY; Rock Creek Ravine, Montgomery Co., PA.

FLIGHT PERIOD & ABUNDANCE   B: LU, late June–early Aug.   **N:** LU-LC, late June–mid July, mainly to the north and west of NYC, Max. 49, 7/8/89 Bedford, NY.   **P:** LU, late June–early July, to the north.   **W:** X.

MAJOR FOODPLANT   Willows *(Salix sericea* and others).

COMMENTS   Like many hairstreaks, male Acadian Hairstreaks exhibit territorial behavior only at specific times of the day. In the early morning and early evening they perch on willows and defend their territories.

Edwards' Hairstreak *(Satyrium edwardsii)* Plate 9

SIZE   = Banded Hairstreak.

SIMILAR SPECIES   Banded Hairstreak, Acadian Hairstreak.

IDENTIFICATION   Very similar to the Banded Hairstreak but usually browner with HW post-median band broken into **spots surrounded by white.** Note the prominent orange anal spot, more prominent than in Banded Hairstreak. Acadian Hairstreak has a HW post-median band of solid black spots and is grayer.

HABITAT   Woodlands with scrubby oaks and adjacent clearings. These are usually poor soil areas: pine barrens, rocky hill-tops, shale barrens, etc.

RANGE   Entire region. Also, north to Maine, west to North Dakota, and south (in the mountains) to Georgia.

36

SPECIFIC LOCALITIES Blue Hills Reservation, MA; Myles Standish State Forest, MA; West Rock Ridge State Park, CT; Pound Ridge Reservation, NY; Soldiers Delight Natural Environment Area, MD.

FLIGHT PERIOD & ABUNDANCE **B:** LC, late June–July. **N:** LC, mid June–July. Most common on eastern Long Island, Max. 50, 6/22/85 Turkey Mtn., Yorktown, Westchester, NY. **P:** LC, late June–mid July. **W:** LC, late June–mid July.

MAJOR FOODPLANT Small oaks, especially Scrub Oak *(Quercus ilicifolia).*

COMMENTS Usually local but can be abundant where it occurs. For example, over 1000 were reported from Myles Standish State Forest, Plymouth Co., MA, on July 8, 1988. Surprisingly uncommon in the NJ pine barrens.

Banded Hairstreak *(Satyrium calanus)* Plate 9

SIZE 10/16 in.

SIMILAR SPECIES Hickory Hairstreak, Edwards' Hairstreak.

IDENTIFICATION Usually our commonest hairstreak, the Banded Hairstreak has well marked post-median bands on both FWs and HWs. The band is outwardly strongly edged with white while inwardly the white edging varies from absent to strong. The Banded Hairstreak is very similar to the more uncommon Hickory Hairstreak and they can often be found together. Although this species is quite variable and some individuals can stump the "experts," with practice, most can be confidently identified. See Hickory and Edwards' Hairstreaks for discussions.

HABITAT Prefers open fields or glades with nectar sources (especially Common Milkweed, Dogbane, and Sumac) adjacent to oak woodlands.

RANGE Entire region. Also, north to Maine, west to North Dakota and Texas, and south to Florida.

FLIGHT PERIOD & ABUNDANCE **B:** C, late June–early Aug. **N:** U-A, mid June–late July. Max. 140, 6/27/89 Pound Ridge Reservation, NY. **P:** C, mid June–mid July. **W:** C, mid June–mid July.

MAJOR FOODPLANT Oaks *(Quercus)* and Hickories *(Carya).*

COMMENTS Although often common, the abundance of this species can exhibit massive fluctuations. Some years this appears to happen synchronously over our entire region.

Hickory Hairstreak *(Satyrium caryaevorus)* Plate 9

SIZE = Banded Hairstreak.

SIMILAR SPECIES Banded Hairstreak, Edwards' Hairstreak.

IDENTIFICATION Very similar to the Banded Hairstreak. Best separated by the HW blue anal spot. In the Hickory Hairstreak this spot usually (1) extends further inward, breaking the arc of the marginal spots and usually reaching, or almost reaching, the arc of the white post-median band, (2) is usually more pointed inwardly, and (3) is a paler, more shining blue. Also, Hickory Hairstreak almost always has the VFW post-median band bordered by white **on both sides,** Banded usually has this band bordered by white only on the distal side. Lastly, note the HW cell-end double white bar. Hickory Hairstreak usually has these lines aligned with the first lines of the post-median band, just above it. Banded usually has these offset.

HABITAT   Prefers open fields or glades with nectar sources (especially Common Milkweed, Dogbane, and Sumac) adjacent to deciduous woods. Probably prefers richer soil than the Banded Hairstreak.

RANGE   Northeast MA south to the Philadelphia area and in the Appalachians to northern Georgia. Also, west to the Mississippi.

SPECIFIC LOCALITIES   Rock Meadow Park, Belmont, MA.

FLIGHT PERIOD & ABUNDANCE   **B:** U, late June–July.   **N:** U, mid June–mid July. Max. 33, 7/7/90 Bedford, Westchester, NY.   **P:** R or X.   **W:** X.

MAJOR FOODPLANT   Hickories *(Carya)*, especially *C. cordiformis.*

Striped Hairstreak *(Satyrium liparops)* Plate 9

SIZE   = Banded Hairstreak.

SIMILAR SPECIES   Banded Hairstreak.

IDENTIFICATION   On first impression appears to have many more white lines and be "stripier" but actual differences are rather subtle. The white lines are set farther apart and **aligned** so as to form stripes. Also note the **orange cap** on the blue anal "eye-spot."

HABITAT   Thickets, brushy edges of woodlands, and adjacent edges of open areas. This species tends to stay closer to the woodlands than related species.

RANGE   Entire region, but rare toward the south. Also, north to Maine, west to Montana, and south to Texas and Florida.

FLIGHT PERIOD & ABUNDANCE   **B:** C, late June–mid Aug.   **N:** U, mid June–July. Max. 9, 7/7/85 Pound Ridge Reservation, NY.   **P:** U-R, late June–mid July, LC Ocean Co., NJ.   **W:** R, late June–mid July.

FOODPLANT   Wild Cherry *(Prunus)*, Blueberry *(Vaccinium)*, and many others.

COMMENTS   Although widespread, the Striped Hairstreak is rarely common. Unlike related hairstreaks, one will not see a swarm of them. Their occurrence and behavior seems to be much more solitary.

Southern Hairstreak *(Satyrium favonius)* Plate 10

SIZE   ≤ Banded Hairstreak.

SIMILAR SPECIES   White M Hairstreak, Gray Hairstreak.

IDENTIFICATION   This rare hairstreak has a "clean" appearance (as do White M and Gray Hairstreaks) due to the lack of cell-end bars. Note that the large red (orange) and black spot on the HW goes right up to the HW margin. White M Hairstreak has this spot displaced inwardly. Distinguished from Gray Hairstreak by brownish, (rather than gray), ground color. Note the **inwardly directed white chevron over the largest HW marginal orange spot.** Gray Hairstreak has a flat black line over this spot. Also lacks the well-marked black inside edge to the HW post-median line present in Gray Hairstreak.

HABITAT   A variety of woodland-edge situations including pine-oak woodlands and the edges of rich mixed deciduous woods.

RANGE   Entire region. Also, south along the coast to the Gulf States.

SPECIFIC LOCALITIES   Soldier's Delight, MD; Washington & Old Dominion RR, VA.

FLIGHT PERIOD & ABUNDANCE   **B:** LR, late June–mid July.   **N:** R, mid June–mid July. Max. 13, 6/22/89 Pound Ridge Reservation, NY.   **P:** R, mid June–mid July, LU-LC in pine barrens.   **W:** R, mid June–mid July.

MAJOR FOODPLANT   Various Oaks *(Quercus).*

COMMENTS   This species has hitherto usually been placed in the genus *Fixsenia.* Previously called the Northern Hairstreak, it has also usually been given the specific name *ontario* and been considered a separate species from the "Southern Hairstreak" which has been referred to as *favonius.* I place it in the genus *Satyrium* and consider the Southern and Northern Hairstreaks conspecific following Ziegler (1960) and R. K. Robbins of the Smithsonian Institution (personal communication). If you are not thoroughly confused at this point, you may be ready for tropical hairstreaks.

Red-banded Hairstreak *(Calycopis cecrops)* Plate 8

SIZE   < Banded Hairstreak.

SIMILAR SPECIES   None.

IDENTIFICATION   A small dark hairstreak with an **obvious red post-median band** on both the HWs and the FWs below. Above, shows some bright blue in flight.

HABITAT   Brushy, overgrown, sandy fields; especially with Winged Sumac. In late summer, this species can be found in a broader range of habitats.

RANGE   Westchester County, NY south through our area excluding northwestern NJ. Also, west to Texas.

SPECIFIC LOCALITIES   Floyd Bennet Field, Brooklyn, NY; Eldora Preserve, Cape May Co., NJ; Glover Park, Washington, D.C.

FLIGHT PERIOD & ABUNDANCE   **B:** X.   **N:** LU-LC, May–mid June, late July–Sept. Max. 8, 5/29/88 Floyd Bennet Field, Queens, NY, 9; 8/10/91 Assunpink WMA, Monmouth Co., NJ.   P: LU-LC, May, late July–mid Sept.   **W:** LU-LC, May, early Aug.–mid Sept.

MAJOR FOODPLANT   Although reported to feed on a wide variety of detritus (rotting leaves), in the NY area it is most associated with Winged Sumac *(Rhus copallina).* Females have been reported to walk on the forest floor ovipositing on dead leaves.

COMMENTS   Seems to have spread northward recently. Recorded in 1989 from northern Westchester Co., NY. Should be looked for to establish a beachhead on Cape Cod.

Olive Hairstreak *(Callophrys gryneus)* Plate 10

SIZE   ≤ Banded Hairstreak.

SIMILAR SPECIES   Hessel's Hairstreak.

IDENTIFICATION   Its bright green color below separates this little jewel from all our other hairstreaks except its close relative, Hessel's Hairstreak. These two can generally be identified by habitat preference alone. Olive Hairstreaks inhabit dry, often hilly fields with good stands of their host, red cedar. Hessel's inhabits white cedar swamps.

HABITAT   Dry fields (especially hilly ones) or ridge tops with good stands of red cedar, some brushy undergrowth, and nectar sources for both the spring and summer broods, In boom years, can be found on single red cedars.

RANGE   Entire region. Also, north to Maine, west to Wisconsin, and south to Texas and Florida.

SPECIFIC LOCALITIES   Babson Park, Wellesley, MA; West Rock Ridge State Park, CT; Muscoot County Park, Westchester, NY; Target Rock National Wildlife Refuge, Suffolk Co., NY; Higbee Beach WMA, Cape May Co., NJ; McKee-Beshers WMA, MD.

FLIGHT PERIOD & ABUNDANCE   **B:** LC, early May–mid June, mid July–mid Aug.   **N:** LC-LA, late April–May, mid July–early Aug. Max. 122, 7/21/90 Target Rock National Wildlife Refuge, Lloyd Harbor, Suffolk Co., NY.   **P:** LC, late April–mid May, mid July–mid Aug.   **W:** LC, late April–mid May, mid June–July.

FOODPLANT   Red Cedar *(Juniperus virginiana).*

COMMENTS   This butterfly tends to remain very close (usually on) its host. Best found by thumping on the red cedars and watching the Olive Hairstreaks whirl up. Seemingly not as fond of flowers as other hairstreaks, it can sometimes by found on Orange Milkweed but more often on damp sand early in the morning or late in the afternoon.

Hessel's Hairstreak *(Callophrys hesseli)* Plate 10

SIZE   ≤ Banded Hairstreak.

SIMILAR SPECIES   Olive Hairstreak.

IDENTIFICATION   Normally, only found in Atlantic White Cedar swamps (although individuals must disperse to new areas). Brighter, more emerald green than the Olive Hairstreak, Hessel's has the last two white spots of the HW post-median line **both concave outwardly.** Olive Hairstreak has these spots facing in opposite direction and offset. Also note the **brown patches distal to the post-median line,** especially on the HW. Olive Hairstreak lacks these brown patches.

HABITAT   Atlantic White Cedar swamps.

RANGE   Entire region in the limited appropriate habitat. Also, south along the coast to Florida.

SPECIFIC LOCALITIES   Blue Hills Reservation, MA; Great Swamp WMA, RI; Cranberry Bog Co. Park, NY; Chatsworth, NJ.

FLIGHT PERIOD & ABUNDANCE   **B:** LU, May.   **N:** LR, late April–mid May, partial second brood mid July. Has not been seen in the Long Island white cedar swamps since 1985. One May 1991 report from a white cedar swamp in Putnam Co., NY.   **P:** LR-LC, NJ white cedar swamps, late April–mid May, rare partial second brood mid July–early Aug.   **W:** X.

FOODPLANT   Atlantic White Cedar *(Chamaecyparis thyoides).*

COMMENTS   Best searched for very early or late in the day (after 4:00 P.M.) when they will come down from the tops of the White Cedars to nectar on Blue-berries, Sand Myrtles, or Chokecherries.

Brown Elfin *(Callophrys augustinus)* Plate 8

SIZE ≥ Eastern Tailed blue.

SIMILAR SPECIES Henry's Elfin.

IDENTIFICATION A small hairstreak of the early spring and our most widespread Elfin. Flight is weak and low. Rich brown below (fresh individuals have a purplish sheen) with the area inward of the post-median line dark brown and the area outward a brighter reddish-brown. Note the lack of white on the FW post-median line and lack of frosting on the HW margin.

HABITAT Generally distributed in acid, poor-soil woodlands, pine barrens, acid bogs, and extensive rocky outcroppings with its host plant.

RANGE Entire region. Also, north to Canada, west to Alaska, and south (in the mountains) to Georgia.

SPECIFIC LOCALITIES Catoctin Mountain Park, MD.

FLIGHT PERIOD & ABUNDANCE **B:** C, early April–mid May. **N:** LC-LA mainly eastern LI, late April–mid May. Max. 50, 4/26/86 Napeague, Suffolk, NY. **P:** LC-LA in NJ pine barrens, otherwise LR-LU, early April–early May. **W:** LU, early April, early May.

MAJOR FOODPLANT Blueberries, especially Low Bush Blueberry *(Vaccinium vacil-lans)* and related heaths.

COMMENTS A strong hilltopper (congregating on hilltops, presumably to concen-trate populations for mating), this species can often be found by climbing to the top of a rocky outcrop in the appropriate habitat.

Hoary Elfin *(Callophrys polios)* Plate 8

SIZE ≥ Eastern Tailed Blue.

SIMILAR SPECIES Frosted Elfin, Henry's Elfin, Brown Elfin.

IDENTIFICATION A small, very dark Elfin of low sand barrens. Note the "frosting" (grayish-white scales) on the HW margins and the **FW margins.** Frosted Elfin is larger, with much paler ground color and has tail-like protuberances on the HW. Brown Elfin lacks frosting. Henry's Elfin lacks frosting on the FW, has beginning and end of HW post-median band bounded by strong white mark, and normally found in different habitat.

HABITAT Dwarf pine barrens and other barrens with good amounts of its food-plant. Rarely forest edges.

RANGE South to the Philadelphia area in appropriate habitat. Also, west to Alaska.

SPECIFIC LOCALITIES Myles Standish State Forest, MA; Wellfleet Bay Wildlife Sanctuary, MA; Warren Grove, Ocean Co., NJ.

FLIGHT PERIOD & ABUNDANCE **B:** LU-LC, south and east of Boston, X to the north and west, mid April–late May. **N:** LR? should be found on eastern Long Island but has not been seen recently. **P:** LC, late April–mid May, northern & central NJ pine barrens. **W:** X.

MAJOR FOODPLANT   Bearberry *(Arctostaphylos uva-ursi)* and Trailing Arbutus *(Epigaea repens)*.

Frosted Elfin *(Callophrys irus)* Plate 8

SIZE   ≤ Banded Hairstreak.

SIMILAR SPECIES   Brown Elfin, Hoary Elfin, Henry's Elfin.

IDENTIFICATION   A larger than average Elfin, with "frosted" HW margin and short tail-like protuberances. Note the **black spot on the HW near the "tailed" area.** Hoary Elfin is smaller, darker, and has frosting on FW margin also. Henry's Elfin has richer, reddish-brown ground color and more contrast overall. Also note pale area between FW post-median and marginal lines of Frosted Elfin. Henry's Elfin lacks this. Brown Elfin lacks frosting.

HABITAT   Sandy or rocky acidic areas cleared by fire or, much more often, by man such as power-line cuts, railroad right-of-ways, and roadsides with good stands of one of its foodplants.

RANGE   Entire region. Also, north to Maine, west to Michigan, and south in the mountains to Georgia.

SPECIFIC LOCALITIES   Great Swamp WMA, RI; Assunpink WMA, NJ; Nottingham County Park, PA; Washington & Old Dominion RR, VA.

FLIGHT PERIOD & ABUNDANCE   **B:** LU, mid May–early June.   **N:** LU May–mid June. Eastern Long Island and north central NJ, Max. 40, 5/6/90 Assunpink WMA, Monmouth Co., NJ.   **P:** LR-LC late April–May.   **W:** LR, late April–May, Fairfax Co., VA. Formerly in Anne Arundel Cos., MD.

MAJOR FOODPLANT   Wild Indigo *(Baptisia)* in most localities and also Lupine *(Lupinus perennis)* on eastern Long Island.

COMMENTS   Thought by many to be declining over wide areas but abundance fluctuates markedly from year to year.

Henry's Elfin *(Callophrys henrici)* Plate 8

SIZE   ≥ Eastern Tailed Blue.

SIMILAR SPECIES   Brown Elfin, Frosted Elfin.

IDENTIFICATION   A bright brown elfin of woodlands. Note the frosted HW margin and the bold white marks at either end of the HW post-median line. Tail-like protuberances are usually visible. Brown Elfin lacks frosting, white marks, and "tails." Frosted Elfin has a black spot on the HW near the "tailed" area, has duller, paler ground color and little contrast between ground color on either side of post-median line.

HABITAT   Poor, acid soil woodlands with brushy understories. South of NY this is usually pine-oak-American Holly. North of NY it is likely to be swampy woodlands with good stands of high-bush blueberries except in the Boston area where it is more widespread.

RANGE   Entire region. Also, north to Maine, west to Wisconsin, and south to Texas and Florida.

SPECIFIC LOCALITIES   Blue Hills Reservation, MA; Great Swamp WMA, RI; Sandy Hook Unit of Gateway National Recreation Area, NJ; Tuckahoe WMA, Cape May Co., NJ.

FLIGHT PERIOD & ABUNDANCE **B:** U, late April—early June. **N:** LR, known only from Sandy Hook, NJ, where it is U-C in late April—early May. Should be looked for on Fire Island. Max. 23, 5/4/91 Sandy Hook, Monmouth Co., NJ. **P:** LR, but LC-LA in southern NJ, early April—mid May. **W:** LU, April—early May.

MAJOR FOODPLANT American Holly *(Ilex opaca)*, other hollies, and the European Buckthorn *(Rhamnus frangula)* in the Boston area. Also reported on Blueberries *(Vaccinium)*.

COMMENTS Apparently the recent inclusion of the European Buckthorn among foodplants in the Boston area has led to a distribution among more diverse habitats and to an increased population. West of the Appalachians this species (or a sibling) seems to prefer Redbud *(Cercis canadensis)*.

Eastern Pine Elfin *(Callophrys niphon)* Plate 8

SIZE = Banded Hairstreak.

SIMILAR SPECIES None.

IDENTIFICATION Stunningly banded with rich reddish-brown and black, the Eastern Pine Elfin can be mistaken for no other butterfly in our area.

HABITAT Most common in pine barrens, this elfin can also be found in deciduous woodlands with groves of White Pine.

RANGE Entire region. Also, north to Maine, west to Wisconsin, and south to Texas and Florida.

SPECIFIC LOCALITIES Soldier's Delight, MD; Washington & Old Dominion RR, VA.

FLIGHT PERIOD & ABUNDANCE **B:** C, mid April—mid June. **N:** U-LC, late April—mid June mainly in the Long Island pine barrens, R elsewhere. Max. 17, 5/15/88 Easthampton, Suffolk Co., NY. **P:** C, mid April—mid June, especially in NJ pine barrens. **W:** LU, mid April—mid June.

MAJOR FOODPLANT Hard pines; especially Pitch Pine *(Pinus rigida)* but also the soft pine, White Pine *(P. strobus)*.

COMMENTS It appears to be much less common in most areas with White Pine. Whether this is real and due to inefficient utilization of this foodplant or to fewer observations because the butterflies are flying at the tops of 50-ft. pines is not certain.

White M Hairstreak *(Parrhasius m-album)* Plate 10

SIZE ≥ Banded Hairstreak.

SIMILAR SPECIES Southern Hairstreak.

IDENTIFICATION With its flashing iridescent blue upper wings, the White M Hairstreak is a worthy representative of a largely tropical group. Unfortunately for us, its beautiful blue is usually only visible during its rapid and erratic flight. Below, the white spot near the base of the HW will separate this species from all our other hairstreaks except for an occasional Southern. Note the inwardly displaced orange and black spot on the HW. Southern Hairstreak has this spot at the usual position at the HW margin.

HABITAT In our area seems to prefer open brushy areas adjacent to oak woodlands, especially on hilltops.

RANGE   North (very rarely) to southeastern MA. Also, west to Iowa and south to Texas and Florida.

SPECIFIC LOCALITIES   West Rock Ridge State Park, CT; Hook Mt., NY; Higbee Beach WMA, Cape May Co., NJ; Washington & Old Dominion RR, VA.

FLIGHT PERIOD & ABUNDANCE   **B:** R, about seven records in the past ten years.   **N:** R, late April–mid May, late June–July, late Aug.–Sept. Max. 2, 4/26/86 Turkey Mtn., Yorktown, Westchester Co., NY.   **P:** R-U, late April–May, late June–July, late Aug.–Sept.   **W:** U, late April–May, late June–July, late Aug.–Sept.

MAJOR FOODPLANT   Oaks *(Quercus)*.

COMMENTS   This essentially southern species has been extending its range northward as have a number of other butterflies (and birds).

Gray Hairstreak *(Strymon melinus)* Plate 10

SIZE   = Banded Hairstreak.

SIMILAR SPECIES   Acadian Hairstreak, Southern Hairstreak.

IDENTIFICATION   A hairstreak with a true gray ground color below (rarely gray-brown). Note the prominent HW post-median line, white outwardly and black inwardly (often with reddish-orange inwards of the black).

HABITAT   Commonest in coastal dunes and scrub and disturbed open habitat generally, but can be encountered in almost any habitat. A strong hilltopper (males perch in the late afternoon and early evening).

RANGE   Entire region. Also, north to Maine (immigrant), west to California, and south to South America.

FLIGHT PERIOD & ABUNDANCE   **B:** C, mid April–May, late June–late July, Sept.   **N:** U-C, but U-R away from the coast late April–Oct. Max. 28, 9/7/86 Jamaica Bay Wildlife Refuge, NY.   **P:** C, Mid April–Oct. probably three broods.   **W:** C, early April–Oct. probably three broods.

MAJOR FOODPLANT   A great variety.

COMMENTS   Our sole representative of a large tropical genus. *Strymon* sun themselves with their wings open (dorsal basking) and thus allow a view of their topsides. All our other hairstreaks sun themselves by angling their closed wings perpendicularly to the sun's rays (lateral basking). Late in the summer, when this species becomes most common, it tends to spread more widely into suburban areas.

Blues

These gossamer-winged butterflies are, in fact, usually blue. In the Western Hemisphere, although some species are tropical, the Blues are essentially a northern temperate zone group with a number of species restricted to arctic areas. This was the group of butterflies most studied by the famous novelist Vladimir Nabokov. While similar in size and shape to the hairstreaks, they can almost always be distinguished on the wing by their less rapid, easy-to-follow flight and by their blue color.

Eastern Tailed Blue *(Everes comyntas)* Plate 11

SIZE   8/16 in.

SIMILAR SPECIES   Spring Azure.

IDENTIFICATION   A small weak-flying Blue. The "tails" are diagnostic but occasionally are worn. Both above and below note the orange spot by the HW tails. Can usually be distinguished from the Spring Azure by its weak, ground-hugging flight and its darker blue in males and some females and grayish color in other females.

HABITAT   Open area in general, especially disturbed areas.

RANGE   Entire region. Also, north to Maine, west to North Dakota, and south to Texas and Florida.

FLIGHT PERIOD & ABUNDANCE   **B:** C, early May–mid Sept.   **N:** C-A, late April–Oct. Max. 15, 5/15/87 Easthampton, Suffolk Co., NY; 44, 7/8/89 Meyer Sanctuary, Westchester, NY; 48, 9/10/89 Jamaica Bay Wildlife Refuge, NY.   **P:** A, mid April–Oct.   **W:** A, late April–Oct.

MAJOR FOODPLANT   Pea family.

Spring Azure *(Celastrina ladon)* Plate 11

SIZE   ≤ Banded Hairstreak.

SIMILAR SPECIES   Appalachian Azure, Eastern Tailed Blue.

IDENTIFICATION   Clear azure blue above (females with black borders). Unlike the Eastern Tailed Blue, there are no tails and no orange. Flight is usually higher and stronger than Eastern Tailed Blue. Below, ground color is pale with various dark markings. Three forms are found in the spring. "Lucia" has a dark mark in the center of the HW below and has a dark brown margin, "marginata" lacks the central mark but retains the marginal brown, "violacea" lacks both marks. The June brood, form "neglecta," looks similar to "violacea" but above tends to have much white overscaling, often visible in flight. The late summer brood is similar to "violacea."

HABITAT   Because a number of species are undoubtedly subsumed under this name (see Comments), "Spring Azures" are found in a wide variety of habitats, including woodlands in general, bogs, pine barrens, swamps, overgrown fields, and suburban yards.

RANGE   Entire region. Also, most of North America.

FLIGHT PERIOD & ABUNDANCE   **B:** A, April–May; C June–early Aug.   **N:** C-A, April–Sept. Max. 50, 4/26/87 Hook Mtn., Rockland Co., NY; 43, 6/20/87 Pound Ridge Reservation, NY; 50, 7/28/85 Jamaica Bay Wildlife Refuge, NY.   **P:** C, April–Sept.   **W:** C, April–Sept.

MAJOR FOODPLANT   Many.

COMMENTS   A bewildering complex of species and forms. We are still far from unraveling the whole story. Although recent authors have begun treating Appalachian Azure and Dusky Azure (not in our area) as distinct species, there are almost certainly other species throughout the United States being lumped as "Spring Azure." In our area there may be at least three species—the early spring "Spring Azure," appearing in the woodlands in April–May; a "violacea" type Azure appearing in the pine barrens in early May; and what should probably be called the **"Summer Azure"** (form "neglecta") first appearing in mid June (in NY, mid to late May in southern NJ) and then throughout the rest of the season. The "Summer Azure" is found in more open situations then the "Spring Azure." Although some merge our species with the Eurasian Holly Blue *(Celastrina argiolus)*, this is almost certainly incorrect.

Appalachian Azure *(Celastrina neglectamajor)* Plate 11

SIZE ≥ Banded Hairstreak.

SIMILAR SPECIES Spring Azure.

IDENTIFICATION A large azure, shining blue above. Below, ground color is grayish-white with black markings very reduced and pale. Most similar to "violacea" form of the Spring Azure but is larger. Above, lacks the whitish overscaling of the neglecta form of the Spring Azure. Best identified by an intimate knowledge of the local brood sequence of azures (see Comments).

HABITAT Rich transition zone woodlands and their borders.

RANGE Western CT southwest through all of our region northwest of the Fall Line. Also, south in the Appalachians.

SPECIFIC LOCALITIES Pound Ridge Reservation, NY.

FLIGHT PERIOD & ABUNDANCE **B:** X. **N:** LU, Max. 4, 5/29/89 Pound Ridge Reservation, NY. **P:** LC, mid May–mid June, mainly to the north and west. **W:** LU, mid May–mid June.

MAJOR FOODPLANT Black Cohosh *(Cimicifuga racemosa)* (personal communication from David Wright).

COMMENTS Only recently recognized as a distinct species, this species flies between the flights of the Spring and Summer Azures and is much less common.

Silvery Blue *(Glaucopsyche lygdamus)* Plate 40

SIZE ≥ Eastern Tailed Blue.

SIMILAR SPECIES None.

IDENTIFICATION Not normally part of our fauna. A small blue, below with a prominent post-median FW and HW band of large black spots (usually surrounded by some white).

RANGE Maine, northern New Hampshire, Vermont, and NY west to Alaska and south through most of the western U.S. Also found in the Appalachians and in other isolated populations. The Appalachian subspecies formerly occurred in the Philadelphia area. The northern subspecies has been consistently extending its range southward and may eventually reach our area (Dirig and Cryan, 1992).

FLIGHT PERIOD & ABUNDANCE **B:** X. **N:** X. **P:** H. May. **W:** X.

MAJOR FOODPLANT Wood Vetch *(Vicia caroliniana)* for the Appalachian subspecies and Tufted Vetch *(Vicia cracca)* for the northern subspecies.

COMMENTS More than most butterflies, the Silvery Blue seems to be capable of suddenly appearing in an area and establishing a colony. To be looked for in a wide variety of habitats. The northern subspecies flies in June.

Karner Blue *(Lycaeides melissa samuelis)* Plate 40

SIZE ≤ Banded Hairstreak
SIMILAR SPECIES Eastern Tailed Blue.
IDENTIFICATION Not normally part of our fauna. Note the submarginal orange band on both HW and FW below.
HABITAT Sandy barrens.
RANGE New Hampshire west to Wisconsin. Formerly occurred in the New York City area.
FLIGHT PERIOD & ABUNDANCE **B:** X. **N:** H. **P:** X. **W:** X.
FOODPLANT Lupine *(Lupinus perennis).*
COMMENTS The Albany pinebush is the major stronghold of this endangered butterfly.

Metalmarks *(Riodinidae)*

The metalmarks derive their name, naturally enough, from the metallic marks that are often present on their wings. The variety of wing size, wing shape, and wing pattern of this very large tropical group is truly amazing. Some resemble hairstreaks, some resemble skippers, some resemble crescents, and some resemble Helicons! The metalmarks are closely related to the lycaenids and, indeed, some scientists consider them members of the same family. Compared to many of the brilliantly colored and patterned tropical species, our one representative of this family is rather a plain Jane, but still handsome nonetheless.

Little Metalmark *(Calephelis virginiensis)* Plate 40

SIZE = Eastern Tailed Blue.
SIMILAR SPECIES Northern Metalmark.
IDENTIFICATION Not normally part of our fauna. Above, a lighter, richer red-brown than the Northern Metalmark. **Note the vertical reddish-brown and black stripes on the thorax.** Northern Metalmark has a solidly colored dark brown/black thorax.
HABITAT Sandy pine woodlands.
RANGE Southeastern U.S., north along the coast to central Virginia.
FLIGHT PERIOD & ABUNDANCE **B:** X. **N:** X. **P:** X. **W:** X. Has been recorded from Prince Georges Co., MD.
FOODPLANT Yellow thistle *(Cirsium horridulum).*

Northern Metalmark *(Calephelis borealis)* Plate 7

SIZE < Banded Hairstreak.
SIMILAR SPECIES None.
IDENTIFICATION A small orange-brown butterfly. During its slow and weak flight it displays a strong contrast between its dark upper surface and its bright or-

ange under surface. Almost always lands with its **wings held flat.** Note the metallic silvery post-median and marginal bands above.

HABITAT   Very local, usually on relatively open limestone ridges in woodlands near streams or ponds.

RANGE   Known colonies in western Litchfield and Fairfield Cos. in CT, one old record from Orange Co., NY, and well known from the area around Springdale, NJ. Four other colonies in southeastern PA now destroyed due to development. May occur in Dutchess and Orange Cos., NY, and possibly still in PA. Also, disjunct populations in the Appalachians and in Ohio and Indiana.

SPECIFIC LOCALITIES   One well-known Springdale colony is along the power-line cut north of Stickle Pond Rd. The Nature Conservancy is trying to preserve the Springdale and Fairfield Co., CT, sites. Other sites are not detailed because of collection pressure.

FLIGHT PERIOD & ABUNDANCE   **B:** X.   **N:** LR, late June–mid July. Known only from a few sites in the Springdale, NJ, area and in Fairfield Co., CT. Max. 30, 7/1/86 Springdale, NJ.   **P:** LR, probably extirpated, July if still extant.   **W:** X.

FOODPLANT   Round-leaved Ragwort *(Senecio obovatus)*.

COMMENTS   Search for this butterfly in the afternoon when it is much more active, ovipositing on the Ragwort and nectaring on Black-eyed Susans. In cloudy weather it will sometimes pitch under leaves and land, moth-like, upside down—a characteristic behavior of the Metalmark family.

Snout Butterflies *(Libytheidae)*

American Snout *(Libytheana carinenta)* Plate 20

SIZE   > Pearl Crescent.

SIMILAR SPECIES   None.

IDENTIFICATION   The extremely long snout (palps) is obvious on this mainly orange and brown butterfly. It is dimorphic below, either pale or dark and mottled. While its flight can be rapid, it often seems erratic and mothlike.

HABITAT   Thickets and brushy open woodlands with hackberries.

RANGE   North to the NY area. A rare stray to CT, RI, and MA. Also, west to California and south to Argentina.

SPECIFIC LOCALITIES   Conference House Park, NY; Higbee Beach WMA, Cape May Co., NJ.

FLIGHT PERIOD & ABUNDANCE   **B:** S, July–Sept.   **N:** LR, July–Sept. Max. 10, 7/19/87 Jamaica Bay Wildlife Refuge, NY.   **P:** LU, late June–July.   **W:** LU, late June–early Aug.

FOODPLANT   Hackberry *(Celtis)*.

COMMENTS   This butterfly is often enormously abundant in the southwest U.S. and Mexico, sometimes literally darkening the sky with millions of wings.

Nymphalidae, or *Brush-footed Butterflies*

The Nymphalids, sometimes called Brush-footed Butterflies because of the greatly reduced male forelegs, include many of our best known and most conspicuous butterflies. They constitute a very diverse collection of species and some consider a number of the groups included here (such as the Satyrs and the Milkweed Butterflies) as separate families. Quite a few of our species overwinter as adults, which may explain why these are the only butterflies in our region to exhibit classical migration patterns (south in the fall, north in the spring).

Gulf Fritillary *(Agraulis vanillae)* Plate 12

SIZE   ≤ Great Spangled Fritillary.

SIMILAR SPECIES   None.

IDENTIFICATION   A long-winged low flying Nymphalid. Orange above and heavily silvered below. Above, note the black-ringed white spots in the fore-wing cell. Wingbeats shallower than the Greater Fritillaries *(Speyeria).*

HABITAT   Open scrub, coastal areas, and gardens.

RANGE   A very rare immigrant into our region from the south. Recorded at least as far north as Long Island (but not for the past 20 years).

FLIGHT PERIOD & ABUNDANCE   **B:** X.   **N:** X.   **P:** S, Aug.–Sept.   **W:** X.

FOODPLANT   Passion Plants *(Passiflora).*

Variegated Fritillary *(Euptoieta claudia)* Plate 14

SIZE   > American Lady.

SIMILAR SPECIES   None.

IDENTIFICATION   A **dull, orange-brown** fritillary whose behavior and overall appearance is more similar to an American Lady than to the Greater Fritillaries. Our other fritillaries are brighter orange above. Below, it is unlike any of our other butterflies, with a pale, very wide, post-median band on the HW.

HABITAT   Open fields with flowers, coastal scrub.

RANGE   An immigrant into our entire region each year, becoming progressively less common farther north and inland. Also, north to Maine, west to Texas, and south to Argentina.

FLIGHT PERIOD & ABUNDANCE   **B:** R, irregular immigrant to the southeastern, portion of this subregion. June–Nov.   **N:** R, June–Nov. Fairly regular, but very variable immigrant. Max. 2, 7/2/88 Floyd Bennet Field, Brooklyn, NY.   **P:** U, June–Nov. very variable immigrant.   **W:** U, June–Nov.

MAJOR FOODPLANT   Violets *(Viola)* and Passion Plants *(Passiflora).*

Great Spangled Fritillary *(Speyeria cybele)* Plate 13

SIZE   1 11/16 in.

SIMILAR SPECIES   Aphrodite Fritillary, Atlantis Fritillary, Monarch, Viceroy.

IDENTIFICATION With its large size, bright orange color above, and silvered spots below, the Great Spangled Fritillary is one of our most conspicuous summer butterflies. Above, note the dark bands and spots on warm orange ground. Below, note the **wide cream-colored band** between post-median and marginal silvered spot-bands. Females are significantly larger and darker than the males.

HABITAT Open fields and meadows, roadsides, etc. Prefers moist areas on rich soil.

RANGE Entire region. Also, north to Canada, west to California, and south to Georgia.

FLIGHT PERIOD & ABUNDANCE **B:** C, late June–Sept. **N:** C-A, mid June–Sept. but rare on Long Island. Max. 148, 7/8/89 Pound Ridge Reservation, NY. **P:** C, but rare southern NJ, mid June–early Sept. **W:** C, late May–early Sept.

FOODPLANT Violets *(Viola)*.

COMMENTS Most late season individuals are females.

Aphrodite Fritillary *(Speyeria aphrodite)* Plate 13

SIZE ≤ Great Spangled Fritillary.

SIMILAR SPECIES Great Spangled Fritillary, Atlantis Fritillary.

IDENTIFICATION Above, note the black spot at the base of the FW (below the cell). Great Spangled Fritillary lacks this spot. Below, the dark cinnamon-brown ground color **extends past the post-median spot-band** so that the **cream-colored band is narrower** than in Great Spangled. The disc of the FW below is usually noticeably rosy.

HABITAT Prefers more wooded, cooler areas than the Great Spangled Fritillary but often occurs with it.

RANGE In our region, roughly north and west of the Fall Line. Also north to Canada, west to Montana, and south in the Appalachians.

FLIGHT PERIOD & ABUNDANCE **B:** U, early July–mid Sept., mostly west and north of Boston. **N:** R, but regular, late June–Sept. mostly north and west of NYC. Max. 8, 7/8/89 Pound Ridge Reservation, NY. **P:** R, to the north and west, July–Aug. **W:** R, to the north and west, July–Aug.

FOODPLANT Violets *(Viola)*.

COMMENTS Although very similar to the Great Spangled Fritillary, the Aphrodite is more beautiful in a subtle way. The silver below seems to flash with more contrast than in the Great Spangled Fritillary.

Regal Fritillary *(Speyeria idalia)* Plate 12

SIZE ≥ Great Spangled Fritillary.

SIMILAR SPECIES Great Spangled Fritillary, Aphrodite Fritillary.

IDENTIFICATION Distinctive. Above, HW extremely dark brown to black with white spots. Below, HW completely dark brown with white spots. Also note brownish-black body (Great Spangled and Aphrodite Fritillaries have orangish-brown bodies).

HABITAT Formerly, a variety of largely unnatural open situations, such as pastures and hayfields, usually wet.

RANGE   Formerly all of our region north of the Fall Line. Also north to Canada, west to Colorado, and south to North Carolina. Now, in the East, found only on Nantucket and Block Islands and perhaps a few colonies in northeastern and southeastern PA. The colony on Martha's Vineyard collapsed in 1987–88. Prairie states are this butterfly's last stronghold.

SPECIFIC LOCALITIES   Nantucket and Block Islands (gone as of 1992).

FLIGHT PERIOD & ABUNDANCE   **B:** LR, as of 1990, a few individuals remained on Nantucket, July–Aug.   **N:** LR, probably extirpated, until the 1970s it was widespread, until late 1980s found sparingly in Montauk area.   **P:** LR, as of 1990 a few individuals remained in a colony in southeastern PA. The area is being managed by the PA Natural Heritage Program.   **W:** H.

FOODPLANT   Violets *(Viola)*.

COMMENTS   Going, going, almost gone. This magnificent animal, one of our most spectacular butterflies, is endangered throughout its range and is on the verge of extinction in our region. Once found commonly throughout the northeast, it has declined drastically over the past 20 years and now clings to existence. The reasons for its decline are not clear. Dale Schweitzer of The Nature Conservancy thinks that changes in agricultural practices, reforestation, and development have played major roles.

Atlantis Fritillary *(Speyeria atlantis)* Plate 13

SIZE   < Great Spangled Fritillary.

SIMILAR SPECIES   Aphrodite Fritillary, Silver-bordered Fritillary.

IDENTIFICATION   Usually smaller than our other Greater Fritillaries. Solid black borders along most of the FWs distinguish it from most Aphrodite Fritillaries but some Aphrodites do have quite dark borders. The Atlantis Fritillary tends to have only a faint spot at the base of the FW above while the Aphrodite Fritillary has a strong spot. The Silver-bordered Fritillary is smaller and doesn't have brown on the inner portions of the FWs above. Below, unlike Aphrodite, dark ground color rarely extends much, if at all, past the post-median spot-band. Instead, outward of most of the post-median spots are small dark-brown spots that I refer to as **follow-spots.** Aphrodite may sometimes also have follow-spots but because the dark ground color surrounds these spots, they are not so obvious.

HABITAT   Open, mixed-growth woodlands, especially in glades or boggy areas.

RANGE   Southeast to our northwest borders. Probably not part of our fauna. Also, north to Canada and west to British Columbia.

FLIGHT PERIOD & ABUNDANCE   **B:** X.   **N:** X, but one report from Chester, Morris Co., NJ, 7/8/78.   **P:** X, but some strays reported mid June–early Aug. to the northwest. The possibility exists for confusion of this species with female Aphrodite Fritillaries.   **W:** X.

FOODPLANT   Violets *(Viola)*.

COMMENTS   Essentially a species of the north woods (where it is common), the Atlantis Fritillary is rare or absent from our region.

Silver-bordered Fritillary *(Boloria selene)* Plate 14

SIZE > Pearl Crescent.

SIMILAR SPECIES Meadow Fritillary, Harris' Checkerspot.

IDENTIFICATION Smaller than the Greater Fritillaries (genus *Speyeria*) but larger than the Crescents *(Phyciodes)*. Above, the **narrow black borders enclosing orange spots** (especially on the HW) separate this species from all of our others. Below distinctive. Note the median and marginal bands of silvered white.

HABITAT Bogs, wet meadows, marshes.

RANGE South to the northern portion of the Washington, D.C., area. Also, north to Canada and west to Alaska.

SPECIFIC LOCALITIES Babson Park, Wellesley, MA; Great Swamp WMA, RI.

FLIGHT PERIOD & ABUNDANCE **B:** C, early May–mid July, late July–late Aug., early Sept.–early Oct. **N:** LR, May, late June–July, mid Aug.–mid Sept. small colonies in Oxford Depot, Orange Co., NY, and Sussex Co., NJ. Max. 25, 9/1/90 Orange Co., NY. **P:** LU, May, late June–July, late Aug.–early Oct. **W:** H, formerly late June–late July, has declined greatly with no records since the early 1970s.

FOODPLANT Violets *(Viola)*.

COMMENTS Seems to have decreased drastically along with the Bronze Copper. Thirty years ago this species was common in the NY area. Seems to be doing better in the north and west.

Meadow Fritillary *(Boloria bellona)* Plate 14

SIZE > Pearl Crescent.

SIMILAR SPECIES Silver-bordered Fritillary.

IDENTIFICATION Dull orange-brown above. Flight is weak with stiff wingbeats. Note the lack of black borders above and the blunt forewing apex. Below, an indistinct smudged pattern, palest outside the post-median line.

HABITAT Low moist grassy fields.

RANGE Southeast to about the Fall Line. Also, north to Canada, west to British Columbia, and south (in the mountains) to North Carolina.

FLIGHT PERIOD & ABUNDANCE **B:** LU, mid May–early July, mid July–late Aug., early Sept.–early Oct., southwestern portion of the region. X, southeastern MA. **N:** A, late April–May, mid June–July, Aug.–mid Sept. north and west of NYC, not on Long Island. Max. 26, 5/20/89 Pound Ridge Reservation, NY; 200, 7/2/89 Bedford, Westchester, NY; 50, 8/27/88 North Salem, Westchester, NY. **P:** LC-LA, late April–mid May, mid June–mid July, late Aug.–mid Nov. **W:** LU-LC, late April–mid May, mid June–mid July, late Aug.–mid Nov.

FOODPLANT Violets *(Viola)*.

COMMENTS Has expanded its range and become much more common over the past 30 years. Perhaps this has contributed to the Silver-bordered Fritillaries' decline?

Silvery Checkerspot *(Chlosyne nycteis)* Plate 15

SIZE   > Pearl Crescent.

SIMILAR SPECIES   Harris' Checkerspot, Pearl Crescent.

IDENTIFICATION   A small, orange and black Nymphalid of woodland glades. Larger than the Pearl Crescent with **wider FW black borders above.** Below, note the very broad **white median band** on the HW. Also, if seen well, note the white crescent at HW margin and adjacent spot with a pale center. Above, very similar to Harris' Checkerspot. Silvery Checkerspot usually has more extensive orange markings. Note **black palps** (in Harris' Checkerspot, orange-brown).

HABITAT   From northern NJ north, open deciduous woodlands and edges, especially traprock ridges. Farther south, more common along stream edges in open country.

RANGE   Southeast to about the Fall Line. Also, north to Canada, west to North Dakota, and south to Texas and Georgia.

SPECIFIC LOCALITIES   West Rock Ridge State Park, CT; Van Cortlandt Park, NY; Great Falls National Park, MD/VA.

FLIGHT PERIOD & ABUNDANCE   **B:** LR, not recorded since 1985.   **N:** LC, mid June–early July. Max. 48, 6/24/89 Van Cortlandt Park, Bronx, NY.   **P:** LU, mid May–early June, mid July–early Sept.   **W:** LU, mid May–early June, mid July–Aug., along the Potomac River and to the northwest.

MAJOR FOODPLANT   Sunflowers *(Helianthus)* and other Compositae especially Woodland Sunflower *(H. divaricatus)* in the NYC area and Jerusalem Artichoke *(H. tuberosus)* in the Philadelphia area.

COMMENTS   Usually flies within 1 ft of the ground or shrubs. Often difficult to see the underside well.

Harris' Checkerspot *(Chlosyne harrisii)* Plate 15

SIZE   > Pearl Crescent.

SIMILAR SPECIES   Silvery Checkerspot, Pearl Crescent.

IDENTIFICATION   Below, one of our most striking butterflies. Alternating white and orange-brown bands make the Harris' Checkerspot a real show-off. Above, larger and darker than the Pearl Crescent. Usually blacker above than the Silvery Checkerspot. Note the **orange-brown palps** (in Silvery Checkerspot, black).

HABITAT   Wet shrubby meadows and marsh borders with its foodplant.

RANGE   South to northern NJ. Also north to Maine and west to Wisconsin.

SPECIFIC LOCALITIES   Broad Meadow Brook Sanctuary, MA; Wachusetts Meadow, MA; Ward Pound Ridge Reservation, NY; Troy Meadows, Parsippany, Morris Co., NJ.

FLIGHT PERIOD & ABUNDANCE   **B:** LU, June–early July.   **N:** LU, June, Max. 40, 6/14/89 Pound Ridge Reservation, NY.   **P:** X.   **W:** X.

FOODPLANT   Flat-topped White Aster *(Aster umbellatus).*

COMMENTS   Larvae are communal. Forms colonies that are often relatively short-lived. Often comes to damp sand.

Pearl Crescent *(Phyciodes tharos)* Plate 15

SIZE   11/16 in.

SIMILAR SPECIES   Silvery Checkerspot, Harris' Checkerspot.

IDENTIFICATION   Probably our commonest Nymphalid. Small, bright orange (when fresh) with a flight that is low to the ground and often involves gliding. Exact pattern can be quite variable. Males and females and different broods also differ to some degree. Note the orange above with extensive reticulate black markings. Below, note the brown smudge on HW border enclosing a pale crescent.

HABITAT   Widespread in open situations, fields, meadows, power-line cuts, suburbia, etc.

RANGE   Entire region. Also, north to Maine, west to Montana, south to Mexico and Florida.

FLIGHT PERIOD & ABUNDANCE   **B:** A, early May–early Oct.   **N:** A, May–June, July–Oct. Max. 120, 5/23/87 Goose Pond Park, Orange Co., NY; 537, 7/24/88 Christie Estate, Nassau, NY.   **P:** A, late April–early June, late June–early Aug., mid Aug.–mid Nov.   **W:** A, early April–early June, mid June–mid Aug., late Aug.–Nov.

MAJOR FOODPLANT   Asters.

Northern Crescent *(Phyciodes selenis)* Not illustrated

SIZE   ≥ Pearl Crescent.

SIMILAR SPECIES   Pearl Crescent, Tawny Crescent.

IDENTIFICATION   This northern species is very difficult to separate from the overwhelmingly more common and variable Pearl Crescent. The major identifiable difference is that males of this species have orange and black antennal clubs while the antennal clubs of male Pearl Crescents are entirely black. Unfortunately, female Pearl Crescents also have orange and black antennal clubs so that one must be certain that one is looking at a male. General differences are that Northern Crescents tend to be larger and have less prominent black reticulations on the HW above (creating a more open appearance). Females of this species tend to have the FW above post-median band a paler (more yellow) orange than the rest of the wing while Pearl Crescent females tend to have a more uniform orange color. It is probably best to study a whole colony before concluding that this species might be present.

HABITAT   In our area, most likely in barrens. Farther north, more general.

RANGE   Canada south to the edges of our area and, in the Appalachians, south to North Carolina, west to British Columbia and the Rocky Mountains. May occur in Sussex County, NJ, and the northwest border of our region in MA.

FLIGHT PERIOD & ABUNDANCE   **B:** LR? at northwest border. Probably mid June.   **N:** LR? Probably mid June if present.   **P:** X.   **W:** X.

MAJOR FOODPLANT   Asters.

Tawny Crescent *(Phyciodes batesii)* Plate 15

SIZE   = Pearl Crescent.

SIMILAR SPECIES   Pearl Crescent.

IDENTIFICATION This rare crescent, probably gone from our area, can be difficult to distinguish from the Pearl Crescent. It is usually significantly darker above. This is particularly true of the basal one-third of the FW where this species has a smudgy (or suffused) black appearance. Below, the HW markings are greatly reduced.

HABITAT Reported to be dry open grassland areas (often with *Andropogon*) with asters. In central NY populations occurred on limestone ledges while other populations were on shale barrens.

RANGE Central NY and PA west through southern Canada to Alberta. South in the Rockies to Colorado. Isolated populations in the Appalachians.

FLIGHT PERIOD & ABUNDANCE **B:** X. **N:** X. **P:** LR/H, mid June–early July. **W:** X.

MAJOR FOODPLANT Wavy-leaved Aster *(Aster undulatus)*.

COMMENTS This species has apparently declined drastically throughout the northeast. Reported to occur in the Philadelphia area by Shapiro in the 1960s, it was still present at Cresheim, Philadelphia Co., in 1980. No colonies are presently known and its current occurrence in our region is questionable.

Baltimore *(Euphydryas phaeton)* Plate 12

SIZE = American Lady.

SIMILAR SPECIES None.

IDENTIFICATION One of our most dazzling butterflies. Black, white, and orange. The underside is particularly arresting as this insect sits thrusting its orange face (palps) into the air.

HABITAT Usually marshes/wet meadows with Turtlehead but recently found in enormous concentrations in dry fields, feeding on English Plantain. In MA, this is now the habitat in which this species is most frequently found.

RANGE Southeast roughly to the Fall Line. Also, north to Maine, west to Wisconsin, and south to the northern Gulf States.

SPECIFIC LOCALITIES Patapsco County Park, MD; Catoctin Mountain Park, MD.

FLIGHT PERIOD & ABUNDANCE **B:** LC-LA, mid June–late July. **N:** LC, mid June–mid July. Max. 370, 7/3/88 Monroe, Orange Co. NY. **P:** LC, June–early July. **W:** LR-LU, early June–mid July, recent decline.

FOODPLANT Turtlehead *(Chelone glabra)* and English Plantain *(Plantago lanceolata)*.

COMMENTS Even very small areas with turtlehead will often have a population of Baltimores. Named for the orange and black colors of Lord Baltimore.

Question Mark *(Polygonia interrogationis)* Plate 16

SIZE > American Lady.

SIMILAR SPECIES Eastern Comma.

IDENTIFICATION A medium-sized orangish butterfly of the woods and nearby open areas. Flight is rapid but usually not very directional, often returning to same area. Above, the only anglewing *(Polygonia)* with a small black horizontal bar in the subapical FW. Also note the violaceous margin of the HW. Below, note the silvered "question-mark." Above, the black or "summer" form has significant black on the HWs while the orange or "fall" form is mainly orangish-brown. These forms correspond largely, but not completely, with the summer and fall broods. There are also two forms below, either fairly unicolored or heavily mottled. The Question Mark can usually be told from the Eastern Comma, even on the wing, by its generally larger size and more robust flight with slower wingbeats.

HABITAT Woodlands and adjacent open areas. More wide ranging than the Eastern Comma.

RANGE Entire region. Also, north to Canada, west to North Dakota, and south to northern Mexico and Florida.

FLIGHT PERIOD & ABUNDANCE **B:** U, late May–Nov. Occasionally overwintering. **N:** U, but C-A migrating south along the coast in late Sept. and early Oct. (Most individuals migrate). Overwintering adults in early spring, new broods in late May and again in late Aug. Success of overwintering adults depends on the severity of the winter. Max. 800, 9/25/81 Riis Park, Brooklyn, NY. **P:** C, overwintering adults in early spring, new broods in late May and again in late Aug. **W:** C, overwintering adults in early spring, new broods in late May and again in late Aug.

MAJOR FOODPLANT Nettles *(Urtica,)* Elm family (Ulmaceae), Hackberry *(Celtis)*, and others.

COMMENTS Late in the fall Question Marks move south along the coast in a dramatic migration. In the spring, these individuals move back north in a migration that isn't as dramatic as the fall's but is noticeable nonetheless. It is these individuals who are largely responsible for repopulating our region each season. Some do overwinter in our region but their numbers are generally low and vary with the severity of the winters.

Eastern Comma *(Polygonia comma)* Plates 16 & 17

SIZE ≤ American Lady.

SIMILAR SPECIES Question Mark.

IDENTIFICATION Note the size, generally smaller than the Question Mark. Above, very similar to the Question Mark, but it **lacks the horizontal black, subapical spot** of that species. Below, note silvered "comma." Like the Question Mark there is an orange above "fall" form and a "summer" form with black on the HW.

HABITAT More closely restricted to woodlands than the Question Mark, but found in a wide variety of situations.

RANGE Entire region. Also, north to Maine, west to North Dakota, and south to Texas and Florida.

FLIGHT PERIOD & ABUNDANCE **B:** U, late March–Nov. **N:** R-U, late March–Nov. Max. 6, 7/8/89 Ward Pound Ridge Reservation, NY. **P:** U, new broods in late May and late Aug. **W:** U, June–July.

MAJOR FOODPLANT Elms and Nettles.

Green Comma *(Polygonia faunus)* Plate 17

SIZE ≤ American Lady.

SIMILAR SPECIES Eastern Comma, Gray Comma.

56

IDENTIFICATION   Wings usually more jagged than other Anglewings. Above, note the **two black spots** on the inner margin of the FW. Eastern Comma and Gray Comma usually have only the bottom spot or if the top spot is present it is faint. In our region, where the occurrence of the Green Comma is very marginal, this mark shouldn't be used to make a positive ID but rather as an alarm bell indicating the importance of examining the butterfly below. Also note black HW border with yellowish spots. Below, note the **bluish-green sub-marginal band and the comma mark with the thick hooked end.**

HABITAT   Canadian zone forests.

RANGE   Southeast to the borders of our region south to the Philadelphia area. Also, north to Canada, west to Alaska, and south in the Appalachians.

FLIGHT PERIOD & ABUNDANCE   **B:** X, stray? along the northwest margins.   **N:** X, but has occurred in Dutchess Co., NY.   **P:** R, stray? Reported from Montgomery & Chester Cos. Aug.–Sept.   **W:** X.

MAJOR FOODPLANT   Willows *(Salix)* and Birches *(Betula).*

Gray Comma *(Polygonia progne)* Plate 17

SIZE   ≤ American Lady.

SIMILAR SPECIES   Eastern Comma, Green Comma, Compton Tortoiseshell.

IDENTIFICATION   Above, very similar to Eastern Comma. HW black border is usually broader than on other Anglewings ("summer" form Commas have extensive black). Below, **dark gray and often heavily striated. Comma is thin and tapers at both ends.** Very similar below to the much larger Compton Tortoiseshell. Wingbeats slower than other Commas.

HABITAT   Mainly rich deciduous woodlands with northern elements.

RANGE   Southeast to central Mass, southeastern NY, northern NJ, and the Philadelphia area. Also, north to Maine, west to British Columbia, and south in the Appalachians.

FLIGHT PERIOD & ABUNDANCE   **B:** X, but has been recorded along the northwest margin.   **N:** R, stray? not recorded most years. Most recent record 10/15/88 Oakwood Cemetery, Mt. Kisco, Westchester, NY.   **P:** LR, two broods, June and October. Most records from October.   **W:** X.

MAJOR FOODPLANT   Currants *(Ribes).*

COMMENTS   As is the case with other Commas, the summer brood of the Gray Comma has more extensive black borders on the HW above than does the fall brood. The American Museum of Natural History, in New York, has a fair number of specimens of this species from Hunterdon Co., NJ, from the late 1950s. This suggests that, like other anglewings, this species might undergo periodic population increases; or that Hunterdon Co. is a particularly good area to look for this species; or that this species is often overlooked because it is most common in woodlands in October when butterfliers become rare.

Compton Tortoiseshell *(Nymphalis vau-album)* Plate 18

SIZE   < Mourning Cloak.

SIMILAR SPECIES   Gray Comma.

IDENTIFICATION   The aristocratic and boldly patterned reddish-brown, black, and orange Compton Tortoiseshell often glides through the woodlands, seemingly surveying its realm. Above note the white spot on the HW. Below, dark gray and heavily striated. Often comes to tree sap. The Gray Comma, similar below, is much smaller.

HABITAT   A wide variety of wooded situations.

RANGE   South to about the Philadelphia area. Also, north to Maine and west to Washington State.

FLIGHT PERIOD & ABUNDANCE   **B:** U, hibernators in late March, new brood early July.   **N:** R-U, hibernators in late March, new brood late June. Max. 10, 3/13/90 Bedford, Westchester Co., NY.   **P:** R, immigrant from the north. Hibernators in early spring, new brood late June.   **W:** S, two records in recent years.

MAJOR FOODPLANT   Birches *(Betula)* and Willows *(Salix)*.

COMMENTS   Subject to cyclical population explosions and range expansions, the Compton Tortoiseshell has been present continuously in the NYC area since at least 1981. This follows A. M. Shapiro's statement in 1972 that it was "perhaps extinct in the entire New York metropolitan area." Recently, individuals even were seen in southern NJ (Port Norris), and Calvert Co., MD!

Mourning Cloak *(Nymphalis antiopa)* Plate 18

SIZE   1 10/16 in.

SIMILAR SPECIES   None.

IDENTIFICATION   Unmistakable. A large, dark Nymphalid. Dark brown above with yellow borders and blue submarginal spots. Below, dark, striated brown with pale yellow borders. Often glides in flight.

HABITAT   One of our most widespread butterflies. Can be found in almost any habitat including, woodlands, field, suburbs, and downtown Manhattan!

RANGE   Entire region. Also, all 49 continental states, Canada, and Mexico.

FLIGHT PERIOD & ABUNDANCE   **B:** C, hibernators on warm winter days, new brood in early July. Adults found in Sept. probably are reappearing aestivators but there seems to be at least a partial second brood.   **N:** C, overwintering adults in early spring, new brood in late June. Aestivators and second brood in late summer–fall. Max. 1500, 9/25/81 Riis Park, Brooklyn, NY.   **P:** U-C, overwintering adults in early spring, new brood in mid June. Aestivators and second brood in late summer–fall.   **W:** U-C, overwintering adults in early spring, new brood in mid June. Aestivators and second brood in late summer–fall.

MAJOR FOODPLANT   Willows *(Salix)* and many other trees and shrubs.

COMMENTS   To some extent, migrates south in the fall, especially along the beaches.

Milbert's Tortoiseshell *(Nymphalis milberti)* Plate 18

SIZE   < American Lady.

SIMILAR SPECIES   None.

IDENTIFICATION   This colorful northern Nymphalid has bright orange and yellow FW borders above. Below, dark, striated brown with a pale **submarginal** band. Mourning Cloak is much larger and has pale marginal band.

HABITAT   Open fields, usually moist, near woodlands.

RANGE   Southeast to about central MA, northwestern CT, extreme northwestern NJ, south to the Philadelphia area. Sometimes strays southeastward. Also, north to Maine and west to Alaska.

FLIGHT PERIOD & ABUNDANCE   **B:** U, at northwest margins, otherwise R, west and north of Boston. Overwintering adults early April, new broods in mid June and early Sept.   **N:** X. To be looked for in northwestern Orange Co.   **P:** R, stray, absent most years, overwintering adults early spring, new broods in mid June and late Aug.   **W:** X.

MAJOR FOODPLANT   Nettles *(Urtica).*

COMMENTS   The range of this species seems to have contracted significantly this century since it formerly occurred more commonly to the southeast.

Small Tortoiseshell *(Nymphalis urticae)* Plate 18

SIZE   < American Lady.

SIMILAR SPECIES   Milbert's Tortoiseshell.

IDENTIFICATION   Bright orange above with **black and yellow stripes perpendicular to the FW margin.** Note black spots and orange ground FW above. Milbert's Tortoiseshell has orange spots on black ground.

HABITAT   Open areas.

RANGE   Most of Eurasia.

FLIGHT PERIOD & ABUNDANCE   **B:** X.   **N:** S, recorded three times in recent years: Aug. 1988 and Aug. 1991 at Jamaica Bay Wildlife Refuge and Oct. 1990 in Riverside Park, Manhattan.   **P:** X.   **W:** X.

MAJOR FOODPLANT   Stinging Nettle *(Urtica dioica),* a European plant now found throughout our area.

COMMENTS   This well-known and highly successful Eurasian species is known to aestivate and hibernate in dark crevices and holes. It is not unimaginable that a gravid female entered an airplane somewhere in Europe and was transported to Kennedy Airport in NY. Thus, given the spate of recent sightings, it is probable that a nascent population exists in the NY area (Glassberg, 1992).

American Lady *(Vanessa virginiensis)* Plate 19

SIZE   1 2/16.

SIMILAR SPECIES   Painted Lady.

IDENTIFICATION   A medium-sized dull-orange butterfly with white spots on the black upper FW apex. Below, note the distinctive cobweb pattern on the HW and the pink patch on the FW.

HABITAT   Open spaces, including fields, meadows, roadsides, and coastal dunes.

RANGE   Entire region. Also, north to Maine, west to California, and south to Mexico and Florida.

FLIGHT PERIOD & ABUNDANCE   **B:** C, early May–Oct.   **N:** C, mid April–Oct. Max.

100, 5/3/86 Jamaica Bay Wildlife Refuge, NY. **P:** C, April–early June, late
June–Aug., late Aug.–early Nov. **W:** C, April–early June, late June–Aug.,
late Aug.–Nov.

MAJOR FOODPLANT   Many Compositae including Pearly Everlasting *(Anaphalis margaritacea).*

COMMENTS   Migrates south in the fall, north in the spring; sometimes in numbers.

Painted Lady *(Vanessa cardui)* Plate 19

SIZE   ≥ American Lady.

SIMILAR SPECIES   American Lady.

IDENTIFICATION   This uncommon butterfly is generally larger than the American
Lady with a pinkish suffusion (American Lady is more orange). The median
black FW band is much bolder (in fact, the entire gestalt of the butterfly is
more dramatic). Above, the American Lady has a white spot on the FW orange ground (sometimes small) that the Painted Lady lacks. Below, note four,
roughly equal eye-spots on the HW. The American Lady has two large eye-
spots.

HABITAT   Can be encountered in any type of open habitat.

RANGE   A permanent resident of Mexico, the Painted Lady moves north in the
early spring to colonize much of North America. The abundance of the butterfly in the north varies tremendously from year to year.

FLIGHT PERIOD & ABUNDANCE   **B:** R, variable immigrant. **N:** R-U, variable immigrant. Max. 41, 8/11/91 Bronx Botanical Garden, Bronx, NY. **P:** R-U,
May–Oct. variable immigrant. **W:** R-C, May–Oct. variable immigrant.

MAJOR FOODPLANT   Thistles and many other species.

COMMENTS   The summer of 1991 saw this species become common throughout
our region (and farther north). Finding Painted Ladies nectaring on Buddleia
blossoms in mid-town Manhattan was certainly a new experience.

Red Admiral *(Vanessa atalanta)* Plate 20

SIZE   = American Lady.

SIMILAR SPECIES   None.

IDENTIFICATION   A rapidly flying (often), medium-sized dark Nymphalid. The
reddish-orange bands of both FWs and HWs above make confusion of this
species with any other very difficult.

HABITAT   Open situations with flowers, including fields, beaches, suburbia, and
especially moist meadows near woodlands.

RANGE   Entire region. Also, 48 contiguous states south to Central America.

FLIGHT PERIOD & ABUNDANCE   **B:** C, late April–Oct. **N:** C-A, mid April–Oct.
Max. 6000, 9/25/81 Riis Park, Brooklyn, NY. **P:** C-A, April–Oct. **W:** C,
April–Oct.

MAJOR FOODPLANT   Nettles *(Urtica).*

COMMENTS   Can be strongly migratory. Tens of thousands streamed north
through the New York area in the spring and summer of 1990.

Common Buckeye *(Junonia coenia)* Plate 20

SIZE = American Lady.

SIMILAR SPECIES None.

IDENTIFICATION A brown Nymphalid with **prominent eye-spots** along the margins of both wings and **two orange bars** in the FW cell.

HABITAT Open fields, beaches, and many disturbed situations. Especially fond of sandy areas and paths where it can rest on the ground.

RANGE Entire region as an immigrant. Also, north (rarely) to Maine, west to California, and south to Mexico.

FLIGHT PERIOD & ABUNDANCE **B:** R-U, variable immigrant, June–Oct. **N:** R-C, May–Oct., most common along the coast. Max. 66, 8/26/90 Marine Park, Brooklyn, NY. **P:** C, mid May–Nov. **W:** C, April–Nov.

MAJOR FOODPLANT Gerardias *(Gerardia)*, Toadflax *(Linaria)*, and Plantain *(Plantago)*.

White Peacock *(Anartia jatrophae)* Plate 40

SIZE = American Lady.

SIMILAR SPECIES None.

IDENTIFICATION Not normally a part of our fauna, this essentially subtropical species is basically an off-white color with orange-brown borders.

HABITAT Usually occurs in weedy sites near water. If it strays into our region, it could appear in most any habitat, although it is probably most likely in sandy areas along the coast.

RANGE South Carolina through Florida. Also south from Texas through Mexico and the Caribbean to Venezuela.

FLIGHT PERIOD & ABUNDANCE **B:** X. **N:** X. **P:** X. **W:** X.

COMMENTS Common in its native haunts, the showy White Peacock rarely strays northward. However it has been recorded from both southern NJ and from MA!

Red-spotted Purple, White Admiral

Long considered separate species (and still so regarded by some), the strikingly different Red-spotted Purple and White Admiral hybridize and intergrade along a very broad zone stretching from southern Maine south to MA and southwest through much of New York State and Pennsylvania. In this blend zone, all possible combinations of the traits of the two subspecies can be found. Most, if not all, of the "White Admiral" types found in our region will be hybrids. Because their appearances and distributions are so different, I give each of these a separate treatment, operationally calling individuals with any white banding "White Admirals."

Red-spotted Purple *(Limenitis arthemis astyanax)* Plate 21

SIZE = Mourning Cloak.

SIMILAR SPECIES Pipevine Swallowtail.

IDENTIFICATION   This magnificent butterfly is common in the south, less so in the north. Above, black with extensive iridescent blue. It has no tails. Below **orange spots** both in a marginal band and **at the base of the wings.** Pipevine Swallowtail has tails and lacks the spots at the wing base.

HABITAT   Rich moist woodlands are preferred but the Red-spotted Purple is widely distributed and often found in suburban areas.

RANGE   Entire region. Also, west to about the Mississippi and south to Florida.

FLIGHT PERIOD & ABUNDANCE   **B:** U, early June–early Sept.   **N:** U, mid May–June, July, Sept. Max. 10, 6/19/87 Manorville, Suffolk Co., NY.   **P:** U-C, late May–June, mid July–early Aug., mid Aug.–Sept.   **W:** C, mid May–June, mid July–mid Aug., late Aug.–early Oct.

MAJOR FOODPLANT   Cherry *(Prunus)* and others.

COMMENTS   Often attracted to mud puddles and animal feces.

White Admiral *(Limenitis arthemis arthemis)* Plate 21

SIZE   = Mourning Cloak.

SIMILAR SPECIES   None.

IDENTIFICATION   The white bands on the velvet-black ground color are striking and give rise to the alternate name Banded Purple. The alternately gliding and flapping flight usually affords an opportunity for good views.

HABITAT   Northern forests, especially along watercourses, and adjacent open areas.

RANGE   Southeast to the northwestern limits of our area south to the Philadelphia area. Also, north to Canada and west to Alaska.

FLIGHT PERIOD & ABUNDANCE   **B:** U, to the northwest, June–Aug.   **N:** X, but has been recorded to the northwest.   **P:** R, to the northwest.   **W:** X.

MAJOR FOODPLANT   Birch *(Betula)*, Poplar *(Populus)*, and many others.

Viceroy *(Limenitis archippus)* Plate 21

SIZE   ≤ Mourning Cloak.

SIMILAR SPECIES   Monarch.

IDENTIFICATION   Fairly large and **uniformly orange.** Distinguished from the Monarch by the black post-median band on the HW. The Viceroy can be readily separated from the Monarch in flight by its smaller size and less powerful wingbeats. It often glides on flat wings while the Monarch "sails" with its wings in a "V."

HABITAT   Open areas adjacent to watercourses or wet areas with willows.

RANGE   Entire region. Also, north to Maine, west to Washington State, and south to Mexico and Florida.

FLIGHT PERIOD & ABUNDANCE   **B:** C, late May–mid July, late July–early Sept.   **N:** C, but R-U on LI. June, July–mid Aug., late Aug.–early Oct. Max. 14, 7/19/89 Tottenville, Staten Island, NY.   **P:** C-A, mid May–mid June, July–early Aug., mid Aug.–mid Sept.   **W:** C, mid May–mid June, July–early Aug., mid Aug.–early Oct.

MAJOR FOODPLANT   Willows *(Salix)*, especially small shrubby species.

62

COMMENTS   Well known as a mimic of the Monarch. For a long time it was thought that birds avoided eating the palatable Viceroy because they confused it with the distasteful Monarch. Recent evidence suggests that, at least in Florida, the Viceroy is also distasteful to birds. Presumably, a greater number of similar-looking, unpalatable individuals in an area results in a faster learning curve for birds, sparing more butterflies.

Hackberry Emperor *(Asterocampa celtis)* Plate 19

SIZE   = American Lady. Females significantly larger than males.

SIMILAR SPECIES   Tawny Emperor.

IDENTIFICATION   A nervous, rapidly flying Nymphalid that often appears quite pale in flight as the sun flashes off the creamy gray-brown undersurface. Above, dark brown. On both surfaces note the **white subapical FW spots** and the **black FW marginal eye-spot.** Tawny Emperor is a warm orange-brown on both surfaces and lacks the white subapical spots and the black FW eyespot.

HABITAT   Closely tied to Hackberry Trees.

RANGE   Northeast to the Springfield, MA, area and central CT and then south through the rest of our region. Also, west to Arizona and south to Mexico and Florida.

SPECIFIC LOCALITIES   Forest Park, Springfield, MA., West Rock Ridge State Park, CT; Inwood Hill Park, NY; Conference House Park, NY; Higbee Beach WMA, Cape May Co., NJ.

FLIGHT PERIOD & ABUNDANCE   **B:** X, but LU-LR in the Springfield area.   **N:** LU-LC, mid June–mid July, mid Aug.–mid Sept. Max. 43, 7/8/90 Tottenville, Staten Island, NY.   **P:** LU, July, late Aug.–early Sept. LC-LA southern NJ mid June–mid July, late July–Sept.   **W:** LU-LC, June, mid Aug.–early Sept.

FOODPLANT   Hackberry *(Celtis occidentalis).*

COMMENTS   An infrequent flower visitor, the Hackberry Emperor can, not surprisingly, most often be found flying around the Hackberry Tree. When not on Hackberry Trees they often alight on people in search of the salts in our perspiration.

Tawny Emperor *(Asterocampa clyton)* Plate 19

SIZE   = American Lady. Females significantly larger than males.

SIMILAR SPECIES   Hackberry Emperor, Painted Lady (below).

IDENTIFICATION   Warm orange-brown both above and below. Note the prominent series of eye-spots on the HW on both surfaces. Hackberry Emperor has white spots above and is much paler and grayer below. Painted Lady is much paler below.

HABITAT   Closely tied to Hackberry Trees but seems to disperse more than Hackberry Emperor.

RANGE   Northeast to the Springfield, MA, area and central CT and then south through the rest of our region. Also, west to Wisconsin and south to Mexico and Florida.

SPECIFIC LOCALITIES   Forest Park, Springfield, MA; Conference House Park, NY.

FLIGHT PERIOD & ABUNDANCE   **B:** X, but LR in the Springfield area.   **N:** LR-LU, July, mid Aug.–mid Sept. Max. 7, Mt. Pleasant, Westchester, NY.   **P:** LU, late May–Sept.   **W:** LR, June, Aug.–Sept.

FOODPLANT   Hackberry *(Celtis occidentalis).*

Satyrs or Browns (subfamily *Satyrinae*)

The satyrs are a group of brown, medium-sized butterflies with a characteristic jerky flight. They tend to remain low and weave among the grasses or sedges which are their larval food plants. All of our species have eye-spots.

Northern Pearly Eye *(Enodia anthedon)* Plate 22

SIZE   > Little Wood Satyr, < Common Wood Nymph.

SIMILAR SPECIES   Appalachian Brown.

IDENTIFICATION   A large, dark, woodland satyr. Below, note the prominent HW submarginal eye-spots that are **surrounded as a group, by one continuous pale white line.** Appalachian Brown is much paler brown and has HW submarginal eye-spots that are **individually surrounded by white circles.**

HABITAT   Prefers the edges and glades of rocky deciduous woodlands in the vicinity of brooks and other water sources.

RANGE   Southeast to about the Fall Line. Very rare or absent on Cape Cod and Long Island. Also, north to Maine, west to North Dakota, and south to Alabama.

SPECIFIC LOCALITIES   Blue Hills Reservation, MA; Great Falls National Park, MD/VA.

FLIGHT PERIOD & ABUNDANCE   **B:** U, late June–mid Sept.   **N:** U, late June–July, partial brood late Aug. Max. 3, 7/8/89 Meyer Sanctuary, Westchester Co., NY.   **P:** R, July. Not in central and southern NJ.   **W:** R-U, June and Aug., especially along the Potomac River.

FOODPLANT   Grasses.

COMMENTS   Look for this elegant Satyr near the end of the day in the dappled light of dirt roads and trails through rocky damp woodlands. Often alights on tree trunks with its head facing downward.

Eyed Brown *(Satyrodes eurydice)* Plate 22

SIZE   > Little Wood Satyr.

SIMILAR SPECIES   Appalachian Brown, Little Wood Satyr.

IDENTIFICATION   See discussion under Appalachian Brown.

HABITAT   Very wet meadows/marshes with sedges.

RANGE   South to southern NJ and northern Delaware where it is very rare. Also, north to Canada and west to about North Dakota.

SPECIFIC LOCALITIES   Lynnfield Marsh, MA; Pound Ridge Reservation, Westches-
ter, NY.
FLIGHT PERIOD & ABUNDANCE   **B:** LC, late June–mid Sept.   **N:** LR, late June–
July. Max. 17, 7/8/89 Cross River Town Park, Westchester, NY.   **P:** LU,
June–early Aug.   **W:** X.
MAJOR FOODPLANT   Sedges *(Carex)*.

Appalachian Brown *(Satyrodes appalachia)* Plate 22

SIZE   > Little Wood Satyr.
SIMILAR SPECIES   Eyed Brown, Northern Pearly Eye, Little Wood Satyr.
IDENTIFICATION   Our two Browns are easily distinguished from the Little Wood
Satyr by their larger size and large HW eye-spots below. They can be distinguished from the Northern Pearly Eye by their paler more subdued coloration
and below, by the presence of a white outer ring around each HW eye-spot.
Separating Appalachian Brown from Eyed Brown can be tricky. Although the
preferred habitats differ, wet wooded habitats tend to intergrade with wet
open habitats so that often both species can be found on the same patch of
land. Usually, Appalachian Browns are darker; have more jagged post-
median lines on the FW and HW below; and have the FW eye-spots below of
unequal size and intensity (at least one of the middle two usually being
smaller and paler). These marks sometimes fail. The best marks are these: (1)
Below, note the HW post-basal line. Appalachian has this line straight, Eyed
has an inward directed "tooth" at the 2nd vein; (2) Below, Appalachian has
lowest FW eye-spot surrounded by a white ring thus making this spot look
like a bull's eye. Eyed has this (and the other FW spots as well) only partially
surrounded by white—thus looking like a pea pod.
HABITAT   Wet wooded situations adjacent to open areas.
RANGE   Entire region. Also, west to Wisconsin and south to Alabama and Florida.
SPECIFIC LOCALITIES   Piney Run County Park, MD.
FLIGHT PERIOD & ABUNDANCE   **B:** U, early July–mid Aug.   **N:** C, mid June–early
Aug., partial brood late Aug. Max. 9, 7/9/88 Ward Pound Ridge Reservation,
NY.   **P:** LC, June–mid Aug.   **W:** LC, June–mid Aug.
MAJOR FOODPLANT   Sedges *(Carex)*.

Gemmed Satyr *(Cyllopsis gemma)* Plate 23

SIZE   < Little Wood Satyr.
SIMILAR SPECIES   Little Wood Satyr.
IDENTIFICATION   A small, inconspicuous Satyr. When seen well, the HW gray
patch enclosing four marginal, compressed eye-spots, is distinctive.
HABITAT   Wet grassy areas in woodlands, especially in pine flats.
RANGE   In our area, an old report from northeastern MD and a more recent one
from Fairfax Co., VA. Also, west to Oklahoma and Texas and south to Florida.
FLIGHT PERIOD & ABUNDANCE   **B:** X.   **N:** X.   **P:** X.   **W:** X, but two reports.
FOODPLANT   Grasses.

Carolina Satyr *(Hermeuptychia hermes sosybius)* Plate 23

SIZE < Little Wood Satyr.

SIMILAR SPECIES Little Wood Satyr.

IDENTIFICATION A small southern Satyr, barely entering our area. Below, very similar to the Little Wood Satyr but note the HW cell-end bar. FW lacks the lower large eye-spot of Little Wood Satyr. Above, uniform dark brown, lacking the eye-spots of the Little Wood Satyr.

HABITAT A variety of wooded habitats in the south. In southern NJ found in various shaded bogs.

RANGE North to southeastern MD and southern NJ. Also, west to Oklahoma and south to South America and Florida.

SPECIFIC LOCALITIES In 1990, found at Flag Ponds Nature Park, Calvert Co., MD.

FLIGHT PERIOD & ABUNDANCE **B:** X. **N:** X. **P:** H, July—early Aug., southern NJ. **W:** LR, July, Sept.—early Oct., Calvert and Charles Cos., MD.

FOODPLANT Grasses.

COMMENTS Colonies in our area may be transient. Not found in southern NJ recently.

Georgia Satyr *(Neonympha areolatus)* Plate 23

SIZE = Little Wood Satyr.

SIMILAR SPECIES None.

IDENTIFICATION A constantly bobbing Satyr of bogs and boggy pine woods. When it can be seen, the orange-brown ring surrounding the HW below post-median eye-spots is distinctive.

HABITAT In our area, restricted to open bogs in pine barrens.

RANGE Southern NJ. Also, southeastern VA south to Florida and west to Texas.

SPECIFIC LOCALITIES Lakehurst Bog, NJ.

FLIGHT PERIOD & ABUNDANCE **B:** X. **N:** X. **P:** LC, late June—mid July, NJ pine barrens. Partial second brood possible in Sept. **W:** X.

MAJOR FOODPLANT Probably sedges although grasses have also been reported.

Mitchell's Satyr *(Neonympha mitchellii)* Plate 23

SIZE = Little Wood Satyr.

SIMILAR SPECIES Georgia Satyr.

IDENTIFICATION Note the presence of **round, post-median eye-spots on both the FW and the HW.** Georgia Satyr lacks the FW spots and has the HW spots much more oval and elongated.

HABITAT **Alkaline** open bogs (fens).

RANGE Until the late 1980s occurred in northern NJ. Also, isolated colonies in North Carolina, Ohio, Indiana, and Michigan.

SPECIFIC LOCALITIES None now known. Formerly at a number of sites in Sussex Co., NJ.

FLIGHT PERIOD & ABUNDANCE **B:** X. **N:** formerly LR, almost certainly extirpated. **P:** X. **W:** X.

FOODPLANT Sedges *(Carex).*

COMMENTS This is one of the real horror stories of American butterflies. This beautiful and mysterious little butterfly was literally hunted to extinction. A group of greedy, immoral individuals returned day after day, year after year, to the few, very small fens where it was found. They illegally collected and killed these animals for their own "amusement" and in some cases profit. In 1991 the subspecies *N. m. mitchellii* was listed as federally endangered due to similar problems throughout its range.

Little Wood Satyr *(Megisto cymela)* Plate 23

SIZE   13/16 in.

SIMILAR SPECIES   Carolina Satyr.

IDENTIFICATION   A medium-brown butterfly that "bounces" along the tops of the grasses, shrubs, and just inside the canopy of small trees. Its characteristic flight, color, and size make it immediately recognizable on the wing. This is good because it rarely rests. When it does, note the two large eye-spots on each wing both above and below.

HABITAT   Most at home in the grassland/woodland interface, this Satyr may be found in the middle of quite large open field or (more rarely) deep in the woods.

RANGE   Entire region. Also, north to Maine, west to North Dakota, and south to Texas and Florida.

FLIGHT PERIOD & ABUNDANCE   **B:** A, mid May–early July; U, mid July–mid Aug.   **N:** A, mid May–June. Max. 400, 5/28/86 Purchase, Westchester Co., NY; C, late June–July. Max. 100, 6/28/87 Goose Pond Park, Orange Co., NY.   **P:** C, mid May–June; U, early July–mid Aug.   **W:** C, mid May–June; U, late June–mid Aug.

FOODPLANT   Grasses.

COMMENTS   The "second brood" may be a separate species that is phenotypically indistinguishable from the spring species. Although the spring "brood" is usually more abundant, there are localities in the New York area in which only the summer "brood" appears.

Common Ringlet *(Coenonympha tullia)* Plate 23

SIZE   < Little Wood Satyr.

SIMILAR SPECIES   Little Wood Satyr.

IDENTIFICATION   A small, **very pale,** Satyr with an orange-red flush that bounces through the grasses, continually stopping to nectar at flowers (unlike other Satyrs). The gray-brown HW below has a white post-median line and no eye-spots. Little Wood Satyr is larger, much darker, and has prominent eye-spots on the HW below.

HABITAT   Low grassy fields. Seems to prefer moist fields, at least in the NY area.

RANGE   As of 1991, south to New York City (see Comments). Also, north to Canada and west to California.

FLIGHT PERIOD & ABUNDANCE   **B:** C-A, June and Aug.   **N:** probably will be C, June and Aug.   **P:** X.   **W:** X.

FOODPLANT   Grasses.

COMMENTS   The Common Ringlet has dramatically expanded its range over the last 30 years. Starting in Canada, year by year it has moved steadily southward. In 1990 it was found for the first time in Westchester, NY. It can be expected to continue pushing southward.

Common Wood Nymph *(Cercyonis pegala)* Plate 22

SIZE 1 4/16 in.

SIMILAR SPECIES None.

IDENTIFICATION A large, very dark Satyr of open, brushy fields. Note the yellow-orange post-median FW patch.

HABITAT Shrubby fields, woodland edge, power-line cuts, etc.

RANGE Entire region. Also, north to Maine, west to California, and south to Texas and Florida.

FLIGHT PERIOD & ABUNDANCE **B:** C-A, early July–late Sept. **N:** C-A, late June–early Sept. Max. 540 7/8/89 North Salem, Westchester Co., NY. **P:** C-A, late June–early Sept. **W:** C, late June–early Sept.

FOODPLANT Grasses.

COMMENTS Farther north and inland, some races of the Common Wood Nymph lack the yellow-orange FW patch. Unlike many of our other Satyrs, this species not uncommonly does nectar at flowers.

Milkweed Butterflies (subfamily *Danainae*)

The Milkweed Butterflies are found throughout the tropical world. We are fortunate to have such a glorious representative of this family in North America. Many of the species of Milkweed Butterflies are distasteful to predators because of the accumulation of toxic chemicals derived from their larval foodplants. They signal this distastefulness to potential predators by sporting bold coloration. For a thorough treatment of this group, see Ackery and Vane-Wright (1984).

Monarch *(Danaus plexippus)* Plate 21

SIZE 2 in.

SIMILAR SPECIES Viceroy, Great Spangled Fritillary.

IDENTIFICATION Probably the best known butterfly of North America. A large orange butterfly with a powerful flight. Often sails with its wings held in a "V." The male has a black scent patch on a HW vein above. The Viceroy is smaller and has a weaker flight on shallower wingbeats, often gliding on flat wings. The Viceroy has a black post-median line on the HW.

HABITAT Open fields, roadsides, suburban areas. While migrating it can be anywhere, but strongly concentrates on the immediate coast.

RANGE Entire region. Also, all of North America, south to South America. Now established on New Zealand, Australia, Canary Islands, India, etc.

FLIGHT PERIOD & ABUNDANCE **B:** C, June–early Nov. **N:** U-A, late May–Nov. Max. 50,000, 10/7/70 Great Kills, Staten Island, NY. **P:** U-C, May–Nov. **W:** U-C, late April–Nov.

FOODPLANT   Milkweeds *(Asclepias)*.

COMMENTS   Tens of thousands of Monarchs move south along our coast in September–October. The spectacle at congregation points is awe-inspiring. Millions of Monarchs from North America eventually overwinter in communal sites in the Mexican mountains. These enormous roosts are rapidly becoming a major tourist attraction. In very early spring, the overwintering adults mate and begin to move north and lay eggs. Their offspring then continue moving north, reaching our region in April or May. See Comments under Viceroy for a discussion of mimicry.

Queen *(Danaus gilippus)* Plate 40

SIZE   ≤ Monarch.

SIMILAR SPECIES   Monarch.

IDENTIFICATION   Not normally a part of our fauna, the Queen is a rich mahogany brown, darker than the Monarch. This closely related species lacks the Monarch's black subapical band and has **white spots in the FW post-median area** that are visible either from above or below.

RANGE   Extreme southern U.S. (including Florida) south to Argentina. Range expands northward in the summer, sometimes reaching North Carolina in the east. Very unlikely, but possible in our region.

FLIGHT PERIOD & ABUNDANCE   **B:** X.   **N:** X.   **P:** X.   **W:** X.

The Skippers (superfamily *Hesperioidea*)

Skippers, which derive their name from their characteristic rapid darting flight, can be the agony and the ecstasy of butterflying. The agony results from trying to identify individual species in the many difficult (some would say impossible) to identify groups. Ecstasy is the result of success. With roughly 3500 species worldwide, there is ample opportunity for pleasure. Skippers are generally distinguishable from the true butterflies by their relatively large bodies (compared to their wings), their relatively small, very angular wings, and by the presence of a thin extension (the apiculus) of the antennal club. There are two subfamilies of skippers in our area. The spread-winged skippers are generally large (for skippers). When these skippers alight they generally hold their wings open flat—thus the name spread-winged skippers. Although they sometimes hold their wings closed or partially open, the FWs and the HWs are always moved in unison. In contrast, the folded-wing skippers either alight with their wings completely closed (often) or with the HWs more or less completely open but with the FWs only partially opened, forming a V or U.

Spread-winged Skippers *(Pyrginae)*

Almost all of our species are essentially dark brown with some spotting. This includes two of our most difficult groups, the Cloudywings and the Duskywings.

Silver-spotted Skipper *(Epargyreus clarus)* Plate 24

SIZE   1 2/16 in.

SIMILAR SPECIES   Hoary Edge.

IDENTIFICATION   A large powerful skipper that flashes its **silvered spot in the middle of the HW below** even as it flies. Above, the brown-gold FW spots are in an open configuration. The somewhat smaller Hoary Edge has these spots enclosing some dark brown ground color. The Hoary Edge also has a large white patch below, but it is located on the HW margin.

HABITAT   Wide ranging in open habitats. Fields, gardens, meadows, etc.

RANGE   Entire region. Also, north to Maine, west to California, and south to Texas and Florida.

FLIGHT PERIOD & ABUNDANCE   **B:** C, late May–mid Aug.   **N:** C-A, May–Sept. Max. 100, 7/22/89 Christie Estate, Nassau Co., NY.   **P:** C-A, early May–late June, early July–early Sept.   **W:** C-A, late April–early July, early July–mid Oct.

MAJOR FOODPLANT   Black Locust *(Robina pseudacacia).*

COMMENTS   One of our most widespread and conspicuous butterflies.

Long-tailed Skipper *(Urbanus proteus)* Plate 24

SIZE   ≤ Silver-spotted Skipper.

SIMILAR SPECIES   None.

IDENTIFICATION   The long, broad "tails" on this large Skipper are distinctive. The iridescent green on the upper body and basal portions of the wings above is striking.

HABITAT   Open fields, especially disturbed and brushy situations.

RANGE   A rare stray into our region from the south. Has been recorded north to MA but not to be expected north of Philadelphia and southern NJ for years on end. Also, west to Mexico and south to Argentina.

FLIGHT PERIOD & ABUNDANCE   **B:** X, but two recorded in 1990 for the first time.   **N:** X, but two seen in 1990 and 1991 after 40-year absence.   **P:** S, most frequent in Sept.   **W:** S.

MAJOR FOODPLANT   Legumes (Fabaceae).

COMMENTS   This species is sometimes viewed as a pest by bean farmers in the south.

Golden-banded Skipper *(Autochton cellus)* Plate 24

SIZE   ≥ Northern Cloudywing.

SIMILAR SPECIES   Hoary Edge.

IDENTIFICATION   A large, dark skipper with very broad yellow FW bands. FW band of Hoary Edge is a series of orange-brown spots. Below, the Golden-banded Skipper has no white patch. It is also very rare in our region.

HABITAT   Wooded ravines with a stream or other water.

RANGE   North to about the Washington area and northern Delaware. Strays to central NJ. Also south to Florida and west to Arkansas, and southeastern Arizona south into Mexico.

SPECIFIC LOCALITIES   Difficult Run region of Great Falls National Park, Fairfax, Co., VA.

FLIGHT PERIOD & ABUNDANCE   **B:** X.   **N:** X.   **P:** H, a few old records from west central NJ, early–mid June.   **W:** LR, late April–June, partial 2nd brood late July–late Aug. Montgomery Co., MD; Fairfax Co., VA.

MAJOR FOODPLANT   Hog Peanut *(Amphicarpa bracteata).*

Hoary Edge *(Achalarus lyciades)* Plate 24

SIZE   < Silver-spotted Skipper.

SIMILAR SPECIES   Silver-spotted Skipper.

IDENTIFICATION   A large dark skipper with a conspicuous white patch on the margin of the HW below. Silver-spotted Skipper has more angled wings and its silvered spot is in the middle of the HW below. Above, note the brown-gold spot-band enclosing dark brown ground.

HABITAT   Widespread in open areas near woodlands. Prefers sandier areas than the Silver-spotted Skipper.

RANGE   North sparingly to the Boston area. Also, west to Iowa and south to Texas and Florida.

SPECIFIC LOCALITIES   Broad Meadow Brook Sanctuary, MA.

FLIGHT PERIOD & ABUNDANCE   **B:** LU, southwest of Boston, June–late July.   **N:** U-C, mid June–mid July. Max. 42, 6/24/89 Van Cortlandt Park, Bronx, NY.   **P:** LU-LC, late May–mid July.   **W:** LU-LC, early May–June, July (partial 2nd brood).

MAJOR FOODPLANT   Tick-trefoils *(Desmodium).*

Southern Cloudywing *(Thorybes bathyllus)* Plate 25

SIZE   = Northern Cloudywing.

SIMILAR SPECIES   Northern Cloudywing, Confused Cloudywing.

IDENTIFICATION   A large brown, spread-wing skipper with prominent white markings above and complex dark markings and frosting below. Often lands with its wings folded over its back. Separable from the Duskywings by its uniformly brown ground color above (Duskywings are heavily mottled) and the bright white line behind the eye. The Southern Cloudywing has more extensive and aligned spots than the Northern Cloudywing. Note especially the second spot from the FW margin. This spot is prominent and hourglassed shaped in the Southern Cloudywing but is usually a small dot or absent in the Northern Cloudywing. Below, note the white or pale gray "face" of the Southern. Northern has a dark brown or dark gray "face."

HABITAT   Open areas, especially dry hillside fields with low brushy areas (for perching).

RANGE   Entire region. Also, north to Maine, west to Nebraska, and south to Texas and Florida.

SPECIFIC LOCALITIES   Broad Meadow Brook Sanctuary, MA; Oakwood Cemetery, NY.

FLIGHT PERIOD & ABUNDANCE   **B:** LU, mid June–mid July.   **N:** LU, mid June–

mid July. Max. 9, 6/28/90 Oakwood Cemetery, Mt. Kisco, Westchester Co., NY. **P:** C, June–early July, mid Aug.–early Sept. **W:** C, June–mid July, Aug.

MAJOR FOODPLANT Legumes.

COMMENTS Males often behave territorially, returning again and again to the same perch.

Northern Cloudywing *(Thorybes pylades)* Plate 25

SIZE 12/16 in.

SIMILAR SPECIES Southern Cloudywing, Confused Cloudywing.

IDENTIFICATION A large skipper, evenly brown above with restricted white spots. See Southern Cloudywing for further discussion of differences.

HABITAT Widespread in open situations, such as power-line cuts, *Andropogon* fields, moist meadows, etc.

RANGE Entire region. Also, north to Maine, west to California, and south to Texas and Florida.

FLIGHT PERIOD & ABUNDANCE **B:** C, late May–mid July. **N:** C, late May–mid July. Max. 15, 6/4/89 Ward Pound Ridge Reservation, NY. **P:** C-A, mid May–mid July. **W:** C, mid May–mid July, late July–Sept. (partial).

MAJOR FOODPLANT Legumes.

Confused Cloudywing *(Thorybes confusis)* Plate 25

SIZE = Northern Cloudywing.

SIMILAR SPECIES Northern Cloudywing, Southern Cloudywing.

IDENTIFICATION Called the Confused Cloudywing for good reason, the identification of this essentially southern butterfly should probably be left to experts. Spot pattern above seems to vary from usually very restricted (like Northern Cloudywing) to extensive (like Southern Cloudywing). "Face" (palps) tends to be grayish white. Males lack a fold (costal fold) on the front margin of the FW that Northern Cloudywing males have, but this is very difficult to ascertain in the field (and Southern Cloudywing males also lack this fold). The genitalia are diagnostic but, for most people, this is even more difficult (actually impossible) to determine in the field (examination of genitalia, usually with a microscope, for species determinations is standard fare for lepidopterists). Although, as indicated above, most individuals cannot be identified to species, individuals strongly exhibiting the following combination of markings can probably be assigned to this species. (1) Above with very reduced white markings. In the grouping of the lower three white spots, the central mark (if present at all) is a very thin, pale white line aligned with the costal spot (Southern Cloudywing has this spot much thicker and more prominent). (2) Face (palps) white (Northern Cloudywing has dark gray or brown palps). (3) On the HW below, the dark median band runs up from the lower wing margin merging (or almost merging) with the more distal of the two costal dark spots. (In Southern and Northern Cloudywings this band stops far short of the costal margin and is positioned between the two costal margin spots.)

HABITAT   Dry open areas.

RANGE   North to the Philadelphia area and southern NJ. Also, west to Missouri and south to Texas and Florida.

FLIGHT PERIOD & ABUNDANCE   **B:** X.   **N:** X.   **P:** R (apparently), late May–early July, Aug.   **W:** R, late May–June, Aug.

MAJOR FOODPLANT   Probably legumes.

Hayhurst's Scallopwing *(Staphylus hayhurstii)* Plate 28

SIZE   = Common Sootywing.

SIMILAR SPECIES   Common Sootywing.

IDENTIFICATION   A small, very dark spread-winged skipper with even **darker bands forming concentric semicircles on the HW above.** Above, **variably strewn with tiny pale silver or gold flecks.** Also note the **scalloped HW margin.** Common Sootywing lacks the gray or gold flecks and scalloped HW, has bright white spots above and on the head, and is more uniformly black.

HABITAT   Formerly restricted to moist open woodlands but now also adapted to disturbed areas and gardens due to utilization of an introduced foodplant.

RANGE   Now north to the Philadelphia area and southern NJ (recently expanded range).

SPECIFIC LOCALITIES   Higbee Beach, Cape May Co., NJ; Nottingham County Park, PA.

FLIGHT PERIOD & ABUNDANCE   **B:** X.   **N:** X.   **P:** R-U and erratic to the south and west, late May–Sept.   **W:** R-U, late May–June, Aug.–Sept.

MAJOR FOODPLANT   Lambsquarters *(Chenopodium album).*

COMMENTS   This species is our only member of the large and easily recognizable (due to the scalloped HW and metallic flecking) tropical genus *Staphylus.*

Duskywings

The Duskywings constitute one of our most difficult identification problems. Many of our species are so similar that it is common to find misidentified museum specimens. Thus the astute observer will often say "That's a Duskywing," or "That's a Wild Indigo group Duskywing." Essentially there are three "groups" of species in our area. First there are the large, well-marked Duskywings with large pale spots on the FWs, Juvenal's and Horace's Duskywings. Second there are the medium-sized species with less extensive pale spots on the FWs, Wild Indigo, Columbine, Persius, Mottled, and Zarucco Duskywings. The first three of these species are particularly closely related and difficult to identify. Lastly there are the smaller species, Dreamy and Sleepy Duskywings, which lack white on the FWs (although even these species occasionally have small white spots at the FW subapices).

Dreamy Duskywing *(Erynnis icelus)* Plate 27

SIZE < Wild Indigo Duskywing.

SIMILAR SPECIES Sleepy Duskywing.

IDENTIFICATION Dreamy and Sleepy Duskywings lack white spots above and have broad, chain-like post-median bands. Dreamy Duskywing is (1) smaller, (2) has a bright silver-gray spot on the FW costa above as its most conspicuous feature (Sleepy females are brown in this area, males have some gray but not so bright and silvered), (3) has the last segment of the palps significantly longer than does Sleepy Duskywing, (4) has the inner one-third of the FW above blacker than the rest of the ground color, (5) flies later in the year (although there is overlap), (6) tends to fly lower to the ground (about 1 ft above the ground as compared with 2–3 ft for Sleepy) with a less powerful flight than the Sleepy Duskywing.

HABITAT Open woodlands and areas adjacent to woodlands.

RANGE Southeast to about the Fall Line. Also, north to Canada, west to California, and south in the mountains to Arizona and Georgia.

FLIGHT PERIOD & ABUNDANCE **B:** C, mid May–early July. **N:** C, mid May–late June. Max. 57, 5/24/86 Chappaqua, NY. **P:** C-A, mid May–June. **W:** C, late April–early June.

MAJOR FOODPLANT Willows *(Salix)* and Poplars *(Populus)*.

Sleepy Duskywing *(Erynnis brizo)* Plate 27

SIZE = Wild Indigo Duskywing.

SIMILAR SPECIES Dreamy Duskywing.

IDENTIFICATION A medium-sized Duskywing, without white spots above and with a broad chain-like post-median band of the FW above. See Dreamy Duskywing for comparison.

HABITAT Poor soil areas with oaks, especially barrens, such as pine barrens, burn scars, and shale barrens.

RANGE Entire region. Also, north to southern New Hampshire, west to California, and south to Florida.

FLIGHT PERIOD & ABUNDANCE **B:** C, late April–mid May. **N:** R-U, late April–May. Max. 10, 5/11/91 Easthampton, Suffolk Co., NY. **P:** U, early April–mid May. **W:** R-U, early April–early May.

MAJOR FOODPLANT Scrub Oak *(Quercus ilicifolia)*.

Juvenal's Duskywing *(Erynnis juvenalis)* Plate 26

SIZE = Northern Cloudywing.

SIMILAR SPECIES Horace's Duskywing.

IDENTIFICATION A large, strong-flying Duskywing that is very common and widespread. Males are territorial and will "police a beat," often returning to the same perch. Larger size and extensive white spots above (especially the one in the FW cell) separate this species from all our other Duskywings but Horace's.

RANGE   Entire region. Also, north to Maine, west to North Dakota, and south to Texas and Florida.

FLIGHT PERIOD & ABUNDANCE   **B:** C, mid April–late June.   **N:** C-A, mid April–mid June. Max. 150, 5/17/87 Easthampton, Suffolk Co., NY.   **P:** C, mid April–early June.   **W:** C, early April–early June.

MAJOR FOODPLANT   Oaks *(Quercus).*

Horace's Duskywing *(Erynnis horatius)* Plate 26

SIZE   = Northern Cloudywing.

SIMILAR SPECIES   Juvenal's Duskywing, Wild Indigo Duskywing.

IDENTIFICATION   A large Duskywing, very similar to Juvenal's. Below, Horace's lacks the two pale subapical spots on the HW that Juvenal's **almost** always has. Best distinguished from the far more common Juvenal's in the summer when Juvenal's doesn't fly. Large, boldly marked summer female Wild Indigo Duskywings can be mistaken for Horace's. Try to note the margin of the HW below. Horace's has large dark spots, Wild Indigo has small pale spots.

HABITAT   Oak woodlands, especially those on poor soils and adjacent open areas.

RANGE   Range extends northwest just to the northwest limits of our region. Also, west to Iowa and south to Texas and Florida.

FLIGHT PERIOD & ABUNDANCE   **B:** U, early May–mid June, early July–mid Aug.   **N:** U, R off the coastal plain late April–early June, early July–early Aug. Max. 4, 7/11/89 Sea View, Staten Island, NY.   **P:** U, C southern NJ, late April–May, mid July–early Aug.   **W:** C, mid April–May, mid July–Aug.

MAJOR FOODPLANT   Oaks *(Quercus).*

Mottled Duskywing *(Erynnis martialis)* Plate 27

SIZE   = Wild Indigo Duskywing.

SIMILAR SPECIES   Wild Indigo Duskywing, Columbine Duskywing, Persius Duskywing.

IDENTIFICATION   A brighter, more mottled skipper than our other Duskywings, especially on the HW above. Usually has gray-white apical markings on the FW above that Wild Indigo Duskywing lacks. **Note the narrow and relatively sharply delineated HW post-median dark band.** Fresh individuals have a strong purplish sheen.

HABITAT   Open wooded areas with sites for hilltopping such as hilly pine-oak woodlands or barrens.

RANGE   Historically, east to southwestern CT and southeastern NY south through northern NJ and the Philadelphia area to the Washington area. Has declined greatly in the northeast. Also, west to Wisconsin and south to Texas and Georgia.

SPECIFIC LOCALITIES   Nottingham County Park, PA.

FLIGHT PERIOD & ABUNDANCE   **B:** H, not recorded this century.   **N:** H, not recorded in 30 years.   **P:** LR, late April–mid May, early July–Aug.   **W:** H, late April–mid May, early July–Aug. Apparently no records since the early 1970s though still possible at Soldier's Delight, Natural Environmental Area, Owings Mills, MD.

MAJOR FOODPLANT   New Jersey Tea *(Ceanothus americanus)*.

COMMENTS   Best chance is to look at ridges or hilltops near extensive stands of New Jersey Tea.

Zarucco Duskywing *(Erynnis zarucco)* Plate 27

SIZE   = Northern Cloudywing.

SIMILAR SPECIES   Wild Indigo Duskywing.

IDENTIFICATION   A very dark Duskywing with angled wings, slightly larger than the Wild Indigo. Above, both the FW and HW are dark. Note the **paler patch** at the end of the FW cell and the **absence of gray overscaling** anywhere. The dark area on the FW extends all the way down to the lower margin. Wild Indigo Duskywing is somewhat paler and more mottled, usually shows at least some gray overscaling, and has a pale patch at the middle of the FW lower margin.

HABITAT   Brushy fields and roadsides.

RANGE   A rare immigrant into our region, north to the Philadelphia area. Also, south to Florida and then west to Texas.

FLIGHT PERIOD & ABUNDANCE   **B:** X.   **N:** X.   **P:** S, Aug.   **W:** R-U, April–June, July–Sept.

MAJOR FOODPLANT   Black Locust *(Robina pseudacacia)* and other legumes.

Columbine Duskywing *(Erynnis lucilius)* Not illustrated

SIZE   ≤ Wild Indigo Duskywing.

SIMILAR SPECIES   Wild Indigo Duskywing.

IDENTIFICATION   Cannot be distinguished on the basis of appearance from Wild Indigo Duskywing. Averages smaller. A small dark duskywing of the Wild Indigo group, flying around Columbine plants, is probably this species. But even then, who knows?

HABITAT   Rich, rocky woodlands with Columbine.

RANGE   MA (except Cape Cod), southwest through central CT, southeastern NY and northern NJ to the Philadelphia area. Also north into Canada, west to Minnesota, and south in the Appalachians to Virginia.

SPECIFIC LOCALITIES   Hanging Hills State Park, CT.

FLIGHT PERIOD & ABUNDANCE   **B:** LR, May, Aug.–early Sept. No recent records.   **N:** LR, May, Aug.–early Sept. Only one report in the past ten years.   **P:** R, May, late July–Aug.   **W:** X.

MAJOR FOODPLANT   Columbine *(Aquilegia canadensis)*.

Wild Indigo Duskywing *(Erynnis baptisiae)* Plate 27

SIZE   11/16 in.

SIMILAR SPECIES   Horace's Duskywing, Columbine Duskywing, Mottled Duskywing, Zarucco Duskywing.

IDENTIFICATION   A medium-sized, very variable Duskywing, usually with three or four small white spots just past the FW "wrist" above. The basal one-half of the FWs is usually very dark and appears "oily." Females are more mottled with more contrast than males. Large, well-marked females sometimes can be mistaken for Horace's Duskywing. Note the small pale spots on the HW margin below.

HABITAT   Widespread in open areas, especially along roadsides and railroad embankments with plantings of Crown Vetch.

RANGE   Entire region. Also, west to Minnesota and south to Texas and Georgia.

FLIGHT PERIOD & ABUNDANCE   **B:** C, mid May–mid June, Late July–early Sept.   **N:** C-LA, mid May–mid June, early July–early Aug., late Aug.–Sept. Max. 117, 7/27/86 Chappaqua RR Station, Westchester Co., NY.   **P:** C-LA, late April–Sept.   **W:** C, late April–mid June, early July–Aug., Sept.

MAJOR FOODPLANT   Crown Vetch *(Coronilla varia)* and Wild Indigo *(Baptisia tinctoria)*.

COMMENTS   Until fairly recently this butterfly was quite uncommon. Having adapted to the widely planted Crown Vetch within the past twenty years, the Wild Indigo Duskywing has undergone a tremendous population explosion and an increase in flight period as well.

Persius Duskywing *(Erynnis persius)* Not illustrated

SIZE   = Wild Indigo Duskywing.

SIMILAR SPECIES   Wild Indigo Duskywing, Columbine Duskywing.

IDENTIFICATION   Reportedly identifiable by the presence of short grayish-white hairs on the FW of the male. In actuality, a highly significant percentage of specimens in museums are misidentified. This doesn't give one much confidence for field identification. Then again, maybe the live butterflies are **easier** to identify once we've figured out the right field marks!

HABITAT   Barrens; pine barrens, power lines through xeric woods, mountain balds, etc. (personal communication from Dale Schweitzer).

RANGE   Presumably similar to Columbine Duskywing.

FLIGHT PERIOD & ABUNDANCE   **B:** LR May.   **N:** H May.   **P:** H May.   **W:** X.

MAJOR FOODPLANT   Lupines *(Lupinus)*.

Grizzled Skipper *(Pyrgus centaureae wyandot)* Plate 28

SIZE   = Common Sootywing.

SIMILAR SPECIES   Common Checkered Skipper.

IDENTIFICATION   A brownish Checkered Skipper with reduced white markings. Note the **inwardly displaced middle spot** of the three lower white spots of the FW post-median band. The HW above lacks a strong median white band. Common Checkered Skipper has more extensive white markings but only one spot at the base of the FW above and its FW post-median band has no inwardly displaced spot.

HABITAT   Open hilltops and grassy hillsides in barrens areas.

RANGE   Northern NJ (formerly, Great Notch, Patterson, Montclair, Pompton) and southeastern Pennsylvania (Lancaster Co.). Also southwest through western Maryland to western Virginia.

FLIGHT PERIOD & ABUNDANCE **B:** X. **N:** H, Formerly LR in northern NJ, Ramapo Mtns., etc., and adjacent NY, late April–mid May. Now probably extirpated. **P:** LR or H to the west in the Blue Ball, Ephrata area. **W:** H.

MAJOR FOODPLANT Dwarf Cinquefoil *(Potentilla canadensis)* (Dale Schweitzer, personal communication).

COMMENTS This butterfly is now close to extinction. Although the reasons for its decline are not known, intensive spraying for gypsy moths is suspected (at least in northern NJ). Many authorities believe that *Pyrgus centaureae wyandot* is a different species from the nominate *Pyrgus centaureae.*

Common Checkered Skipper *(Pyrgus communis)* Plate 28

SIZE ≥ Common Sootywing.

SIMILAR SPECIES Grizzled Skipper.

IDENTIFICATION The extensive white spots on the black ground coupled with the blue-tinged hair create the effect of a blue-gray blur as this little skipper whirs by you.

HABITAT Open, disturbed areas.

RANGE North to the New York area (occasionally straying farther north). Also, west to California and south to Florida and Argentina.

FLIGHT PERIOD & ABUNDANCE **B:** X. **N:** R immigrant, very occasionally overwintering, late May (very rare), July, late Aug.–Sept. Max. 10, 9/14/86 Goose Pond Park, Orange Co., NY. **P:** C, mid May (rare), mid July–mid Aug., late Aug.–Sept. **W:** C, late April–May, late June–early Aug., late Aug.–Oct.

MAJOR FOODPLANT Mallow family *(Malvaceae).*

COMMENTS Often does not survive the winter north of Virginia. Everywhere, the late summer–fall brood is by far the commonest.

Common Sootywing *(Pholisora catullus)* Plate 28

SIZE 9/16 in.

SIMILAR SPECIES Hayhurst's Scallopwing, Wild Indigo Duskywing.

IDENTIFICATION A very small, black spread-winged skipper with a variable number (but usually many) of small, bright white dots on the wings and head.

HABITAT Disturbed open areas, urban lots, railroad yards, etc.

RANGE Entire region. Also, north to Maine, west to Washington State, and south to Texas and Florida.

FLIGHT PERIOD & ABUNDANCE **B:** C, May–Sept. in urban areas, otherwise R-U. **N:** C, mid May–mid Sept. Max. 45, 7/19/87 Jamaica Bay Wildlife Refuge, NY. **P:** C, early May–Sept. peaking in early June, mid July and late Aug. **W:** C, late April–Sept.

MAJOR FOODPLANT Lamb's Quarters *(Chenopodium album)* and others.

COMMENTS Shapiro (1965) describes this as "perhaps the only butterfly to benefit appreciably from urbanization."

Folded Wing Skippers *(Hesperiidae)*

Our folded wing skippers are generally smaller than the spread-wing skippers and their flight is harder to follow. Generally brown to pale orange, many of these are the LBJs (little brown jobs) of the butterfly world. In many species the males have specialized scent patches or stigmas on the FWs.

Arctic Skipper *(Carterocephalus palaemon)* Plate 28

SIZE = Tawny-edged Skipper.

SIMILAR SPECIES None.

IDENTIFICATION A small, but choice, gift from the north. Marked rather like a miniature Fritillary. Above checked orange and very dark brown. Below, rows of gray-white spots on an orange-brown ground.

HABITAT Moist, grassy open areas within or adjacent to oak-pine transition forest.

RANGE In scattered colonies southeast to about 30 miles west of Boston, MA (reported from Blue Hills Reservation, Norwood, MA), possibly northwestern CT, and extreme northwestern NJ. Also, north to Canada and circumpolar.

FLIGHT PERIOD & ABUNDANCE **B:** LR, June, north and west of Boston. **N:** X. **P:** X. **W:** X.

MAJOR FOODPLANT Grasses.

Swarthy Skipper *(Nastra lherminier)* Plate 31

SIZE ≥ Least Skipper.

SIMILAR SPECIES Tawny-edged Skipper.

IDENTIFICATION A very small **dark yellowish-brown** skipper with **slightly paler veining below.** Small worn Tawny-edged Skippers can look very dark below but they usually have pale subapical spots on the FW and lack the paler veining. Above the Swarthy Skipper is plain dark brown while the Tawny-edged Skipper has extensive markings.

HABITAT Barren fields with low vegetation and bluestem grasses.

RANGE North to Cold Spring, Putnam Co., NY, and eastern Rhode Island. Also, west to Kansas and south to Texas and Florida.

SPECIFIC LOCALITIES Iona Island, Rockland Co., NY; Jamaica Bay Wildlife Refuge, Queens, NY. Widespread further south.

FLIGHT PERIOD & ABUNDANCE **B:** X. **N:** C-A, but R in CT and RI mid June–early July. Max. 60, 6/12/89 Iona Island, NY; 119, 9/7/86 Jamaica Bay Wildlife Refuge, NY. **P:** C, mid June–early July, early Aug.–mid Sept. **W:** C, May–June, Aug.–Sept.

MAJOR FOODPLANT Little Bluestem Grass *(Andropogon scoparius).*

Clouded Skipper *(Lerema accius)* Plate 36

SIZE ≥ Zabulon/Hobomok Skipper.

SIMILAR SPECIES Zabulon Skipper (female), Dusted Skipper.

IDENTIFICATION A very dark southern skipper. When fresh has significant frosting below. The HW frosting (or, when worn, paler areas) at the margin and at the lower middle of the wing sets off a dark band that extends from the center of the HW inner margin. Male above, dark brown with a darker stigma and a few inconspicuous white spots. Female above dark brown with seven white spots on the FW; three in a diagonal row near the middle of the FW, three strong contiguous subapical spots, and **one smaller ovate cell spot.** Female Zabulon Skipper has white costal margin of the HW below and much more extensive spotting above. Dusted Skipper has white "eye-brows."

HABITAT   Could be found in almost any open habitat, including open woodland, but prefers moist grassy areas.

RANGE   A regular immigrant to the southern portions of our area and a rare stray to the northern portions. Also south to Florida, Texas, and South America.

SPECIFIC LOCALITIES   Mattawoman Natural Environment Area, MD.

FLIGHT PERIOD & ABUNDANCE   **B:** S, recorded only a few times.   **N:** S, not present for many years at a time.   **P:** R-U, immigrant, Aug.–Sept.   **W:** U, immigrant, Aug.–Oct.

MAJOR FOODPLANT   Grasses.

COMMENTS   The fall of 1991 saw a major irruption of this species into the northeast, with it actually becoming abundant in southern NJ. The movement proceeded north to at least New York City, where five individuals were seen.

Least Skipper *(Ancyloxypha numitor)* Plates 28 & 35

SIZE   8/16 in.

SIMILAR SPECIES   European Skipper.

IDENTIFICATION   A tiny, bright orange skipper weakly weaving through the grass is sure to be this species. Contrasting black wings above can be detected in flight. European Skipper is larger, duller orange below and orange above.

HABITAT   Wet meadows and marshes, roadside ditches, etc.

RANGE   Entire region. Also north to Maine, west to North Dakota, and south to Texas and Florida.

FLIGHT PERIOD & ABUNDANCE   **B:** C, early June–early July, mid July–early Aug., & late Aug.–early Oct.   **N:** C-A, June–mid July, mid July–early Aug., mid Aug.–early Oct. Max. 200, 6/11/91 Goose Pond Park, Orange Co., NY; 300, 8/24/86 Goose Pond Park, Orange Co., NY.   **P:** A, early May–early July, July–early Aug., mid Aug.–mid Oct.   **W:** A, early May–late June, July–early Aug., early Aug.–mid Oct.

MAJOR FOODPLANT   Grasses.

European Skipper *(Thymelicus lineola)* Plate 35

SIZE   ≤ Tawny-edged Skipper.

SIMILAR SPECIES   Delaware Skipper, Least Skipper.

IDENTIFICATION   A small, weak-flying skipper that is completely orange (usually with a fair amount of white dusting below). Note the short reddish antennae with blunt ends. Delaware Skipper is larger (usually), a much more powerful, faster flyer, with longer antennae with hooked, pointed ends. Least Skipper is smaller, brighter orange.

HABITAT   Dry grassy fields, especially those with tall grasses.

RANGE   Entire region. Also, north to Canada, west to the Rocky Mountains, and south to Virginia.

FLIGHT PERIOD & ABUNDANCE **B:** A, June–mid July. **N:** A, June–early July. Max. 1350, 6/20/89 Meyer Sanctuary, North Castle, Westchester Co., NY. **P:** C, but U southern NJ, early June–early July. **W:** C, late May–June.

MAJOR FOODPLANT Timothy *(Phleum pratense).*

COMMENTS A native of Europe, this skipper was introduced into Ontario in 1910 and has since spread throughout the northeast.

Fiery Skipper *(Hylephila phyleus)* Plate 29

SIZE ≤ Zabulon/Hobomok Skipper.

SIMILAR SPECIES Whirlabout.

IDENTIFICATION The male is an orange skipper with many small spots below. These can vary from faint dull brown to sharp black. The Whirlabout has fewer, larger brown to black blotches. Note the **very wavy black borders on the HW above.** Whirlabout has HW border smooth. The female Fiery Skipper is similar to the male but the ground color is dull yellow-brown with a greenish tinge. Above, she is brown with yellow spots. Note **five spots on the diagonal from FW apex to the middle of the wing base.**

HABITAT Primarily lawns but also other low open grassy areas such as dry fields and roadsides.

RANGE An immigrant into our area north to at least southeastern NY and southern CT. Also, west to California and south to Chile.

FLIGHT PERIOD & ABUNDANCE **B:** X, but recorded from Rockport 9/8–9/12/91. **N:** R, immigrant, but probably present most years in Sept. Max. 9, 9/2/91 Snug Harbor, Staten Island (usually no more than 1) **P:** R, late June–July; U, late Aug.–Sept. **W:** R, May; C, Aug.–Oct.

MAJOR FOODPLANT Bermuda Grass *(Cynodon dactylon).*

COMMENTS 1991 saw an unprecedented invasion by this species as it blazed a trail through our region.

Leonard's Skipper *(Hesperia leonardus)* Plate 30

SIZE ≥ Zabulon/Hobomok Skipper.

SIMILAR SPECIES None.

IDENTIFICATION A large reddish-brown skipper bombing around large open fields in very late summer is almost certainly this species. Note the very conspicuous white post-median spot band on the HW below.

HABITAT Open fields with thick low vegetation and nectar sources. Seems to prefer a combination of dry *Andropogon*-covered hillside juxtaposed with moist open meadow.

RANGE Entire region. Also, north to Maine, west to Minnesota, and south to Arkansas and northern Georgia.

SPECIFIC LOCALITIES Broad Meadow Brook, MA; Wellfleet Bay Wildlife Sanctuary, MA; Nottingham Barrens, PA; Soldier's Delight, MD.

FLIGHT PERIOD & ABUNDANCE **B:** U, late Aug.–Sept. **N:** LU, late Aug.–Sept. Max. 12, 9/16/87 Somers, Westchester Co., NY. **P:** LU, late Aug.–Sept. **W:** LU, Sept.

MAJOR FOODPLANT   Grasses.

COMMENTS   Our only fall flying, single-brooded butterfly. Unlike most of our other skippers and butterflies, when disturbed, Leonard's Skipper will most likely fly rapidly out of sight. Now listed as extirpated in CT.

Cobweb Skipper *(Hesperia metea)* Plate 30

SIZE   = Tawny-edged Skipper.

SIMILAR SPECIES   Female Sachem.

IDENTIFICATION   A small, often inconspicuous, dark springtime skipper. Usually flies low among or at the top of *Andropogon* grasses. Note the pale, chevron-shaped post-median band on the HW below. Female Sachem also has a chevron-shaped band but is larger, much paler yellowish-brown, and unlikely to be found in much of our region in May.

HABITAT   Dry open fields with bluestem grasses, often on hillsides but also power-line cuts, open hilltops, etc.

RANGE   Entire region. Also, north to Maine and south in the Appalachians to Georgia and discontinuously west to Minnesota and south to Texas.

SPECIFIC LOCALITIES   Soldier's Delight, MD.

FLIGHT PERIOD & ABUNDANCE   **B:** C, early May–early June.   **N:** C, May. Max. 19, 5/10/85 Bedford, Westchester Co., NY.   **P:** C, mid May–late May. Late April–mid May in southern NJ.   **W:** U, May.

MAJOR FOODPLANT   Bluestem Grasses *(Andropogon).*

Dotted Skipper *(Hesperia attalus slossonae)* Plates 30 & 31

SIZE   ≥ Zabulon/Hobomok Skipper.

SIMILAR SPECIES   Crossline Skipper.

IDENTIFICATION   Large. Below, quite variable, from rich yellowish-brown with bold white spots forming a post-median chevron on the HW to dull pale brownish-yellow with weak pale dots. Boldly marked individuals are unmistakable (Leonard's Skipper is red-brown and flies a month and a half later) but individuals with weak spots could be confused with Crossline Skipper. Note the presence of **two subapical FW spots** that Crossline Skipper lacks.

HABITAT   Sandy barrens often along railroad tracks, airport runways, and power-line cuts.

RANGE   This rarely encountered skipper is little known. Although individuals have been recorded from Nantucket, Staten Island, and the Washington area, the only area north of Florida where one can reasonably expect to see this skipper is the NJ pine barrens. Also, Texas north to Kansas (although these populations may not be conspecific).

SPECIFIC LOCALITIES   Lakehurst, NJ, especially the Lakehurst Naval Air Engineering Station.

FLIGHT PERIOD & ABUNDANCE   **B:** S, recorded from Nantucket.   **N:** S, stray, recorded from Long Island.   **P:** LU, early July–early Aug. south–central NJ.   **W:** S, stray.

MAJOR FOODPLANT   Unknown.

COMMENTS   Look for this skipper before 2 P.M. while it is nectaring.

Indian Skipper *(Hesperia sassacus)* Plate 30

SIZE ≤ Zabulon/Hobomok Skipper.

SIMILAR SPECIES Long Dash.

IDENTIFICATION A spring skipper with an indistinct orange pattern below. HW below has a pale yellow post-median chevron that is usually indistinct but sometime obvious. Note that the chevron spots are **somewhat concave distally.** Above, note clear orange HW with black border. Long Dash pattern below is more distinct and spots are not concave distally. Above, bright orange with thin black stigma. Long Dash has black "cobwebbing" in the center of HW.

HABITAT Brushy fields and open meadows near woodlands, both dry and moist.

RANGE Southeast to the Philadelphia area. Rare or absent on Cape Cod, eastern Long Island, and southern NJ. Also, north to Maine, west to Minnesota, and south in the Appalachians to southern Virginia.

SPECIFIC LOCALITIES Catoctin Mountain Park, MD.

FLIGHT PERIOD & ABUNDANCE **B:** C, late May–early July. **N:** C, mid May–mid June. Max. 30, 6/4/89 Ward Pound Ridge Reservation, NY. **P:** LU, to the north and west. R or absent in central and southern NJ, mid May–mid June. **W:** LR, in Frederick Co.

MAJOR FOODPLANT Grasses.

COMMENTS You may have noticed that many of the scientific names of American skippers are based on Native-American names.

Peck's Skipper *(Polites peckius)* Plate 32

SIZE = Tawny-edged Skipper.

SIMILAR SPECIES Long Dash, Tawny-edged Skipper (above).

IDENTIFICATION HW below has two "patches" of yellow separated by the warm brown ground color but bridged by yellow. The amount of the brown between the two patches is quite variable. **HW surfaces of both sexes have post-median spot-bands with the central spot extending outward toward the wing margin.** Male above, note the prominent black stigma separating orange FW margin from the dark distal two-thirds of the wing. Tawny-edged Skipper is similar above but note dark HW. Long Dash has less contrast below with more of a post-median band and less of a "patch."

HABITAT Any open grassy areas with nectar sources, including meadows, power-line cuts, suburban habitats, and roadsides.

RANGE Entire region. Also north to Canada, west to Washington State, and south to Kansas and Georgia.

FLIGHT PERIOD & ABUNDANCE **B:** A, late May–early July, early Aug.–mid Sept. **N:**A, late may–June, late July–Sept. Max. 50, 6/4/89 Oakwood Cemetery, Mt. Kisco, Westchester Co., NY; 239, 7/28/91 Chappaqua Rd. power-line cut, Mt. Pleasant, Westchester Co., NY. **P:** A, but R-U southern NJ, mid May–late June, late July–late Sept. **W:** A, early May–mid June, early July–early Oct.

MAJOR FOODPLANT Grasses.

COMMENTS One of our most common skippers, this active butterfly is very fond of clovers.

Tawny-edged Skipper *(Polites themistocles)* Plate 31

SIZE   9/16 in.

SIMILAR SPECIES   Crossline Skipper.

IDENTIFICATION   A small, dull to darkish skipper below. Below, usually unicolorously drab olive except for tawny orange FW margin and three white spots on the FW subapex (sometimes HW has faint post-median band). Male above has intense **thick black stigma** bordering bright orange FW margin. Rest of FW and HW dull brown. HW below usually lacks a post-median band but occasionally a faint band is seen. Below, usually has sharp contrast between HW color and the brighter FW costal margin. See Crossline Skipper.

HABITAT   Open grassy areas with nectar sources, including suburban habitats and roadsides.

RANGE   Entire region. Also, north to Canada, west to Washington State and south to Texas and Florida.

FLIGHT PERIOD & ABUNDANCE   **B:** A, late May–early July, early Aug.–mid Sept.   **N:** A, late May–early July, late July–Sept. Max. 25, 5/31/86; 126, 7/28/91 Chappaqua Rd. power-line cut, Mt. Pleasant, Westchester Co., NY.   **P:** C, but R-U southern NJ, early June–mid July, late July–late Sept.   **W:** U, late May–early July, late July–Oct.

MAJOR FOODPLANT   Grasses.

Crossline Skipper *(Polites origenes)* Plate 31

SIZE   ≥ Tawny-edged Skipper.

SIMILAR SPECIES   Tawny-edged Skipper, female Sachem, Dotted Skipper.

IDENTIFICATION   A small to medium-sized dull skipper. Below, distinguished from Tawny-edged Skipper by (1) Larger size (usually), (2) lighter ground color, yellowish-brown, often with a "brassy" look (compared to dull olive for Tawny-edged), (3) presence (usually) of at least some (often marked) post-median spot-band (Tawny-edged Skipper usually lacks a HW post-median spot band), and (4) less contrast between the HW color and the color of the FW costal margin. Above, the male is distinguished from the Tawny-edged Skipper by the **less intense stigma that narrows significantly toward the base of the FW** and by the presence of an **additional pale yellow spot distally adjacent to the stigma.** Female above is very similar to Tawny-edged Skipper but on the HW usually has a broad dark border and a hint of orange. Tawny-edged females lack these features.

HABITAT   Dry grassy fields, power-line cuts, especially in poor soil areas.

RANGE   Entire region. Also north to Maine, west to Nebraska, and south to Texas and Florida.

FLIGHT PERIOD & ABUNDANCE   **B:** U, late June–late July.   **N:** C, late June–July. Max. 35, 7/8/91 Somers, Westchester Co., NY.   **P:** C, June–mid July, mid Aug.–Sept. Only one brood, late June–late July, in the NJ pine barrens.   **W:** U-C, late May–June, early Aug.–Sept.

MAJOR FOODPLANT   Purple Top *(Tridens flavus)* and other grasses.

COMMENTS   More restricted in habitat than the Tawny-edged Skipper, the Cross-line Skipper still often flies in the same locality. Attracted to Knappweed and Viper's Bugloss.

Long Dash *(Polites mystic)* Plates 30 & 32

SIZE   ≤ Hobomok Skipper

SIMILAR SPECIES   Indian Skipper, Peck's Skipper.

IDENTIFICATION   Clear orange-brown and yellow pattern below with wide yellow-spotted post-median band and yellow cell spot. Usually separable from Indian Skipper by much sharper pattern. HW post-median spot-band smoother than Indian Skipper. Occasionally has yellow spots almost as extensive as Peck's Skipper. On the FW, note the three elongated subapical spots with the lowest of the three closest to the wing margin (straight in Indian and Peck's Skippers) and the elongated FW post-median spot.

HABITAT   Toward the south, wet meadows and marshes, often with Blue Flag. More tolerant of drier condition in the north where it is more common.

RANGE   South to the northern Washington, D.C., area. Also, north to Maine, west to Washington, and south in the mountains to southern Virginia.

FLIGHT PERIOD & ABUNDANCE   **B:** C, June, partial brood Aug.–Sept. **N:**LC, June. Max. 25, 6/11/89 Ward Pound Ridge Reservation, NY. **P:** LU, late May–June, absent southern NJ.   **W:** LR, Carroll Co., MD.

MAJOR FOODPLANT   Grasses.

COMMENTS   Often nectars at Blue Flag.

Whirlabout *(Polites vibex)* Plate 29

SIZE   ≥ Tawny-edged Skipper.

SIMILAR SPECIES   Fiery Skipper.

IDENTIFICATION   Male below, orange-yellow with **large smudged brown or black spots.** These spots are larger and not as numerous as in Fiery Skipper. Male above, note smooth black border on the HW (Fiery Skipper has jagged black border). Female below, dull greenish-gray with smudged brown spots.

RANGE   A very rare late summer immigrant and stray into our area, north at least to Staten Island, NY. Also, south to Florida, west to Texas, and south to Argentina.

FLIGHT PERIOD & ABUNDANCE   **B:** X.   **N:** S, not recorded for many years at a time.   **P:** S, not recorded most years, late Aug.–mid Oct.   **W:** S, not recorded most years, late Aug.–mid Nov.

MAJOR FOODPLANT   Grasses.

Southern Broken Dash *(Wallengrenia otho)* Plate 33

SIZE   ≥ Tawny-edged Skipper.

SIMILAR SPECIES   Northern Broken Dash, Black Dash.

IDENTIFICATION   Similar to Northern Broken Dash but **ground color is a rich reddish brown.** Note the **broad gray FW fringe** contrasting with the buffy

HW fringe. Northern Broken Dash has a yellowish-brown ground color and brownish fringes on both wings. The Black Dash below is quite similar but larger. The Black Dash male above has extensive orange on both sides of the FW black stigma.

HABITAT   Moist woodland trails and edges.

RANGE   Another rare immigrant into our region, occurring in northern MD. Also, south to Florida, west to Texas, and south to Argentina.

SPECIFIC LOCALITIES   Mattawomen Natural Environment Area, MD.

FLIGHT PERIOD & ABUNDANCE   **B:** X.   **N:** X.   P: X.   **W:** R-U, recorded from MD east and south of Baltimore-Washington, especially Charles Co., MD.

MAJOR FOODPLANT   Grasses.

Northern Broken Dash *(Wallengrenia egeremet)* Plates 33 & 34

SIZE   ≥ Tawny-edged Skipper.

SIMILAR SPECIES   Little Glassywing, Dun Skipper, Black Dash, Southern Broken Dash.

IDENTIFICATION   Below, ground color **yellowish-brown** often with a **violaceous sheen.** HW has a fairly wide, but often indistinct, cream-colored spotband that is usually **vaguely in the shape of a 3.** Male above, usually has tawny FW margin. Note the two-part **black stigma and adjacent pale elongate spot.** Female above is mainly dark brown. Note **distinctive elongated pale yellow spot near wing center.** Below, Little Glassywing and Dun Skipper have darker brown ground colors and narrower HW post-median spot-bands with smaller spots. Black Dash and Southern Broken Dash have reddish brown ground colors. Distinguish worn Black Dash with brown ground color by "chunky" post-median mark as opposed to a spot-band.

HABITAT   Open field and meadows, most common in moist but not wet situations.

RANGE   Entire region. Also, north to Maine, west to Minnesota, and south to Texas and Florida.

FLIGHT PERIOD & ABUNDANCE   **B:** C, July–mid Aug.   **N:** A, late June–July. Max. 250, 7/8/89 Ward Pound Ridge Reservation, NY.   **P:** C-A, early June–mid July, Aug.   **W:** C, early June–July, mid Aug.–Sept.

MAJOR FOODPLANT   Panic Grasses *(Panicum).*

COMMENTS   Along with Little Glassywing and Dun Skipper, one of the "three witches." Switches from single to double brooded just south of New York City although the second brood is normally much less common.

Little Glassywing *(Pompeius verna)* Plates 33 & 34

SIZE   = Tawny-edged Skipper.

SIMILAR SPECIES   Dun Skipper, Northern Broken Dash.

IDENTIFICATION   Below, dark brown ground color with post-median line of discrete pale spots. Above, dark brown with a large square (female) or rectangular (male) pale spot. Female also has a white spot **in** the cell (but this can be small). **Note white areas just before antennal clubs.** Other similar skippers lack these white areas. Dun Skipper below has HW spot-band usually less extensive, usually lacks FW subapical white spots along costa (usually prominent in Little Glassywing), and usually has a "veined" look. Northern Broken Dash has a somewhat paler yellowish-brown-mauve ground color and wider post-median band usually forming a 3.

HABITAT   Moist brushy fields near woodlands, rarer in poor soil areas.

RANGE   Entire region. Also, west to Minnesota and south to Texas and Florida.

FLIGHT PERIOD & ABUNDANCE   **B:** C, late June–early Aug.   **N:** C, late June–July. Max. 350, 7/8/89 Ward Pound Ridge Reservation, NY.   **P:** C, June–early July, sometimes partial in Aug.   **W:** C, late May–early July, Aug.–Sept.

MAJOR FOODPLANT   Purple Top Grass *(Tridens flavus)*.

Sachem *(Atalopedes campestris)* Plate 32

SIZE   = Zabulon/Hobomok Skipper.

SIMILAR SPECIES   Cobweb Skipper, Hobomok Skipper.

IDENTIFICATION   Male below, note the **squarish brown patch at center of HW bottom margin surrounded by yellow.** Broad borders are similar to Hobomok Skipper but Sachem lacks the large brown patch at the base of the HW. Male above, the **large rectangular stigma** is unmistakable. Female below, very large, pale yellow post-median chevron on the HW. Cobweb Skipper is much smaller and flies only in the spring. Female above, note the two very large, white hyaline spots on the FW.

HABITAT   Open disturbed fields, roadsides, suburban and urban lots, barrens.

RANGE   Usually an immigrant into our area on very rare occasions overwintering in the south or straying north to Long Island.

FLIGHT PERIOD & ABUNDANCE   **B:** X.   **N:** S, not recorded for many years at a time.   **P:** R-C, variable immigrant, May (very rarely), July–Oct., most records in Sept.   **W:** U-A, May–Oct. Abundance increases greatly in late summer.

MAJOR FOODPLANT   Bermuda Grass *(Cynodon dactylon)* and Crabgrass *(Digitaria)*.

Arogos Skipper *(Atrytone arogos)* Plate 35

SIZE   = Tawny-edged Skipper.

SIMILAR SPECIES   Delaware Skipper.

IDENTIFICATION   Above, note **broad brown borders** and absence of black veining. Below, very similar to Delaware Skipper but veining somewhat paler. Midwest populations have white fringes but our population seems to have yellow-orange fringes.

HABITAT   In our region, barrens and dry grassy pine woods.

RANGE   Formerly occurred on Staten Island on serpentine outcrops and in the NJ pine barrens. It has not been found recently despite much searching. Also, a few disjunct populations in the southeast U.S. and Minnesota south to Texas.

SPECIFIC LOCALITIES   Formerly known from the serpentine grassland at the intersection of Bradley and Brielle Aves., Sea View, Staten Island, NY.

FLIGHT PERIOD & ABUNDANCE   **B:** X.   **N:** formerly LR, now probably extirpated.

Present into the 1980s. July. **P:** formerly LR, now possibly extirpated. July. A few records in Aug.–Sept. **W:** X.

MAJOR FOODPLANT Probably Bluestem Grasses *(Andropogon)*.

Delaware Skipper *(Atrytone logan)* Plate 35

SIZE = Hobomok Skipper, but very variable.

SIMILAR SPECIES European Skipper, Arogos Skipper, Rare Skipper.

IDENTIFICATION An active skipper, **clear bright unmarked yellow-orange below.** Above, orange with black borders and **black FW cell-end bar** and at least some **black veining.** Fringes orange. European Skipper has short reddish antennae and is duller orange, usually with some whitish overscaling and whitish fringes.

HABITAT Open brushy fields, moist meadows, sedge marshes, and coastal marshes.

RANGE Entire region. Also, north to southern Maine, west to Montana, and south to Texas and Florida.

FLIGHT PERIOD & ABUNDANCE **B:** C, late June–late July. **N:** C-A, July. Max. 205, 7/8/89 Pound Ridge Reservation, NY. **P:** C, July–Aug. In the southern NJ salt marshes there are two broods, mid June and Aug. **W:** U, July.

MAJOR FOODPLANT Grasses.

Rare Skipper *(Problema bulenta)* Plate 35

SIZE > Hobomok Skipper.

SIMILAR SPECIES Delaware Skipper.

IDENTIFICATION Very similar to the tremendously more common and widespread Delaware Skipper. Below, unmarked bright yellow-orange but not so bright or so orange as the Delaware Skipper. Of course, worn Delaware Skippers quickly fade in brightness! On average Rare Skippers are larger than Delaware Skippers. This is especially true of the females where there is little, if any, size overlap. On males, note the FW black cell-end bar that can often be seen clearly from below. This spot is generally not seen in Delaware Skipper both because it tends to be weaker and less distinct below and because when the Delaware Skipper sits with its wings folded this spot is almost always hidden by the HW. Above, the male is a glowing golden-orange with wide black FW borders. The female above has extensive black markings. In both sexes, note the **white lines separating the abdominal segments.** Delaware Skipper is deep orange above with narrower black FW borders and has a dull-orange abdomen whose segments are not separated by white lines.

HABITAT Brackish coastal tidal marshes.

RANGE Coastal marshes of NJ north to at least Burlington Co. Also, Dorchester Co., MD, and a number of disjunct populations south to Georgia.

FLIGHT PERIOD & ABUNDANCE **B:** X. **N:** X. **P:** LC, July. **W:** X.

MAJOR FOODPLANT Probably Intertidal Cordgrass *(Spartina cynosuroides)* (personal communication from Dr. Jamie Cromartie and Dr. Dale Schweitzer).

COMMENTS Until recently, this rarely encountered skipper was known only from marshes near the mouths of five southern rivers, the farthest north being on the eastern shore of MD. Very recently, Dr. Cromartie of Stockton State College and Dr. Schweitzer of The Nature Conservancy discovered a number of colonies along the NJ coast. At some locations this skipper can be common but only because the colonies are so intensely localized and the individual butterflies concentrate on flowers. The exact location of colonies is not being released by Drs. Cromartie and Schweitzer because of fears of collection pressure. One behavioral trait of these skippers that I noticed deserves mention. When an individual is standing on a leaf (not nectaring on a flower) it will usually rotate its body to the left or take a few steps forward, just before taking off.

Mulberry Wing *(Poanes massasoit)* Plate 37

SIZE = Tawny-edged Skipper.
SIMILAR SPECIES None.
IDENTIFICATION The distinctive bright yellow patch on the reddish brown HW below is striking. Very rarely (but frequently in southern NJ), individuals are entirely suffused with the reddish-brown color below. Above, males are black with a purplish sheen when fresh (like a mulberry) and females are black with a few small white spots. The black upper surface is often visible during its low and weak flight.
HABITAT Wet meadows, open freshwater marshes, fens, or bogs.
RANGE In the east, largely limited to our region. Entire Region, but rare or absent from Cape Cod, southern NJ, and south of Washington, D.C. Also, western NY west to Minnesota.
SPECIFIC LOCALITIES Ward Pound Ridge Reservation, NY.
FLIGHT PERIOD & ABUNDANCE **B:** LU, but rare or absent from Cape Cod. mid July–mid Aug. **N:** LC, but rare or absent LI. early July–early Aug. Max. 85, 7/14/91 Pound Ridge Reservation, NY. **P:** LC, but uncommon southern NJ. Late June–July. **W:** LU, late June–July.
MAJOR FOODPLANT Sedges *(Carex).*
COMMENTS Almost everywhere associated with the Black Dash.

Hobomok Skipper *(Poanes hobomok)* Plate 36

SIZE 10/16 in.
SIMILAR SPECIES Zabulon Skipper.
IDENTIFICATION Males and most females below—mainly yellow with **extensive brown patch at base of HW** and **broad brown borders.** Zabulon Skipper has narrower borders and yellow within a smaller basal brown patch. Some females below (form pocahontas) are suffused with dark brown but usually retain some of the usual pattern. Distinguish from female Zabulon by lack of silvery white on the HW costal margin. Female above, dark with pale spots. Note **pale cell spot,** lacking in female Zabulon.
HABITAT Deciduous woodland edges and openings.
RANGE Southeast to about the Fall Line. Also, north to Maine, west to North Dakota, and south to Arkansas and Georgia.

FLIGHT PERIOD & ABUNDANCE   **B:** C-A, late May–early July.   **N:** C, late May–
early July. Max. 30, 6/11/89 Caumsett State Park, Suffolk Co., NY.   **P:** C, to
the northwest, LU, to the southeast, rare or absent in the pine barrens, late
May–mid July.   **W:** LU, late May–mid June, north and west of Washington,
D.C.

MAJOR FOODPLANT   Grasses.

COMMENTS   Although this species is territorial and the males fly rapidly along the
edges of trees lining woodland trails and edges, they do not appear to return
to the same perch as frequently as Zabulon Skippers do.

Zabulon Skipper *(Poanes zabulon)* Plate 36

SIZE   10/16 in.

SIMILAR SPECIES   Hobomok Skipper.

IDENTIFICATION   Male below, mainly yellow with HW post-basal **brown patch
enclosing yellow at wing base.** Female below, dark rusty brown with
vague darker blotches. Note **silvery white HW costal margin.** Dark female
Hobomok Skippers lack this mark. Dark female above, dark brown with extensive white spots on the FW but not in the cell. Female Hobomok Skipper
has spot in the cell.

HABITAT   Woodland openings, edges, and adjacent fields, including suburban
habitats.

RANGE   North to the northern New York area and north along the Connecticut
River Valley barely to the Springfield area. Also, west to Kansas and south to
Texas and Florida.

FLIGHT PERIOD & ABUNDANCE   **B:** X, but R in the Springfield area, Late May–early
June, Aug.   **N:** C, late May–June, late July–early Sept. Max. 12, 6/6/87 For-
est Hills, Queens, NY; 35, 8/10/86 Tottenville, Staten Island, NY.   **P:** C late
May–late June, late July–mid Sept.   **W:** C-A, late May–June, late July–Sept.

MAJOR FOODPLANT   Grasses.

COMMENTS   Males are highly territorial, patrolling along a woodland trail and
returning to the same perch.

Aaron's Skipper *(Poanes aaroni)* Plate 37

SIZE   = Zabulon/Hobomok Skipper.

SIMILAR SPECIES   Broad-winged Skipper, Dion Skipper.

IDENTIFICATION   A large dingy orange skipper of the salt marsh and adjacent
fields. Below, note the **pale HW ray flanked by two pale dots.** Broad-
winged Skipper similar but has two, well-defined white spots on the FW below. Dion Skipper is usually brighter orange and lacks spots flanking HW ray.

HABITAT   Salt marshes.

RANGE   North, on the coast, to about the Forked River area just south of Toms
River, NJ. South along the coast (including Delaware and Chesapeake Bays)
discontinuously to Florida.

FLIGHT PERIOD & ABUNDANCE   **B:** X.   **N:** X.   **P:** LC, June, Aug.–Sept. southern
NJ coast.   **W:** LU-LC, June, Aug.

90

MAJOR FOODPLANT   Possibly Saltgrass *(Distichlis spicata).*
COMMENTS   Often found nectaring outside of marshes.

Broad-winged Skipper *(Poanes viator zizaniae)* Plate 37

SIZE   > Zabulon/Hobomok Skipper.
SIMILAR SPECIES   Aaron's Skipper, Mulberry Wing.
IDENTIFICATION   A very large, dull-colored, weak-flying Skipper. Below, dull orangish-brown with a somewhat paler ray. Usually **lands with its head up** and its body oriented perpendicularly to the ground. Mulberry Wing is much smaller with much sharper contrasting pattern.
HABITAT   Formerly only tidal marsh but now following phragmites into inland fresh-water marshes.
RANGE   Recently expanded northward into the Boston area and southern Maine (1991). Now present in the entire region but usually rare and local away from the coast. Also, south along the coast to Florida and Texas and a disjunct inland population from western NY west to North Dakota.
FLIGHT PERIOD & ABUNDANCE   **B:** LC, mid July–late Aug.   **N:** A, July–Aug. Max. 220, 7/28/85 Jamaica Bay Wildlife Refuge, NY.   **P:** A, July, along the Delaware.   **W:** LA, July–Aug.
MAJOR FOODPLANT   Phragmites *(Phragmites communis).*

Dion Skipper *(Euphyes dion)* Plate 38

SIZE   ≥ Zabulon/Hobomok Skipper.
SIMILAR SPECIES   Delaware Skipper, Broad-winged Skipper, Aaron's Skipper.
IDENTIFICATION   A large wetland skipper. Bright orange to duller reddish-orange below with **one or two pale rays on the HW.** Delaware Skipper lacks pale rays and is smaller. Aaron's Skipper is duller, flies in different habitat at a different time. Broad-winged Skipper has a vague pale HW ray but is duller orange, its wings are more rounded, and the pale ray is flanked by two pale spots.
HABITAT   Calcareous fens and other alkaline to neutral wetlands from northern NJ north; bogs and other acidic wetlands from southern NJ south.
RANGE   (1) Western CT (Fairfield and western Litchfield Cos.), southeastern NY (Dutchess and Westchester Cos.), and northern NJ. (2) Central and southern NJ. (3) Washington, D.C., area. Also, south along the coast to Florida then west to Texas, and western NY west to Minnesota.
SPECIFIC LOCALITIES   Wingdale, Dutchess Co., NY; Spingdale, Sussex Co., NJ; Lakehurst bog, NJ; Mattawoman Natural Environment Area, MD; Huntley Meadows, Fairfax Co., VA.
FLIGHT PERIOD & ABUNDANCE   **B:** X.   **N:** LR, late June–mid July. Max. 5, 7/13/87 Wingdale, NY.   **P:** LU-LC, mid July–early Aug., south-central NJ.   **W:** LR, June–early July, Aug.–early Sept., Calvert & Charles Cos., MD, and Fairfax Co., VA.
MAJOR FOODPLANT   Sedges *(Carex).*
COMMENTS   The northern populations are not only found in different habitat than

the southern populations but they fly at a different time (earlier!) and they behave differently. They are very nervous and active, powerful flyers. In contrast, the southern populations seem to be sluggish. Perhaps these are sibling species.

Black Dash *(Euphyes conspicua)* Plate 38

SIZE = Zabulon/Hobomok Skipper.

SIMILAR SPECIES Northern Broken Dash.

IDENTIFICATION A rusty-yellow-brown marsh skipper with a characteristic pale chunky post-median HW patch. Northern Broken Dash is smaller and is not reddish below.

HABITAT Wet meadows and fresh-water marshes.

RANGE Eastern populations are essentially restricted to our region. Rare or absent on Cape Cod, Long Island, and southern NJ. Also, disjunct population from Ohio west to Minnesota.

FLIGHT PERIOD & ABUNDANCE **B:** LU, mid July–mid Aug. **N:** LC, July–early Aug. Max. 117, 7/8/89 Pound Ridge Reservation, NY. **P:** LU, early July–late July. **W:** LR, late June–July.

MAJOR FOODPLANT Sedge *(Carex stricta).*

COMMENTS Usually flies with the Mulberry Wing. The presence of Swamp Milkweed is a good indicator for these species.

Two-spotted Skipper *(Euphyes bimacula)* Plate 38

SIZE ≥ Hobomok Skipper.

SIMILAR SPECIES None.

IDENTIFICATION A bold orange skipper below with **paler veining** and striking **white ray along HW inner margin.** Above, male has dull orange on both sides of the stigma.

HABITAT Wet acid-soil areas such as bogs, acid marshes, and meadows with sedges.

RANGE Entire region except southern NJ and south and east of Washington, D.C. Also, north to Maine, west to Minnesota, and south in the mountains to southern Virginia.

SPECIFIC LOCALITIES Lebanon State Forest, NJ, Lakehurst Bog, NJ.

FLIGHT PERIOD & ABUNDANCE **B:** LR, late June–early July. **N:** LR, mid June–early July. no extant colonies known. **P:** LU, mid June–early July, most common in NJ pine barrens. **W:** LR, June.

MAJOR FOODPLANT Sedges *(Carex).*

Dun Skipper *(Euphyes vestris)* Plates 33 & 34

SIZE = Tawny-edged Skipper.

SIMILAR SPECIES Little Glassywing, Northern Broken Dash.

IDENTIFICATION Dark brown all over. Above, male is **all dark brown** with black stigma. In many populations, the **head is bright orange.** Female is all dark brown above with **two small pale spots.** Little Glassywing has a better defined HW spot-band, white at base of antennal clubs, and is very different above. Northern Broken Dash has paler yellow-brown ground color and HW post-median band in the shape of a 3. Northern Broken Dash female above has distinctive elongated white spot past the FW cell.

RANGE   Entire region. Also, north to Maine, west to Washington, and south to Arizona, Texas, and Florida.

FLIGHT PERIOD & ABUNDANCE   **B:** C, July.   **N:** C-A, late June–early Aug., mid Aug.–early Sept. (S.I. and NJ). Max. 1350, 7/8/89 Pound Ridge Reservation, NY.   **P:** C, mid May–early July, late Aug.–late Sept.   **W:** C, June, late July–Aug.

MAJOR FOODPLANT   Sedges *(Carex)*.

Dusted Skipper *(Atrytonopsis hianna)* Plate 39

SIZE   ≥ Zabulon/Hobomok Skipper.

SIMILAR SPECIES   Female Zabulon Skipper, Cloudywings, Common Roadside Skipper, Clouded Skipper.

IDENTIFICATION   A large dark folded-wing skipper with much frosting of the marginal wing areas below. When (usually) present, the **white spot at the base of the HW below** is diagnostic. Its **"masked" appearance,** due to its dark eye being bordered by the white palps below and a **white eye stripe** above, separates this species from our other dark skippers with frosting.

HABITAT   Dry fields, barrens, and power-line cuts in association with its foodplant.

RANGE   Entire region. Also, west to North Dakota and south to Texas and Florida.

SPECIFIC LOCALITIES   West Rock Ridge State Park, CT; Nottingham County Park, PA. (common); Soldier's Delight, MD.

FLIGHT PERIOD & ABUNDANCE   **B:** C, mid May–late June.   **N:** U, late May–mid June. Max. 5, 5/29/88 Floyd Bennet Field, Brooklyn, NY.   **P:** LU-LC, late May–June.   **W:** LU, late May–June.

MAJOR FOODPLANT   Blue Stem Grasses *(Andropogon)*.

COMMENTS   Widespread but often local, the few individuals present in an *Andropogon* field are usually easy to see because this skipper is active over a wide area. Generally, an area good for Dusted Skippers will have had a greater number of Cobweb Skippers flying a few weeks earlier. In its courtship flight as the female flies forward the male comes from behind and loops over and then under her a number of times.

Pepper and Salt Skipper *(Amblyscirtes hegon)* Plate 39

SIZE   = Least Skipper.

SIMILAR SPECIES   None.

IDENTIFICATION   Below, yellowish tinged gray-brown ground with prominent cream-colored HW post-median band. Note the relatively short wings and the abdomen segments faintly ringed with white. Above, dark brown with a few pale spots on the FW. Holds its wings in characteristic Roadside Skipper fashion, with the **FWs held almost perpendicularly to the flat HWs** (other folded-wing skippers hold the FWs at a much more oblique angle).

HABITAT   Edges of northern woodlands, especially along grass-lined watercourses.

RANGE   Normally entering our region only at its northwestern margins, the Pepper and Salt Skipper ranges southeast to the Boston area and then west through MA. It has been recorded from western CT and the Ramapo Mtns of northern NJ as well as northwest of Philadelphia. Also, north to Maine, west to Minnesota, and south to Texas and northern Georgia.

FLIGHT PERIOD & ABUNDANCE   **B:** LR, south and east to just southeast of Boston, early June–mid July.   **N:** X. Possibly occurs in the Hudson Highlands.   **P:** LR, at the northwest margins, June.   **W:** X.

MAJOR FOODPLANT   Grasses.

Common Roadside Skipper *(Amblyscirtes vialis)* Plate 39

SIZE   = Least Skipper.

SIMILAR SPECIES   Dusted Skipper, female Zabulon Skipper.

IDENTIFICATION   A **very small black** skipper. Below, frosted on outer portions of the wings. Note **strongly checked fringes.** Above, mainly dark brown. Holds its wings in characteristic Roadside Skipper fashion, with the **FWs held almost perpendicularly to the flat HWs.** Dusted and Zabulon Skippers are much larger and lack checkered fringes.

HABITAT   Roadsides and other edge areas where woodlands meet grasslands. Barrens.

RANGE   Recorded from most of our region but very rare (or absent) in southeastern MA, most of CT, the NY area, and southern NJ. Also, north to Maine, west to northern California, and south to Texas and Florida.

SPECIFIC LOCALITIES   Nottingham County Park, PA; Soldiers Delight, MD.

FLIGHT PERIOD & ABUNDANCE   **B:** LR, north and west of Boston, late May–June.   **N:** LR, has been recorded from eastern Long Island and northern NJ but hasn't been seen in many years.   **P:** LU, mid May–early June, a few reports late July–early Aug.   **W:** U, May, late July–early Aug.

MAJOR FOODPLANT   Grasses.

Eufala Skipper *(Lerodea eufala)* Plate 40

SIZE   = Tawny-edged Skipper.

SIMILAR SPECIES   Swarthy Skipper, Little Glassywing, Tawny-edged Skipper.

IDENTIFICATION   A small, brown, nondescript skipper that is not normally part of our fauna. Eufala Skipper has a series of three white spots on the FW subapex (visible from above and below) that Swarthy Skipper lacks. There is an additional white spot on the FW above. Distinguish from Little Glassywing by the less extensive white spots above, paler gray-brown ground color below, and the narrower wings.

RANGE   Southern U.S. south to southern South America. Range expands northward in the summer, especially through the middle of the country. In the East, ranges northward to southern VA with occasional individuals straying farther northward.

FLIGHT PERIOD & ABUNDANCE   **B:** X.   **N:** X.   **P:** S, recorded in southern NJ in 1991.   **W:** S, a few records.

94

Twin-spot Skipper *(Oligora maculata)* Plate 40

SIZE = Hobomok/Zabulon Skipper.
SIMILAR SPECIES Brazilian Skipper.
IDENTIFICATION Not normally a part of our fauna. Note the three bold white spots on the HW below tending toward having the same curvature as the HW margin. The Brazilian Skipper, another rare stray into our region, is much larger and has bold white HW spots that angle outward.
RANGE Southeastern U.S. coastal plain from North Carolina to Texas.
FLIGHT PERIOD & ABUNDANCE **B:** X. **N:** X. **P:** S, a few records. **W:** S, a few records.

Brazilian Skipper *(Calpodes ethlius)* Plate 40

SIZE >> Hobomok/Zabulon Skipper.
SIMILAR SPECIES Twin-spot Skipper.
IDENTIFICATION This very large folded-wing skipper (about the size of the Hoary Edge) is a rich reddish-tinged brown below with **three large white spots in an angled line on the HW below.**
HABITAT Suburban gardens with Cannas.
RANGE Resident of southern Florida and Texas south to Argentina. Periodically irrupts northward to a greater or lesser degree. Recorded (extremely rarely) north to NY.
FLIGHT PERIOD & ABUNDANCE **B:** X. **N:** X, but there are a few old records. **P:** S, not seen for many years at a time. Occasionally seen in the Cape May area. **W:** S, not seen for many years at a time.
MAJOR FOODPLANT Cannas *(Canna).*

Salt Marsh Skipper *(Panoquina panoquin)* Plate 39

SIZE = Zabulon/Hobomok Skipper.
SIMILAR SPECIES None.
IDENTIFICATION A very long-winged, yellow-brown skipper with **paler yellow veining** and **a cream-colored streak distal to the HW cell below.** Note the **dark line running down the side of the abdomen.** This, along with the very long wings, is characteristic of Panoquins.
HABITAT Salt marsh and adjacent fields.
RANGE North to the south shore of Long Island. Also, south to Florida and then west to Texas.
FLIGHT PERIOD & ABUNDANCE **B:** X. **N:** LR, late June–mid July, Aug.–mid Sept. Max. 18, 9/3/91 Lido Beach, Nassau Co., NY. **P:** LU-LA, mid June–mid July, Aug.–Sept. **W:** LC.
MAJOR FOODPLANT Saltgrass *(Distichlis spicata).*

Ocola Skipper *(Panoquina ocola)* Plate 39

SIZE ≥ Zabulon/Hobomok Skipper.
SIMILAR SPECIES Little Glassywing.
IDENTIFICATION Note the long and narrow wings. Plain, dull yellowish-brown

below with **distal one-quarter of wings darker brown.** Note the **striped abdomen.** Little Glassywing doesn't have the distal one-third of its wings below sharply darker and lacks the striped abdomen.

HABITAT   Almost any open moist areas, including salt marsh and open pine woodlands and gardens.

RANGE   A very variable immigrant from the south into our region. Not normally found north of the Philadelphia area, it has been recorded from Long Island. Also, south to Florida, then west to Texas, and south to Argentina.

FLIGHT PERIOD & ABUNDANCE   **B:** X.   **N:** S, not recorded for many years at a time.   **P:** R, immigrant, mid Sept.–mid Oct.   **W:** R, immigrant, mid Aug.–mid Oct.

MAJOR FOODPLANT   Unknown in our area.

Appendix A

Descriptions and Checklists for Selected Butterflying Localities

The following localities have been chosen for the diversity and abundance of their butterfly fauna as well as for their easy accessibility to a large percentage of the people of our region. They should serve as excellent starting points for your butterflying experiences. Most of the species recorded from our region have been seen in at least one of these localities. Butterflies found at the localities listed in this section should not be harmed. In almost all cases they are protected by law. In the few cases where they are not, it would be unethical to deny other butterfliers the pleasure of seeing these butterflies.

Middlesex Fells Reservation
Middlesex County, MA
Robert K. Robbins

DESCRIPTION   This park of approximately 3000 acres is 10 to 15 minutes north of Boston surrounding Interstate 93 in the towns of Stoneham, Medford, Winchester, Melrose, and Malden. It was established in the late 1800s and consists mostly of forested uplands with poor soil. Water drains quickly from the rocky hillsides, making ideal conditions for Blueberries, Pitch Pines, and Scrub Oaks. Large ponds (some are reservoirs) and numerous temporary ponds are scattered over the reservation, but there are few streams.

BUTTERFLIES   The richest area for butterflying is the Nike Field-Observatory Hill-Whitmore Brook area, which is on the left-hand (south) side of South Border Road—1 to 1.3 miles from the I-93 exit. A carriage trail parallels Whitmore Brook from South Border Road to Winthrop Street, and this is where I have seen wetland associated butterflies such as Harvesters, Baltimores, and Mulberry Wings. A marsh to the south of this trail—and just east of Winthrop Street—is probably the most likely area in the Fells to find previously unrecorded species. The large open dry meadow to the south of Whitmore Brook and South Border Road was apparently a Nike missile base during World War II. Beginning about the second week of May, there is a succession of annual flowers and butterflies that lasts for the remainder of the summer. Some years, the diversity and abundance of skippers and hairstreaks are remarkable. The usually rare Southern Hairstreak can be common in late June on flowers about 5 P.M., but it has been rare for the last decade because the field is becoming overgrown. In fact, an open area south of Wenepoykin Hill on the east side of South Border Road has been a better site for hairstreaks the last few years. Parts of the Nike Field need to be mowed regularly if it is to retain its diversity.

Just to the SE of the Nike Field, a radar station was located on top of small, wooded Observatory Hill. Some ruins remain, and there is a good view of Boston. Before the trees leaf out in spring, this is an excellent area for Spring Azures, Elfins, and Duskywings. Later in the year, males of many species, such as Roadside Skippers and Red-spotted Purples, set up mating territories along the carriage trail just to the NE of the summit. Northern Pearly Eyes are sometimes seen in woods to the west of Observatory Hill, walking toward Whitmore Brook.

Just to the west of I-93 are Pine and Bear Hills, located at the south and north extremes of the Fells, respectively. Each has an observation tower on its summit with fantastic views. The top of Pine Hill is rocky and excellent in the late afternoon for hilltopping males of Red Admirals and American Ladies. There are Red Cedars on the north slope of Bear Hill, which is one of the best areas for Olive Hairstreaks.

SPECIES LIST   Black Swallowtail U, Eastern Tiger Swallowtail C, Spicebush Swallowtail A, Cabbage White A, Clouded Sulphur A, Orange Sulphur C, Harvester R, American Copper C, Coral Hairstreak U, Acadian Hairstreak R, Edwards' Hairstreak C, Banded Hairstreak A (some years U), Striped Hairstreak C, Olive Hairstreak C, Brown Elfin A, Frosted Elfin R, Henry's Elfin R, Eastern Pine Elfin C, Southern Hairstreak U-C, Gray Hairstreak U, Eastern Tailed Blue C, Spring Azure C, Great Spangled Fritillary C, Pearl Crescent A, Baltimore R (some years A), Question Mark C, Eastern Comma R, Compton Tortoiseshell R, Mourning Cloak C, American Lady C, Painted Lady R, Red Admiral U, Common Buckeye R, Red-spotted Purple C, Viceroy C, Northern Pearly Eye U, Appalachian Brown R, Little Wood Satyr A, Common Ringlet A, Common Wood Nymph C, Monarch C, Silver-spotted Skipper C, Hoary Edge C, Southern Cloudywing U, Northern Cloudywing C, Dreamy Duskywing C, Sleepy Duskywing A, Juvenal's Duskywing A, Horace's Duskywing R, Wild Indigo Duskywing U, Least Skipper U-C, European Skipper A, Leonard's Skipper R, Cobweb Skipper U, Indian Skipper C, Peck's Skipper C, Tawny-edged Skipper C, Crossline Skipper U, Long Dash C, Northern Broken Dash C, Little Glassywing A, Delaware Skipper C, Mulberry Wing R, Hobomok Skipper C, Dun Skipper A, Dusted Skipper U, Pepper and Salt Skipper R, Roadside Skipper U.

DIRECTIONS   Exit I-93 at Fellsway West (Exit 33), and follow the signs to Winchester, which will put you on South Border Road. A map of the Fells can be obtained from the Metropolitan District Commission office.

Great Swamp Management Area
West Kingston, RI
Harry Pavulaan

DESCRIPTION   This is perhaps the best single location in southeastern New England to find such a diversity of habitats within a half-day's walk. The Management Area, maintained by the RI Department of Environmental Management, covers several square miles containing dry upland transition zone forest and extensive woodland swamps dominated by various species of Oaks and Red Maple. Some primary natural features are: Atlantic White Cedar swamps, cranberry bogs, Red Maple swamps, sedge marshes, Scrub Oak thickets, and one of the last remaining large natural stands of American Holly in New England. Man-made and maintained features include a large impoundment pond and several large fields that display an abundance of native wildflowers throughout the season.

BUTTERFLIES   From the main parking area, looking west beyond the Oaks bordering the parking area, one will see a stand of Atlantic White Cedar trees. This is home to a colony of Hessel's Hairstreak. While this butterfly can be common, it is one of the most elusive resident species because of its habit of remaining high up in the tops of the cedars. It can be found nectaring on the Highbush Blueberries that ring the swamp, especially in the morning and late afternoon. As you walk in from the gate at the end of the main parking area, follow the main dirt road through the swamp. In the spring, one will see multitudes of Spring Azures as well as Dreamy and Juvenal's Duskywings. In the summer this is a good spot to find Appalachian Brown. Take the first roadway to the right and follow it to the first rise and sharp bend to the left; there is a small cutoff to the right. In the spring, follow this cutoff a few feet to the end and turn right along an old trail. Follow this old trail into the field, but bear left and keep to the left side of the field. Follow this trail to the railroad tracks. Either to the left or to the right, you will see extensive growths of Wild Indigo along the tracks and the sandy areas nearby. In this area you can find Frosted Elfins, Wild Indigo Duskywings, and Cobweb Skippers. Follow the railroad tracks to the right until you see the Atlantic White Cedar swamp on the right. Watch for Hessel's Hairstreak feeding on Wild Cherry blossoms in the spring. The Little Yellow has been seen here in summer, though it only appears some years. Carefully retrace your steps back to the left-bend along the main dirt roadway, turn right, and continue along the roadway. The small dry field on the left holds Coral Hairstreak in summer. Continuing along, there is a large field on your right. This field is filled with the blooms of Common Milkweed in summer, providing nectar for a multitude of butterflies. Edwards' Hairstreak is often seen by the thousands along with Banded, Striped, and Southern Hairstreaks, Great Spangled and Aphrodite Fritillaries, Common Wood Nymph, and a large variety of skippers. Continuing along, bear right at the powerline and follow the roadway, keeping left at the first fork. Where the roadway enters the woods you will note several large roadside clearings that are filled with Milkweed flowers. The Spicebush Swallowtail may be found here in summer. Follow this roadway past the large fields on the right. These fields are filled with flowers throughout the summer and fall, with Joe-pye Weed being the most prominent in late summer, Goldenrod in the fall. One will see large numbers of the Common Wood Nymph here in summer, as well as the well-known Viceroy. Later in the summer, Leonard's Skipper can be found on the Joe-pye Weed. As you make the first left, and then another left farther down, the trail takes you through mixed transition zone forest in which American Holly abounds as an understory tree. Numerous Red-spotted Purples can be found in this area, some showing traces of white bands. In spring, less common or rare species such as Henry's Elfin and the White M Hairstreak are found here. Follow the roadway back to the power line where you will make a right turn. Along the sandy powerline road is a colony of American Coppers. Follow the power line to where you pass thickets of Phragmites (Giant Reed) and where Broadwinged Skippers can be seen coursing back and forth within and along the edges of the reeds. Turn back as the power line turns to the right and return to the main dirt roadway. There, turn right and continue to the main parking area. Drive back toward the ranger compound. Just before reaching the compound, turn right onto the rifle range roadway. On the left you will pass a large patch of Common Milkweed. Gray, Olive, and Acadian Hairstreaks have been seen here. Drive to the rifle range, park, and continue along the foot trail to the power line. Cross the power line and continue along a trail that has become overgrown with Sweet Pepperbush in recent years. In summer, this trail can be quite choked, but still recognizable. After about 200 feet, look for a small, indistinct trail (also overgrown) going to the left, into a large cranberry bog. One can safely walk through this bog, on a cushion of bog plants, but expect to sink ankle-deep into the water with each step. The bog itself has a colony of Bog Coppers that fly in July and the Atlantic White Cedars around the fringes of the bog support another colony of Hessel's Hairstreak. To return, retrace your route carefully back to the rifle range.

SPECIES LIST   Pipevine Swallowtail R, Black Swallowtail U, Eastern Tiger Swallowtail U, Spicebush Swallowtail C, Cabbage White C, Clouded Sulphur A, Orange Sulphur A, Little Yellow R-C, American Copper C, Bog Copper U, Coral Hairstreak U, Acadian Hairstreak R, Edwards' Hairstreak A, Banded Hairstreak A, Striped Hairstreak C, Olive Hairstreak U, Hessel's Hairstreak C, Brown Elfin C, Frosted Elfin C, Henry's Elfin C, Eastern Pine Elfin U, Southern Hairstreak U, White M Hairstreak R, Gray Hairstreak U, Eastern Tailed Blue A, Spring Azure A, Variegated Fritillary R, Great Spangled Fritillary C, Aphrodite Fritillary C, Silver-bordered Fritillary U, Pearl Crescent A, Baltimore R, Question Mark U, Eastern Comma U, Mourning Cloak C, American Lady C, Painted Lady R-C, Red Admiral U, Common Buckeye R, Red-spotted Purple C, Viceroy C, Appalachian Brown C, Little Wood Satyr I U, Little Wood Satyr II A, Common Wood Nymph A, Monarch C, Silver-spotted Skipper A, Southern Cloudywing U, Dreamy Duskywing C, Sleepy Duskywing R, Juvenal's Duskywing A, Horace's Duskywing C, Wild Indigo Duskywing A, Common Sootywing C, Least Skipper C, European Skipper C, Leonard's Skipper C, Cobweb Skipper C, Indian Skipper C, Peck's Skipper C, Tawny-edged Skipper C, Crossline Skipper U, Northern Broken Dash C, Little Glassywing A, Delaware Skipper C, Mulberry Wing U, Hobomok Skipper C, Broad-winged Skipper U, Black Dash U, Dun Skipper C, Dusted Skipper C.

DIRECTIONS   Either from the north or south, take I-95 to RI Exit 3 (Route 138). Take Route 138 east toward West Kingston for about 8 miles. After crossing the Route 138 overpass over the railroad tracks, continue about one-half-mile and watch for Liberty Lane on the right. There is a small general store on the near corner, where food and drink can be obtained. Turn right onto Liberty Lane (if you pass the turn, you will come to a traffic light on Route 138; turn around and go back and make your first left turn). Follow Liberty Lane to its end at the railroad tracks and follow the gravel roadway that continues toward the left, marked Great Neck Rd. Take this past the ranger compound and make note of the left turn cutoff for the rifle range, for your return trip. Continue along Great Neck Rd. to the very end where there is a parking area. All areas of the Management Area are accessible by foot, from the gated dirt road at the end.

West Rock Ridge State Park
New Haven County, CT
Larry Gall

DESCRIPTION   This is the larger of two majestic trap-rock ridges that flank the city of New Haven, and is one link in a series of geologically related ridges that extend from the Palisades of New Jersey through Mount Tom in Massachusetts. West Rock was established as a state park only in the late 1980s, having been principally in the domain of the city for many decades prior. In addition to the typical plants found in southern New England forests, West Rock supports a number of normally more southerly plants than the surrounding areas. This is due to the high heat-retaining capacity of the trap-rock (which imparts the xeric flavor to the ridge system). Accordingly, the diverse West Rock flora support a diverse butterfly fauna, with over 80 species so far recorded. The canopy on West Rock ridge is open and dominated by oaks, hickories, and ashes. Blueberries, serviceberries, and other scrubby plants compose the rather sparse understory. A few of the West Rock plants more characteristic of southerly climates include prickly pear cactus, hackberry, redbud, and dwarf chestnut oak. There are only occasional vernal ponds and streams on the ridge itself, although several large lakes occur at the western and northern bases of the park.

BUTTERFLIES   The richest area for butterflies is along the westernmost loop of the ridgetop hiking trail that leads northwest from the Judges' Cave car turnaround. The Judges' Cave area can be reached by following Park Drive (the only open road) for about two-thirds mile from the park entrance kiosk and taking the right-hand spur, which is marked (note that Baldwin Drive appears on many maps as another available car road running for about 10 miles along the ridge from the park entrance to the town of Hamden, but vehicles are barricaded from Baldwin both at the park entrance and at the other terminus in Hamden). The Judges' Cave hiking trail begins as a wide gravel path, but splits into two footpaths about one hundred yards in. After about one-half mile the paths reconnect with one another in a small ravine that sits directly atop the Route 15 (Merritt Parkway) tunnel. You can return to Judges' Cave by backtracking along the other loop, or continue north and west up the steep hill in front of you for more ridgetop butterflying, or exit onto Baldwin Drive near the large circular tower that vents the car tunnel (the ridgetop trail will also eventually meet up with Baldwin Drive). If you walk downhill to the right on Baldwin Drive, you will make a single large switchback and reach the park entrance kiosk in about one-quarter mile.

On warm days in February and March, waking Mourning Cloaks and Compton Tortoiseshells can be seen along the ridgetop. The latter species has been present regularly since the early 1980s. Later on, in late April and early May, Falcate Orangetips fly throughout the park but most densely along the ridgetop hiking trail. At the same time, swift kicks to the Red Cedars along the western loop of the hiking trail will send Olive Hairstreaks swirling—but watch closely for the occasional White M Hairstreak that will be among them. Brown Elfins hold territories in the late afternoon on the scrub oaks overlooking the southwestern flank of the ridgetop. Look for Cobweb Skippers in the Baldwin Drive switchbacks in early May, with a follow-up several weeks later for Dusted Skippers.

Edwards', Banded, Striped, and Coral Hairstreaks begin flying during the last 1 to 2 weeks of June. The latter three are found rather generally in the park, but Edwards' Hairstreaks tend to be localized in two large scrub oak thickets along the western hiking trail, and along a dirt path leading north and west from the large parking lot/overhang at the extreme southeastern end of Park Drive. On a crisp day, much of southern New Haven County, Long Island Sound, and northern Long Island will be visible from this parking lot. Hackberry Emperors and Northern Pearly Eyes can be seen occasionally on the stone retaining walls at the parking lot, and the area can also be productive for hilltopping/territorial species such as Red Admirals and American Ladies. The scattered milkweeds, New Jersey Teas, and sumacs are preferred nectaring grounds in early summer.

SPECIES LIST Pipevine Swallowtail R, Black Swallowtail C, Canadian Tiger Swallowtail U, Eastern Tiger Swallowtail C, Spicebush Swallowtail U, Cabbage White A, Falcate Orangetip C, Clouded Sulphur C, Orange Sulphur C, Cloudless Sulphur R (fall migrant only), Little Yellow R, Harvester R, American Copper C, Coral Hairstreak C, Edwards' Hairstreak C, Banded Hairstreak C, Hickory Hairstreak R, Striped Hairstreak U, Olive Hairstreak C, Brown Elfin U, Frosted Elfin R, Eastern Pine Elfin R, Southern Hairstreak R, White M Hairstreak U, Gray Hairstreak U, Eastern Tailed Blue C, Spring Azure C, Variegated Fritillary R, Great Spangled Fritillary R, Silver-bordered Fritillary H, Meadow Fritillary R, Silvery Checkerspot U, Harris' Checkerspot R, Pearl Crescent A, Question Mark U, Eastern Comma U, Compton Tortoiseshell U, Mourning Cloak A, American Lady C, Painted Lady R, Red Admiral C, Common Buckeye R, Red-spotted Purple U, Viceroy U, Hackberry Emperor U, Tawny Emperor R, Northern Pearly Eye U, Appalachian Brown U, Little Wood Satyr A, Common Wood Nymph C, Monarch C, Silver-spotted skipper C, Hoary Edge U, Southern Cloudywing R, Northern Cloudywing R, Dreamy Duskywing U, Sleepy Duskywing R, Juvenal's Duskywing C, Horace's Duskywing R, Columbine Duskywing R, Wild Indigo Duskywing R, Common Sootywing C, Swarthy Skipper R, Least Skipper U, European Skipper C, Leonard's Skipper R, Cobweb Skipper U (to C), Indian Skipper U, Peck's Skipper C, Tawny-edged Skipper U, Crossline Skipper U, Long Dash C, Northern Broken Dash A, Little Glassywing U, Delaware Skipper U, Mulberry Wing R, Hobomok Skipper U, Zabulon Skipper R, Broad-winged Skipper R, Black Dash U, Dun Skipper C, Dusted Skipper U.

DIRECTIONS Either from the north or south, take Route 15 (= Merritt Parkway) to Interchange 59 (= exit for Routes 63/69). Go southeast (toward New Haven) on Route 63 (= Whalley Avenue) just over a mile to Blake Street. Turn left on Blake, go about one-quarter mile to left turn onto Farnham Avenue. At end of Farnham turn left onto Wintergreen (you are on the campus of Southern Connecticut State University). A little under one-half mile, as you pass a cemetary on left and landfill on right, angle left off of Wintergreen to an almost immediate stop sign at Springside Avenue. Turn right onto Springside, continue to next stop sign. Turn left (this is Wintergreen again), and look for marked entrance to West Rock State Park on your left about one-quarter mile up the hill (you've overshot if you go under the Merritt Parkway).

Ward Pound Ridge Reservation
Cross River, Westchester, NY
Jeffrey Glassberg

DESCRIPTION   A magnificent park and one of the best areas in the NYC area to find butterflies. Its six square miles are mainly deciduous woodlands, but there are significant areas of wooded swamps, open upland fields, wet meadows, and marshes. A program of annual mowing maintains prime butterfly habitat.

BUTTERFLIES   Eighty-one species have been recorded from the Reservation and at least four or five more certainly will be found here. As you drive out on Michigan Rd., Acadian Hairstreaks are commonly seen on dogbane in an open field on your left. The damp soil around the parking area at the end of Michigan Rd. is usually attractive to a variety of species including Appalachian Azure in late May. The trail leading into the woods curves left through some Bluestem Grass and ends at a small pond. Cobweb Skippers can be seen in the Bluestem field and Appalachian Browns around the pond. When you return to the parking area, you'll find the marsh-meadow stretching east is good for Mulberry Wings, Black Dashes, and Harris' Checkerspots. The park's only record of Silver-bordered Fritillary is from here. The Swamp Milkweed and, farther east at the juncture of the meadow with the woods, the large stands of Common Milkweed and Dogbane are attractive to an enormous number of butterflies in late June and July. In addition to the more widespread Hairstreaks and Skippers, Southern and White M Hairstreaks have been found here.

Back on Boutonville Rd., the area adjoining the Meadows Parking Area on your left is good for Long Dashes in early summer and Aphrodite Fritillaries and Leonard's Skippers in late summer/early fall. Another excellent spot is just across from the Trailside Museum (go on in and say hello to the helpful staff). In the marsh here, Baltimores and Meadow Fritillaries can be found along with good numbers of Black Dashes, Delaware Skippers, and others.

The top of Pell Hill can be good for Silvery Checkerspots and Northern Cloudywings in early July, while one of Westchester's few real colonies of Brown Elfins is found on Fire Tower Hill.

The eastern side of Boutonville Rd. has good numbers of Scrub Oaks and one of the two known Westchester colonies of Edwards' Hairstreak. The barrens area on the south side of the road has Dusted Skippers while the marsh at the end of Boutonville Rd. can have Browns, Black Dash, and, once, even a Dion Skipper!

SPECIES LIST   Pipevine Swallowtail R, Black Swallowtail U, Eastern Tiger Swallowtail C, Spicebush Swallowtail C, Cabbage White U, Clouded Sulphur C, Orange Sulphur C, Harvester R, American Copper C, Coral Hairstreak C, Acadian Hairstreak C, Edwards' Hairstreak C, Banded Hairstreak A, Hickory Hairstreak U, Striped Hairstreak U, Olive Hairstreak R, Brown Elfin U, Eastern Pine Elfin R, Southern Hairstreak R, White M Hairstreak R, Gray Hairstreak R, Eastern Tailed Blue C, Spring Azure C, Appalachian Azure U, Variegated Fritillary R, Great Spangled Fritillary A, Aphrodite Fritillary U, Regal Fritillary H, Silver-bordered Fritillary S, Meadow Fritillary C, Silvery Checkerspot U, Harris' Checkerspot U-C, Pearl Crescent A, Baltimore U, Question Mark U, Eastern Comma U, Compton Tortoiseshell R, Mourning Cloak U, American Lady U-C, Painted Lady R, Red Admiral U, Common Buckeye R, Red-spotted Purple R, Viceroy U, Tawny Emperor R, Northern Pearly Eye U, Eyed Brown R, Appalachian Brown U-C, Little Wood Satyr A, Common Ringlet (probably will soon be) C, Common Wood Nymph A, Monarch C, Silver-spotted Skipper A, Hoary Edge R, Southern Cloudywing R, Northern Cloudywing U-C, Dreamy Duskywing U, Juvenal's Duskywing C, Wild Indigo Duskywing U, Swarthy Skipper R, Least Skipper U, European Skipper A, Leonard's Skipper U, Cobweb Skipper U, Indian Skipper C, Peck's Skipper C, Tawny-edged Skipper C, Crossline Skipper U-C, Long Dash C, Northern Broken Dash A, Little Glassywing A, Delaware Skipper A, Mulberry Wing A, Hobomok Skipper C, Zabulon Skipper U, Broad-winged Skipper R, Dion Skipper S, Black Dash A, Two-spotted Skipper S, Dun Skipper A, Dusted Skipper U.

DIRECTIONS   Either from the north or south, take Route 684 till the exit for Route 35. Take 35 East, toward Cross River, about 5 miles. Turn right onto Route 121 south then quickly turn left. The park entrance is about 1 mile down this road. Telephone number for Trailside Museum is (914) 763-3993.

Gateway National Recreation Area
NY/NJ
Don Riepe and Guy Tudor

DESCRIPTION   Gateway consists of 26,000 acres divided into three distinct units: Jamaica Bay/Breezy Point (in Brooklyn and Queens, NY), Staten Island, and Sandy Hook, NJ. The varied coastal habitats include salt marsh, fresh-water ponds, grasslands, holly forest, developing woodlands, shrub thicket, urbanized fields, and spoil grounds. All units are managed to some degree for butterflies by mowing and/or planting butterfly bush *(Buddleia)*, milkweeds, etc.

BUTTERFLIES   Approximately 60 species have been recorded from the park with most records from the Jamaica Bay/Breezy Point Unit. The best area for species diversity is the Jamaica Bay Wildlife Refuge District located in the boroughs of Brooklyn and Queens. The refuge has an active management program and many *Buddleia* bushes have been planted around the visitor's center. The south field, adjacent to the center, is a good area for several locally common species, such as Gray Hairstreak, Common Buckeye, and Swarthy Skipper. An occasional Salt Marsh Skipper wanders from the high tide zone to nectar at flowers in June, and again in August (when favoring the abundant camphorweed). At the south end of this field lies a wide trail that doubles back to Cross Bay Boulevard. Search along here in late summer for Red-banded Hairstreaks nectaring at Winged Sumac flowers. A bit farther south, behind a VFW building on Cross Bay Blvd., is a small ballfield where the clover edges may be productive at times. In general, these various fields are prime spots to search for southern strays in late summer/early fall: Checkered White, Cloudless Sulphur, Little Yellow, Variegated Fritillary, Common Checkered Skipper, and Fiery Skipper. Pipevine Swallowtail and White M Hairstreak have also been found here. The Checkered White is a specialty at the refuge but not always reliably found. The best area to search is just east of the train tracks along the North Dike Rd.

Hackberry trees near the visitor's center are good spots to look for American Snouts and other, but much rarer *Celtis* specialists, the Tawny Emperor and the Hackberry Emperor. The extensive garden areas and trailsides of the refuge contain an assortment of commoner "woodland" species, including Zabulon Skipper. A butterfly impossible to overlook in July and early August is the Broad-winged Skipper; it swarms abundantly over the *Buddleia* plantings.

Another good area within the Jamaica Bay District is Floyd Bennett Field, a 1200-acre former historic airfield where there is an abundance of open grassland and weedy edge. Here too, the National Park Service has planted *Buddleia* around buildings to attract butterflies. The best spot however is the Ecology Village Pine camping area, which contains a mix of old fields, open grassland, and sections of pine plantings. Here, Red-banded Hairstreaks nectar in clumps of Winged Sumac, American Coppers are everywhere, and the only known colony of Coral Hairstreak in the unit can usually be found on Orange Milkweed. Other good spots for Common Checkered Skippers and other "southerners" include the greenhouse site and the Return-A-Gift Pond in the North 40 section of the field. The 100-plus acre Breezy Point tip is a good fall migratory site for Monarchs, Question Mark, Red Admiral, and both Ladies.

The Staten Island Unit includes Miller Field and Great Kills. At Miller Field there is a small, swamp white oak forest that has some edge and glades where one can find Spicebush Swallowtail and a smattering of other species. Great Kills is known for its Monarch migration. Otherwise, not much data is available on butterflies from this unit.

The Sandy Hook, NJ, unit is basically a barrier island spit of land with typical dune species of plants present. The area does have a sizable holly forest *(Ilex opaca)* and here occurs the only known colony of Henry's Elfin in the NY metropolitan area. The dense stands of red cedars harbor Olive Hairstreaks in May and August. Falcate Orangetips have been recorded at this site as well.

Together, the three units of Gateway contain a good diversity of resident butterfly species and the possibility of seeing southern strays. All units are within a one-hour drive from Manhattan (albeit through sometimes heavy city traffic).

SPECIES LIST Pipevine Swallowtail R-U, Black Swallowtail C, Eastern Tiger Swallowtail C, Spicebush Swallowtail U, Checkered White R-U, Cabbage White A, Falcate Orangetip R (Sandy Hook), Clouded Sulphur C, Orange Sulphur A, Cloudless Sulphur R, Little Yellow R, Harvester R, American Copper C-A, Coral Hairstreak U, Red-banded Hairstreak U, Olive Hairstreak C (Sandy Hook), Henry's Elfin C (Sandy Hook), White M Hairstreak R, Gray Hairstreak U, Eastern Tailed Blue C-A, Spring Azure C, Summer Azure A, American Snout U, Variegated Fritillary R, Aphrodite Fritillary S, Pearl Crescent C, Question Mark C-A, Eastern Comma R, Mourning Cloak C, Compton Tortoiseshell R, Small Tortoiseshell S (or R?), American Lady C-A, Painted Lady R-U, Red Admiral C-A, Common Buckeye U, Red-spotted Purple R, Viceroy R, Hackberry Emperor R, Tawny Emperor R, Little Wood Satyr R, Common Wood Nymph R, Monarch C-A, Silver-spotted Skipper C, Juvenal's Duskywing U, Wild Indigo Duskywing R, Common Checkered Skipper R, Common Sootywing U-C, Swarthy Skipper C, Clouded Skipper S, Least Skipper U-C, European Skipper U, Fiery Skipper S, Cobweb Skipper R (Floyd Bennett), Peck's Skipper C, Tawny-edged Skipper U, Crossline Skipper U, Northern Broken Dash C, Delaware Skipper R-U, Zabulon Skipper C, Broad-winged Skipper A, Dun Skipper R, Dusted Skipper R (Floyd Bennett), Salt Marsh Skipper R-U.

DIRECTIONS   Jamaica Bay Wildlife Refuge: Take the Belt Parkway to Exit 17S and proceed south on Cross Bay Blvd. about 4 miles to the refuge entrance on the right.

Floyd Bennet Field and Breezy Point: Take the Belt Parkway to Exit 11S and proceed south on Flatbush Ave. to Floyd Bennet Field on the left. Follow signs to Breezy Point.

The Staten Island Unit is located along the south shore of Staten Island just off of Hylan Blvd.

The Sandy Hook Unit is reached by going south on the Garden State Parkway to Exit 117. Proceed west and follow the signs to Sandy Hook. Park at the visitor's center and use nearby trails through the holly forest.

Telephone numbers for Gateway National Recreation Area Units are as follows: (718) 474-0613 (Jamaica Bay); (718) 474-4600 (Breezy Point); (718) 338-3799 Floyd Bennett; (718) 351-8700 (Staten Island); and (908) 872-0115 (Sandy Hook).

Cape May County
NJ
Patricia Sutton and David Wright

DESCRIPTION AND BUTTERFLIES   Cape May County occupies a relatively small area at the southern tip of New Jersey. In part due to the great diversity of habitats found here, 100 species of butterflies have been recorded in the county. In an afternoon's leisurely drive you can visit saltmarsh, fresh-water marsh, coastal dune forest, white cedar swamp, abandoned cranberry bog, lowland hardwood swamp forest, pine/oak forest, pine barrens, cultivated fields, fallow fields, and natural grasslands. One of the best butterflying areas in the County is in the vicinity of Cape May, the 8-square-mile area south of the Cape May Canal. Here you will find four sizable preserves open to the public and all within a five-minute drive of one another (Higbee Beach Wildlife Management Area = 600+ acres; The Nature Conservancy's Cape May Migratory Bird Refuge = 187 acres; Cape May Point State Park = 190 acres; and the Cape May Bird Observatory's property and butterfly garden = 1 acre). Collecting or disturbance is not permitted on any of these properties, but there are ample opportunities to observe and study butterflies with binoculars and cameras. The New Jersey Audubon Society, the State of New Jersey, and The Nature Conservancy are all actively pursuing preservation of additional acreage in the Cape May area, so there will be even more butterflying opportunities in the future.

The Cape May peninsula is an excellent migrant and vagrant trap. The preserves near Cape May and the dunes and gardens in the town of Cape May Point are excellent for migrant and vagrant butterflies, just as they are famous for migrant and vagrant birds. In fact, these Cape May areas are the best spots for vagrants in all of New Jersey. Some migrants and vagrants that have appeared in varying numbers at Cape May in recent years include Long-tailed Skipper, Fiery Skipper, Clouded Skipper, Brazilian Skipper, Little Yellow, Gulf Fritillary, and Eufala Skipper.

The season begins in February and March when warm weather brings out Mourning Cloaks. Buffered by the warm waters of the Atlantic Ocean and the Delaware Bay, the season on the Cape May Peninsula extends most years until early December. Sixteen species can easily be found in late October, and eleven species might still be enjoyed in mid-November.

Higbee Beach Wildlife Management Area (WMA) is the key butterflying spot in the Cape May area. Five fields to the south (left) of the parking lot are managed for nongame birds by successional tilling and mowing. This management also benefits butterflies. Mustards blooming in late April and early May attract Falcate Orangetips. Each June and July the fields support a healthy stand of Common Milkweed and Dogbane. Goldenrods, asters, Camphorweed, and thoroughworts attract many butterflies from summer through mid-October. Some species to expect include Olive Hairstreak, White M Hairstreak, Redbanded Hairstreak, Spicebush Swallowtail, Sachem, and Hayhurst's Scallopwing. Substantial hedgerows between the fields contain many trees and shrubs attractive as nectar sources and/or essential as a larval food plant (American Hackberry, Red Cedar, Persimmon, American Holly, Sassafras, Wild Cherry, Beach Plum, Winged Sumac, privet, Groundsel-tree, blueberry). The sandy, unpaved parking lot and the sand road to the right of the parking lot, leading out to the Cape May Canal, can be excellent for mud-puddling species. Henry's Elfins can be found on this road in late April and May. American Hackberry trees surround the parking lot, making Hackberry Emperors, Question Marks, and American Snouts sure bets, along with an occasional Tawny Emperor. The last natural dune forest along the entire Delaware Bayshore survives at Higbee Beach WMA, characterized by huge, windswept Red Cedars, American Hollies and oaks, and a mosaic of sprawling Beach Plum bushes and Poison Ivy. A trail runs through the dune forest and is worth visiting for a step back in time to when natural dunes were commonplace on the coastal plain.

The Nature Conservancy's "Cape May Migratory Bird Refuge," also known as the South Cape May Meadows (for the town of South Cape

May with its 60+ homes that once stood one-half mile south of the current beachfront but is now a victim of erosion), is a coastal meadow adjoining "fresh-water" marsh and ponds (brackish after storms). The fresh-water marsh is transitional with extensive stands of cattail and sedges coming in since the mid-1980s, when cattle were no longer pastured here. Access is restricted to a loop trail (beginning and ending at the parking lot) and the beachfront. Several extensive stands of swamp milkweed, visible west of the center road, attract hundreds of Monarchs and other butterflies in July and August. Closer to the trail, Saltmarsh Fleabane, Climbing Hempweed, Seaside Goldenrod and other goldenrods, Mistflower, and the Common Milkweed attract good numbers of butterflies. Seaside Gerardia, one the host plants for the Common Buckeye, grows along the loop trail. Common Buckeye caterpillars are especially plentiful in fall when thousands of Common Buckeyes migrate through the region.

Cape May Point State Park is protected from the Atlantic Ocean by an unstabilized dune and has over three miles of trails running through a series of coastal "fresh-water" ponds and marsh and wooded islands of pines, Red Cedars, hickories, oaks, Sour Gums, Persimmon, and Sassafrass. Many of the migrating Monarch counts have been conducted at the State Park from the Hawk Watch Platform (by Cape May Bird Observatory staff) or from the dune crossover nearby as the Monarchs stream down the man-made dune. Some representative Monarch counts follow: August 13, 1991—30/minute; September 28, 1990—60/minute; and October 3, 1987—37/minute (day after hurricane Gloria passed). Monarch roosts in the State Park sometimes hold thousands of individuals. Common Buckeyes, Red Admirals, Mourning Cloaks, American Ladies, Painted Ladies, Question Marks, and some years countless Cloudless Sulphurs are also noticeable as migrants on certain days at Cape May. The huge numbers of Monarchs and other butterflies in the dunes in September and early October attract an amazing number of praying mantids. Some specific plants to check include the phragmites (for Broad-winged Skipper), Seaside Gerardia in the weedy and grassy areas around the perimeter of the parking lot (for Common Buckeyes), the healthy stand of Tall Sunflowers along the first part of the Yellow Trail (for Monarchs and many other butterflies), and the Pearly Everlasting growing in the dunes and weedy edges of the park (for caterpillars of the American Lady in September and October).

In the middle and northern parts of Cape May County unique habitats occur that are not found south of the Cape May Canal. These include Pine Barrens, White Cedar swamps, abandoned cranberry bogs, and sedge meadows. Sedge meadows support Appalachian

Brown, Mulberry Wing, Black Dash, and Dion Skipper. Look for Hessel's Hairstreak in White Cedar swamps and Bog Copper in cranberry bogs. Power lines through dry upland forests are good for Frosted Elfin, Sleepy Duskywing, Cobweb Skipper, and Cloudywings. Pine Barren areas in the northern part of the County are a stronghold for Southern Hairstreaks.

Belleplain State Forest, Beaver Swamp WMA, the Cape May National Wildlife Refuge, and The Nature Conservancy's Eldora Nature Preserve are all excellent for butterflies. Belleplain State Forest, beyond Dennisville, is largely north of Route 47 but the Jakes Landing Road portion of the forest (south of Route 47) should not be overlooked. The sand roads through Belleplain State Forest and west of Jakes Landing Road course through White Cedar swamps and pine/oak forest, and are edged by blooming Mountain Laurel and Sheep Laurel in May and June and by Sweet Pepperbush in July and August. Henry's Elfin, Brown Elfin, and Eastern Pine Elfin are all likely in April and May.

One part of Beaver Swamp WMA (near South Dennis) can be reached from the end of Beaver Dam Road off of Route 657, just east of Route 47. The sand roads are good for mud-puddling species. Eastern Pine Elfin, Henry's Elfin, numbers of Salt Marsh Skipper, Falcate Orangetip, and numbers of swallowtails and hairstreaks can be expected.

SPECIES LIST   Pipevine Swallowtail R, Zebra Swallowtail S, Black Swallowtail C, Eastern Tiger Swallowtail C, Spicebush Swallowtail C, Palamedes Swallowtail S, Checkered White R, Cabbage White A, Falcate Orangetip C, Clouded Sulphur C, Orange Sulphur A, Cloudless Sulphur C, Little Yellow U, Sleepy Orange R, Harvester R, American Copper C, Bog Copper LU, Bronze Copper R, Great Purple Hairstreak S, Coral Hairstreak C, Banded Hairstreak C, Striped Hairstreak U, Red-banded Hairstreak C, Olive Hairstreak C, Hessel's Hairstreak LC, Brown Elfin C, Frosted Elfin LU, Henry's Elfin C, Eastern Pine Elfin C, White M Hairstreak U, Southern Hairstreak U, Gray Hairstreak C, Eastern Tailed Blue A, Spring Azure A, American Snout C, Gulf Fritillary S, Variegated Fritillary C, Great Spangled Fritillary U, Regal Fritillary H, Silver-bordered Fritillary R, Meadow Fritillary R, Pearl Crescent A, Baltimore LR, Question Mark C, Eastern Comma U, Mourning Cloak C, American Lady C-A, Painted Lady U, Red Admiral C-A, Common Buckeye C-A, Red-spotted Purple C, Viceroy C, Hackberry Emperor U-C, Tawny Emperor U, Northern Pearly Eye H, Eyed Brown H, Appalachian Brown LC, Carolina Satyr H, Georgia Satyr LC, Little Wood Satyr C, Common Wood Nymph C-A, Monarch A,

Silver-spotted Skipper C, Long-tailed Skipper S, Hoary Edge U, Southern Cloudywing C, Northern Cloudywing C, Confused Cloudywing R?, Hayhurst's Scallopwing U, Sleepy Duskywing U, Juvenal's Duskywing C-A, Horace's Duskywing C, Zarucco Duskywing S, Wild Indigo Duskywing U, Common Checkered Skipper C, Common Sootywing C, Swarthy Skipper C, Clouded Skipper S, Least Skipper C, European Skipper U, Fiery Skipper C, Leonard's Skipper U, Cobweb Skipper C, Peck's Skipper U, Tawny-edged Skipper U, Crossline Skipper C, Northern Broken Dash C, Little Glassywing U, Sachem C, Delaware Skipper C, Rare Skipper LU, Mulberry Wing LC, Zabulon Skipper C, Aaron's Skipper C, Broad-winged Skipper C-A, Dion Skipper LC, Black Dash LU, Dun Skipper U, Dusted Skipper R, Eufala Skipper S, Brazilian Skipper S, Salt Marsh Skipper C.

DIRECTIONS   Higbee Beach WMA: Take the Garden State Parkway to its southernmost terminus. Continue into Cape May on Lafayette Street (Rt. 633). Bear right at Collier's Liquor Store. Continue straight through two traffic lights heading toward Cape May Point. The road now becomes Sunset Boulevard (Rt. 606). Turn right onto Bayshore Road (Rt. 607). Continue until stop sign. Turn left onto New England Road (Rt. 641). Continue to Higbee Beach WMA parking lot at end of road.

The Nature Conservancy's "Cape May Migratory Bird Refuge": Retrace steps back to Sunset Boulevard (Rt. 606) and turn right heading to Cape May Point. Park in TNC's parking lot on the left.

Cape May Bird Observatory: From TNC parking lot turn left onto Sunset Boulevard (Rt. 606) heading to Cape May Point. Turn left onto Lighthouse Avenue (Rt. 629). Take second right onto East Lake Drive and park. Has available "Checklist of Butterflies of Cape May County, NJ" by David Wright. Telephone (609) 884-2736.

Cape May Point State Park: Return to Lighthouse Avenue (Rt. 629) and turn right onto it. Park entrance is ahead on the left.

Town of Cape May Point: Exit State Park and wander the many streets running the length of the beachfront and radiating out from the Cape May Point Circle.

Tinicum National Environmental Center
Philadelphia, PA
David Wright

DESCRIPTION   Tinicum is a large wildlife habitat situated in extreme southeastern Philadelphia and adjacent Delaware County. It has long been famous among naturalists and bird students. The name Tinicum is from an Indian word meaning "marshes of islands." The area occupied by the preserve was originally part of a fresh-water tidal plain flooded and exposed with each tide in Darby Creek. Although some of the original tidal marshes remain, much of the land has been altered by diking, dredging, or filling. These disturbances have created a unique variety of butterfly habitats. Tinicum is part of the National Wildlife Refuge System administered by the U.S. Fish and Wildlife Service.

BUTTERFLIES   A total of 75 butterfly species have been recorded from Tinicum. The tidal marsh is characterized by unbroken stands of wild rice in shallow water and is readily accessible via dike trails in the refuge. Only two species are limited to the tidal marshes proper— the Broad-winged Skipper and the Salt Marsh Skipper. The distinctive eastern subspecies of the Broad-winged Skipper was described from Tinicum material. The adults are easily observed on flowers of purple loosestrife and pickerelweed. Adjacent to the tidal marshes are wet meadows and willow thickets. The Viceroy and Mourning Cloak are common here; females can often be seen laying eggs on willow. The Least Skipper is extremely common along the edges of small watercourses throughout the area. Sedgy marsh-meadows (where wet meadows intergrade with dry meadows) are good habitats for Silvery Checkerspots, Bronze Coppers, and Eyed Browns. Colonies of these butterflies fluctuate from year to year. The foot trails around the perimeter of the refuge pass through many old fields with grasses and wildflowers. Butterfly nectaring activity allows close-up observation of swallowtails, Pearl Crescents, Red-spotted Purples, Red Admirals, Sulphurs, and Skippers. The diked pond near the Visitors' Center is rimmed by a dense stand of shrubby swamp dogwoods and Spring Azures lay their eggs on the tiny dogwood flowers in June. Adjacent to the refuge boundaries are disturbed soils and waste places where Checkered Whites are locally abundant. Several immigrant butterflies from southern states have also been recorded from Tinicum in late summer and fall. The Cloudless Sulphur and the Little Yellow can be seen nearly every year. The Variegated Fritillary and Fiery Skipper also appear regularly. Several rarities like the Ocola Skipper, Long-tailed Skipper, Gulf Fritillary, and Southern Dogface show up sporadically.

SPECIES LIST   Pipevine Swallowtail U, Black Swallowtail U-C, Giant Swallowtail R, Eastern Tiger Swallowtail C, Spicebush Swallowtail C, Checkered White C, Cabbage White A, Clouded Sulphur C,

Orange Sulphur A, Southern Dogface R, Cloudless Sulphur U, Sleepy Orange R, Little Yellow U, Harvester R, American Copper U, Bronze Copper U, Banded Hairstreak R, Red-banded Hairstreak R, Gray Hairstreak C, Eastern Tailed Blue C, Spring Azure C, American Snout U, Gulf Fritillary S, Variegated Fritillary R, Great Spangled Fritillary C, Silver-bordered Fritillary R, Silvery Checkerspot U, Baltimore R, Pearl Crescent C, Question Mark C, Eastern Comma C, Mourning Cloak C, American Lady C, Painted Lady U, Red Admiral C, Common Buckeye C, Red-spotted Purple C, Viceroy C, Tawny Emperor U, Eyed Brown U, Appalachian Brown U, Little Wood Satyr U-C, Common Wood Nymph C, Monarch C, Silver-spotted Skipper C, Hoary Edge U, Long-tailed Skipper S, Southern Cloudywing C, Northern Cloudywing U, Confused Cloudywing U, Juvenal's Duskywing U, Horace's Duskywing C, Zarucco Duskywing R, Common Checkered Skipper C, Common Sootywing C, Swarthy Skipper U, Clouded Skipper R, Least Skipper A, European Skipper U, Fiery Skipper R, Cobweb Skipper U, Peck's Skipper C, Tawny-edged Skipper U, Crossline Skipper U, Whirlabout S, Northern Broken Dash C, Little Glassywing U, Sachem R, Delaware Skipper U, Hobomok Skipper U, Zabulon Skipper C, Broad-winged Skipper A, Dun Skipper C, Salt Marsh Skipper C, Ocola Skipper R.

DIRECTIONS   Visitors Center and parking lot are reached by public access road at 86th Street and Lindbergh Blvd. in southwest Philadelphia. Signs are posted. From I-95 take Route 291 exit (near airport) to Bartram Ave. Go north on Bartram Ave, left on 84th St., and left on Lindbergh Ave. Proceed two blocks to Visitors Center access road. An additional parking area is located at the extreme western edge of the preserve in Delaware Co., just north of I-95 on Route 420. Telephone number is (215) 521-0662.

Upper Dogue Creek and Huntley Meadows County Park
Fairfax County, VA
Paul Opler

DESCRIPTION   One of several remnant woodlands in highly developed northern Virginia. The area is increasingly built up with suburban development, but Huntley Meadow Park, Fort Belvoir, and floodplain woodlands upstream constitute a large diverse area for butterfly populations. The natural habitats consist of oak-hickory and red maple woodlands, overgrown fields, slow moving streams, and open swamp.

BUTTERFLIES   80 species have been found in Rose Hill and nearby Huntley Meadows, a Fairfax County park. Butterflies are more common on the power-line right-of-way than in the county park. The power line is mowed about every third year and is best for butterflies when the vegetation is at intermediate growth levels. Huntley Meadows has low butterfly density but has the only colony of Dion Skippers in the county. In the fall, tickseed sunflower beds can be a good place to find Common Buckeyes and colonizing skippers. Slow-moving wood streams are good places in season to seek Appalachian Browns and the rare Northern Pearly Eye. Along the power line there is a seasonal sequence of attractive nectar sources including Winter Cress, New Jersey Tea, Dogbane, Orange Milkweed, Common Milkweed, Joe-pye Weed, and Tickseed Sunflower. The rare Southern Hairstreak has been found on New Jersey Tea and Sumac. Many of the photographs in Opler and Krizek were taken here, and a survey by Paul Opler was published in *Atala* (Vol. 14 [2], 1986).

SPECIES LIST   Pipevine Swallowtail R, Black Swallowtail U, Spicebush Swallowtail C, Eastern Tiger Swallowtail C, Zebra Swallowtail R, Falcate Orangetip C, Cabbage White A, Checkered White R, Orange Sulphur A, Clouded Sulphur A, Cloudless Sulphur R, Sleepy Orange R, Little Yellow U, Harvester U, American Copper C, Eastern Tailed Blue A, Spring Azure A, Coral Hairstreak U, Banded Hairstreak U, Striped Hairstreak U, Red-banded Hairstreak C, Olive Hairstreak U, Brown Elfin R, Henry's Elfin R, Eastern Pine Elfin C, Southern Hairstreak R, Gray Hairstreak U, White M Hairstreak R, American Snout R, Variegated Fritillary R, Great Spangled Fritillary C, Meadow Fritillary R, Baltimore R, Pearl Crescent A, Question Mark C, Eastern Comma C, Mourning Cloak C, American Lady U, Painted Lady R, Red Admiral U, Common Buckeye U, Red-spotted Purple C, Viceroy C, Hackberry Emperor U, Tawny Emperor R, Northern Pearly Eye R, Appalachian Brown C, Little Wood Satyr A, Gemmed Satyr S, Common Wood Nymph C, Monarch C, Silver-spotted Skipper C, Hoary Edge U, Southern Cloudywing R, Northern Cloudywing R, Hayhurst's Scallopwing U, Dreamy Duskywing C, Horace's Duskywing U, Juvenal's Duskywing C, Wild Indigo Duskywing R, Common Checkered Skipper R, Common Sootywing U, European Skipper U, Least Skipper A, Swarthy Skipper C, Clouded Skipper R, Leonard's Skipper U, Sachem A, Fiery Skipper R, Peck's Skipper C, Crossline Skipper C, Tawny-edged Skipper U, Northern Broken Dash A, Little Glassywing C, Delaware Skipper U, Zabulon Skipper C, Dion Skipper R, Dun Skipper A, Dusted Skipper R, Ocola Skipper R.

DIRECTIONS   Take I-495 to Telegraph Road exit. Take Telegraph Road west to Franconia Road. Turn left onto Franconia Road and go 2 miles to Rose Hill Road. Take Rose Hill Road 2 blocks to May Blvd. Take May Blvd. and turn right at first street. Drive to dead end and park. Walk down power line and trail along golf course fence.

McKee-Beshers Wildlife Management Area, Sugarland
Montgomery Co., MD
Richard H. Smith and Philip J. Kean

DESCRIPTION   Although managed primarily for hunting, the area's 2.5 square miles offers a variety of habitats with convenient trails especially favorable for harboring and observing a diversity of butterfly species within 20 miles of Washington, D.C. Habitats consist primarily of wet woods, fresh-water ponds and swamps, and wet meadows, but the perimeter of the area contains both dry fields and hillsides as well as river bottomland. Strip mowing and water level control is practiced to facilitate game species development, but these measures also serve to maintain the butterfly habitats as well.

BUTTERFLIES   At least 81 species have been recorded at McKee-Beshers WMA. These represent a combination of typically transition zone and coastal plain species as well as those characteristic of the Maryland Piedmont Plateau in which McKee-Beshers is located. The area may be entered first at the east end of Hunting Quarter Road. Here on wet sand and mud in June and August one may encounter several Eastern Commas, Question Marks, Hackberry Emperors, and Tawny Emperors—the latter two species often perching immediately on sweaty clothing to probe for salts. At sunny spots in the woodland farther along the road, one may encounter Falcate Orangetips and Zebra Swallowtails in mid April or Silvery Checkerspots in June and August. From muddy spots in the darker areas, groups of 2 or 3 Northern Pearly Eyes and Red-spotted Purples or a Harvester may fly up when disturbed. There are three side trails leading south from Hunting Quarter Road. The first and easternmost trail leads through more swampy woodland and then opens into an alfalfa field with Meadow, Variegated, and Great Spangled Fritillaries in June and swallowtails and skippers in August. The second trail farther west passes between more open wet areas, where the Bronze Copper has been spotted, and then on to scattered clusters of Red Clover, Joe-Pye Weed, and Swamp Milkweed where Checkered Whites have been found. The third trail is near the west end of Hunting Quarter Road where a sizable unpaved parking area often has a few mud puddles where several Question Marks and American Snouts may be spotted. The trail itself leads between a large pond and some smaller water impoundments and then on to weedy field edges and woodland habitats. Here among willow and Indian Hemp blossoms in June one may find Viceroys, Banded and Coral Hairstreaks, and a variety of common skippers such as Peck's, Common Sootywing, and Common Checkered Skipper.

Along River Road on the northern boundary of McKee-Beshars WMA is Sycamore Landing Road. At the north end, for the first one-quarter mile of the road, is open weedy meadow wetland habitat where Buttonbush and Teasel bloom in June and Swamp Milkweed, New York Ironweed, and goldenrods occur later in summer. Although uncommon to rare at this location, a variety of skipper species such as Fiery Skipper, Two-spotted Skipper, and Ocola Skipper have been spotted here. Also located here in previous years have been Appalachian Browns, Bronze Coppers, and Checkered Whites. At the far south end of the road is a parking area and entrance to the Chesapeake and Ohio Canal towpath. Along the towpath at this location is one of the few significant local colonies of the Giant Swallowtail in MD. It is known to utilize Hoptree as a larval foodplant here. Also found along the canal trail have been occasional Sleepy Oranges and Hayhurst's Scallopwings.

SPECIES LIST   Pipevine Swallowtail U, Zebra Swallowtail C, Black Swallowtail C, Giant Swallowtail U, Eastern Tiger Swallowtail C, Palamedes Swallowtail S, Spicebush Swallowtail C, Checkered White R, Cabbage White A, Falcate Orangetip C, Clouded Sulphur C, Orange Sulphur C, Cloudless Sulphur R, Little Yellow U, Sleepy Orange R, Harvester U, American Copper C, Bronze Copper U, Coral Hairstreak U, Banded Hairstreak U, Red-banded Hairstreak C, Olive Hairstreak C, Eastern Pine Elfin U, Henry's Elfin R, White M Hairstreak R, Gray Hairstreak C, Eastern Tailed Blue A, Spring Azure C, American Snout U, Variegated Fritillary C, Great Spangled Fritillary C, Regal Fritillary H, Meadow Fritillary C, Silver-bordered Fritillary H, Silvery Checkerspot C, Pearl Crescent A, Question Mark C, Eastern Comma C, Mourning Cloak C, American Lady C, Painted Lady C, Red Admiral C, Common Buckeye C, Red-spotted Purple C, Viceroy C, Hackberry Emperor C, Tawny Emperor C, Northern Pearly Eye C, Appalachian Brown C, Little Wood Satyr C, Common Wood Nymph C, Monarch C, Silver-spotted Skipper C, Long-tailed Skipper S, Hoary Edge U, Southern Cloudywing U, Northern Cloudywing C, Hayhurst's Scallopwing U, Dreamy Duskywing C, Sleepy Duskywing U, Juvenal's

Duskywing C, Horace's Duskywing C, Wild Indigo Duskywing U, Common Checkered Skipper C, Common Sootywing C, Swarthy Skipper C, Clouded Skipper C, Least Skipper C, European Skipper C, Fiery Skipper U, Peck's Skipper C, Tawny-edged Skipper U, Crossline Skipper C, Northern Broken Dash C, Little Glassywing C, Sachem A, Hobomok Skipper U, Zabulon Skipper C, Two-spotted Skipper R, Dun Skipper C, Ocola Skipper R.

DIRECTIONS   Take the Capital Beltway (I-495) to Exit 39 and proceed west on River Road (Rt. 190) for 11 miles. Turn left at the stop sign, and continue on River Road for 4 miles. The area lies to the left and may be entered either along Hunting Quarter Road, Hughes Road, or Sycamore Landing Road.

Other Localities

Here are some suggestions for increasing the variety of your butterflying experiences. You should be able to find all these localities using a good road map. Additional possibilities, along with detailed directions to many of the localities listed here, can be found in the following books: *The Audubon Society Field Guide to the Natural Places of the Mid-Atlantic States, Inland* by Lawrence and Gross; *A Guide to Bird Finding East of the Mississippi* by Pettingill; *Where to Find Birds in New York State* by Drennan; *A Guide to Bird Finding in New Jersey* by Boyle.

MYLES STANDISH STATE FOREST, PLYMOUTH CO., MA   Mainly barrens butterflies including Edwards' Hairstreak, Hoary Elfin.

BLUE HILLS RESERVATION, NORWOOD, NORFOLK CO., MA   Look along the bog walk through the white cedar swamp for Hessel's Hairstreak and Bog Copper. Arctic Skipper has been seen here once. The Reservation also has Henry's Elfin and Northern Pearly Eye.

WELLFLEET BAY WILDLIFE SANCTUARY, BARNSTABLE CO., MA   Hoary Elfin, Eastern Pine Elfin, Leonard's Skipper.

BROAD MEADOW BROOK WILDLIFE SANCTUARY, 414 MASSASOIT RD., WORCESTER, WORCESTER CO., MA 01604 (508) 753-6087   272 acres. Harris' Checkerspot, Hoary Edge, Southern Cloudywing, Leonard's Skipper, and Broad-winged Skipper. This Massachusetts Audubon Society sanctuary has a good selection of species. Although the sanctuary has a variety of habitats, the best area for butterflies is the power-line cut running through its middle. Surprisingly, despite the address, no Mulberry Wings have been seen yet.

WACHUSETTS MEADOW SANCTUARY, PRINCETON, WORCESTER CO., MA (508) 464-2712   Harris' Checkerspot.

DRUMLIN FARM WILDLIFE SANCTUARY, LINCOLN, MIDDLESEX CO., MA (617) 259-9005   This glacial drumland with a meadow and mixed deciduous forest contains a large variety of butterfly species.

HANGING HILLS STATE PARK, MERIDEN, NEW HAVEN, CO., CT
Columbine Duskywing.

STEEP ROCK RESERVATION, LITCHFIELD CO., WASHINGTON, CT
West Virginia White.

HOOK MOUNTAIN, ROCKLAND CO., NY   Falcate Orangetip. From the Tappan Zee Bridge, take Route 87 west a short distance to Exit 11 (9W north). Go straight past the stop sign and proceed to the stop light at the intersection with 9W. Turn left (north) onto 9W and go 1.8 miles. Pull into the small pull-out on the right (if you get to Rockland Lake you have gone too far). On the ground, note the small flat rock with the words "Hook Mtn" and an arrow painted upon it in yellow. Follow the arrow to the yellow trail. Follow this trail about 0.4 miles to the summit. The Orangetips are most common near the summit. A Columbine Duskywing was once seen on the Columbines just below the south side of the summit.

OAKWOOD CEMETERY, MT. KISCO, WESTCHESTER CO., NY
Southern Cloudywing.

VAN CORTLANDT PARK, BRONX, NY   Silvery Checkerspot, Hoary Edge.

CHRISTIE ESTATE, MUTTONTOWN, NASSAU CO., NY   This county preserve has deciduous woods, brushy fields, and a good selection of butterflies. Enter via the Muttontown Preserve south of North Hempstead Tpke. (Rt. 25A). The best area seems to be along the eastern border, parallel to Route 106 and north of the equestrian area.

STILLWELL WOODS, WOODBURY, NASSAU CO., NY   A general selection.

OCEANSIDE TOWN NATURE PARK, OCEANSIDE, NASSAU CO., NY
Salt Marsh Skipper.

TARGET ROCK NATIONAL WILDLIFE REFUGE, LLOYD, SUFFOLK CO., NY   Olive Hairstreak.

UPLAND FARM, COLD SPRING HARBOR, SUFFOLK CO., NY The deciduous woods and grassy fields harbor a general selection of butterflies with good diversity. Enter this property, the headquarters of the Long Island Chapter of the Nature Conservancy, from Lawrence Hill Road.

QUOGUE BIRD SANCTUARY, QUOGUE, SUFFOLK CO., NY Bog Copper. This privately owned property contains pine barrens habitat (including dwarf pine plains at the northern end) and several ponds.

CRANBERRY BOG COUNTY PARK, RIVERHEAD, SUFFOLK CO., NY Hessel's Hairstreak. As you walk south from Center Drive south (just west of the Suffolk Co. Center), search the white cedar swamp along the north side of Sneezy Pond. Unfortunately, Hessel's Hairstreak has not been seen here since 1983, although it still may be here. The trail from Riverhead-Moriches Rd. north to the south side of Sneezy Pond usually has a selection of pine barren species.

MARINE PARK (GERRITSEN BEACH), BROOKLYN, NY Little Yellow.

INWOOD HILL PARK, MANHATTAN, NY Hackberry Emperor. Contains the largest selection of species on Manhattan.

RIVERSIDE PARK, MANHATTAN, NY Located between Riverside Drive and the Hudson River, between 91st and 94th Streets, this beautiful little flower garden attracts many late summer and fall southern immigrants. Small Tortoiseshell, Long-tailed Skipper, and Clouded Skipper have all been seen here.

SAILOR'S SNUG HARBOR, STATEN ISLAND, NY An attractive site for late summer and fall southern immigrants.

CONFERENCE HOUSE PARK, TOTTENVILLE, STATEN ISLAND, NY American Snout, Hackberry Emperor, Tawny Emperor. Situated on the extreme southwestern corner of Staten Island, Conference House Park contains what is probably the most extensive stand of Hackberry Trees in the New York City area. As recently as twenty years ago, this area had Bronze Copper, Silver-bordered Fritillary, and other unusual species. These have all succumbed to the extensive development.

STICKLESPOND RD., SPRINGDALE, SUSSEX CO., NJ Northern Metalmark, Dion Skipper.

ASSUNPINK WMA, MONMOUTH CO., NJ Frosted Elfin. Take the NJ Turnpike south to Exit 8. Follow Route 33 into the outskirts of Hightstown. At the junction with Route 539 go left. Proceed through the

traffic light at Stockton St. then, shortly, take a sharp left turn following 539 (33 continues to the right). Take a left onto Herbert Rd. Go
about 2 miles to Imlaystown Rd (this is not marked but there is a large
"bait" sign at the corner). Take a left. Proceed just over a mile straight
until you can just see a bit of the lake ahead. An obvious sand road
curves left at this point. Continue along this wide dirt road, skirting
the lake's SW edge, and keep to the main road (ignoring several side
roads). The sand road (which may be impassable by car) passes some
open fields on your left, then takes a 90° left turn at the end of the far
field. Take this left turn and then look for a sand trail that leaves the
main trail perpendicularly to the right and soon comes to an abandoned RR embankment. Frosted Elfins may be found here.

LAKEHURST BOG, LAKEHURST, OCEAN CO., NJ   Bog Copper, Georgia Satyr, Dotted Skipper, Dion Skipper, Two-spotted Skipper. One of
the most famous and historic sites for northeastern butterflies. This
relatively small bog, sandwiched between RR tracks and a school,
should be acquired by the State of New Jersey and formally designated
the Alexander B. Klots Butterfly Sanctuary both to preserve the unusual species present and to honor one of the foremost figures in
American butterfly studies. Take the Garden State Parkway south to
Route 70 (Exit 88). Go west on 70 toward Lakehurst. At the rotary
intersection with Route 37, go south on 37 a short distance to the RR
crossing. Pull off to the right. A small field on your right often has
many skippers including Horace's Duskywing and an occasional Dotted Skipper. Walk to the right along the abandoned RR tracks. Cross
a small bridge. About 50 yards farther along, look for a small trail to
your left that goes into the bog. For best results one needs to plan on
getting wet.

LAKEHURST NAVAL AIR ENGINEERING CENTER   Dotted Skipper.
Although not normally open to the public, it is possible to obtain special permission to look for the Dotted Skipper.

MIDDLE CREEK WMA, LANCASTER, LANCASTER CO., PA
Bronze Copper.

NOTTINGHAM COUNTY PARK, CHESTER CO., PA   Mottled Duskywing, Leonard's Skipper, Common Roadside Skipper. Take the NJ
Turnpike to its southern end. Cross the Delaware Memorial Bridge
and gain I-95 south. Go about 22 miles to Route 272 north, to Bay-
view and Nottingham. Stay on 272 to Nottingham. Just before inter-
secting Route 1 in Nottingham, note the sign for Nottingham County
Park on your left. Turn left onto Herr Drive. If you reach Route 1,

you've gone too far. Follow the signs to the park. Park at the far end of the parking lot and take the trail marked "Nature Trail." Follow it into the serpentine pine barrens or veer right onto the White Trail.

ELK NECK STATE PARK, CECIL CO., MD   Zebra Swallowtail.

PINEY RUN COUNTY PARK, CARROLL CO., MD   Appalachian Brown.

PATAPSCO COUNTY PARK, CATONSVILLE, HILLTOP AND AVALON AREAS, BALTIMORE CO., MD   Diverse habitats with a good selection of species including Baltimore and southern immigrants in fall. Best area is along the power-line cut and associated trails.

SOLDIER'S DELIGHT NATURAL ENVIRONMENT AREA, BALTIMORE CO., MD   Edwards' Hairstreak, Southern Hairstreak, Eastern Pine Elfin, Cobweb Skipper, Leonard's Skipper, Dusted Skipper, Delaware Skipper, Common Roadside Skipper. This 1000+ acre area is largely a serpentine barren. Amid the pine and oak are large open areas with native grasses. Take I-695 to Exit 18 on the west side of Baltimore. Gain Route 26 (Liberty Rd.) and travel westward about 5 miles. Just past the Deer Park shopping center, take a right onto Deer Park Rd. Proceed 3.4 miles to the parking lot for Soldier's Delight.

CATOCTIN MOUNTAIN PARK, FREDERICK CO., MD   West Virginia White, Brown Elfin, Baltimore, and Indian Skipper. Check the mountain trails and the valley marshes. Take Route 70 (from Baltimore) or Route 270 (from Washington, D.C.) west to Frederick. Take Route 15 north to Thurmont. Take Route 77 west through the park.

GREAT FALLS PARK, MONTGOMERY CO. MD AND FAIRFAX CO., VA Zebra Swallowtail, Silvery Checkerspot, Northern Pearly Eye, Hayhurst's Scallopwing, Golden-banded Skipper.

WASHINGTON AND OLD DOMINION RAILROAD TRAIL, FAIRFAX CO., VA   Coral Hairstreak, Frosted Elfin, Eastern Pine Elfin, Southern Hairstreak, White M Hairstreak, Delaware Skipper, Common Roadside Skipper. This essentially linear park with miles of paved trail affords excellent opportunities for butterflying. Dry clay soil and a coincident power-line cut provide a partially open and barren areas with abundant Virginia Pine, Red Cedar, and blackberry. Prevalent butterfly foodplants include Wild Indigo and New Jersey Tea. Enter at the trail crossing along Sunrise Valley Drive in Reston, about 10 miles west of the District of Columbia.

MATTAWOMAN NATURAL ENVIRONMENT AREA, CHARLES CO., MD Zebra Swallowtail, Sleepy Orange, Banded Hairstreak, Clouded Skipper, Southern Broken Dash, Dion Skipper. This park includes both a woodlands and a marsh. At bridge crossings and along power-line cuts, large growths of Common Milkweed, Dogbane, Joe-pye Weed, etc. provide ample nectar sources for butterflies. From the District of Columbia take Route 210 south for about 20 miles to Potomac Heights. From here, take Route 225 southeast about 2 miles through Mason Springs.

Appendix B

Median Times of Appearance of New York Area Butterflies

The first date is the median date of appearance; the following dates give the range of dates of first appearance.

Mourning Cloak	3/16	2/22–4/05
Compton Tortoiseshell	3/25	3/07–3/28
Cabbage White	3/29	3/18–4/05
Eastern Comma	4/07	3/15–5/31
Spring Azure	4/09	3/29–4/19
Falcate Orangetip	4/14	4/05–4/27
American Lady	4/17	4/06–5/16
Juvenal's Duskywing	4/19	4/14–4/20
Red Admiral	4/21	4/11–5/22
Orange Sulphur	4/21	4/09–5/16
Clouded Sulphur	4/22	3/20–5/10
Eastern Tiger Swallowtail	4/23	4/05–4/27
American Copper	4/25	4/06–5/01
Olive Hairstreak	4/26	4/24–5/10
Brown Elfin	4/26	4/17–5/12
Sleepy Duskywing	4/27	4/26–5/09
Hoary Elfin	4/27	4/26–4/28
Eastern Pine Elfin	4/27	4/22–5/10
West Virginia White	4/27	4/26–4/28
Meadow Fritillary	4/27	4/21–5/11
White M Hairstreak	4/27	4/26–5/28

Henry's Elfin	4/28	4/27–4/28
Gray Hairstreak	4/28	4/07–5/17
Spicebush Swallowtail	4/28	4/26–5/05
Eastern Tailed Blue	4/28	4/24–5/12
Black Swallowtail	4/28	4/21–5/15
Hessel's Hairstreak	5/02	5/01–5/03
Pearl Crescent	5/06	4/26–5/12
Frosted Elfin	5/07	5/06–5/14
Question Mark	5/07	3/28–5/26
Silver-spotted Skipper	5/07	4/28–5/18
Cobweb Skipper	5/08	5/07–5/12
Dreamy Duskywing	5/10	5/01–5/14
Wild Indigo Duskywing	5/14	5/10–5/27
Common Sootywing	5/15	5/01–5/19
Red-banded Hairstreak	5/15	5/03–5/29
Appalachian Azure	5/16	5/14–5/20
Northern Cloudywing	5/18	5/12–5/26
Zabulon Skipper	5/19	5/13–5/20
Hobomok Skipper	5/20	5/12–5/24
Peck's Skipper	5/22	5/15–5/28
Little Wood Satyr	5/23	5/15–5/26
Tawny-edged Skipper	5/24	5/22–5/28
Monarch	5/24	5/09–6/13
Red-spotted Purple	5/24	5/16–5/30
C. Checkered Skipper	5/25	5/23–5/26
Dusted Skipper	5/25	5/23–6/13
Indian Skipper	5/27	5/16–6/11
Viceroy	5/27	5/20–6/13
Pipevine Swallowtail	5/30	5/02–6/06
Common Ringlet	6/01	5/29–6/04
Long Dash	6/01	5/23–6/16
European Skipper	6/02	5/27–6/14
Least Skipper	6/02	5/27–6/18
Hoary Edge	6/06	5/31–6/23

Harris' Checkerspot	6/11	5/31–6/18
Swarthy Skipper	6/12	5/27–6/18
Variegated Fritillary	6/12	6/09–6/18
Common Buckeye	6/15	5/24–7/21
Hackberry Emperor	6/15	6/11–6/26
Gr. Spangled Fritillary	6/15	5/31–6/18
Banded Hairstreak	6/16	6/06–6/21
Silvery Checkerspot	6/17	5/21–6/22
Southern Cloudywing	6/19	6/12–6/22
Crossline Skipper	6/19	6/17–6/24
Northern Broken Dash	6/19	5/31–6/21
Little Glassywing	6/20	6/17–6/22
Southern Hairstreak	6/23	6/11–7/08
Coral Hairstreak	6/23	6/15–6/25
Appalachian Brown	6/25	6/18–7/05
Baltimore	6/25	6/10–7/05
Common Wood Nymph	6/25	6/14–6/28
Little Wood Satyr II	6/26	6/21–7/02
Salt Marsh Skipper	6/27	6/19–7/02
Delaware Skipper	6/27	6/20–7/05
Edwards' Hairstreak	6/28	6/15–7/04
Dun Skipper	6/28	5/29–6/30
Hickory Hairstreak	6/28	6/21–7/11
Acadian Hairstreak	6/28	6/21–7/04
Tawny Emperor	7/01	6/22–7/13
Eyed Brown	7/01	6/22–7/11
Northern Pearly Eye	7/02	6/28–7/07
Broad-winged Skipper	7/02	6/28–7/08
American Snout	7/02	5/25–7/19
Black Dash	7/04	6/28–7/07
Dion Skipper	7/04	7/03–7/06
Bog Copper	7/05	6/22–7/17
Aphrodite Fritillary	7/05	6/20–7/13
Northern Metalmark	7/05	6/25–7/12

Mulberry Wing	7/09	7/01–7/12
Checkered White	7/19	7/04–8/21
Little Yellow	8/16	7/11–9/08
Leonard's Skipper	8/28	8/26–9/02
Small Tortoiseshell	8/31	8/25–10/15
Fiery Skipper	9/05	6/29–9/12
Cloudless Sulphur	9/06	9/03–10/9

Appendix C

Phenograms
for New York Area Butterflies

The following phenograms display flight period and abundance information for New York area butterflies as determined from data generated by members of the NYC Butterfly Club. Each of the five years covered is broken into five day blocks. For each species the status actually observed within each of these time periods is depicted as.

| Uncommon | Common | Abundant |

For example, the first phenogram shows that for year one the Pipevine Swallowtail was not seen until June 25; was uncommon between June 25 and July 10; common between July 10 and July 15; uncommon between July 15 and Aug. 5 and then not seen again until Sept. 5. Note that in year two it was abundant between July 15 and July 20.

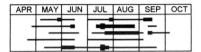

Pipevine Swallowtail

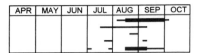

Spicebush Swallowtail

Black Swallowtail

Checkered White

Eastern Tiger Swallowtail

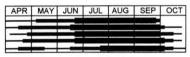

Cabbage White

APR	MAY	JUN	JUL	AUG	SEP	OCT

Falcate Orangetip

APR	MAY	JUN	JUL	AUG	SEP	OCT

Clouded Sulphur

APR	MAY	JUN	JUL	AUG	SEP	OCT

Orange Sulphur

APR	MAY	JUN	JUL	AUG	SEP	OCT

Cloudless Sulphur

APR	MAY	JUN	JUL	AUG	SEP	OCT

Little Yellow

APR	MAY	JUN	JUL	AUG	SEP	OCT

Harvester

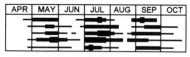

American Copper

APR	MAY	JUN	JUL	AUG	SEP	OCT

Coral Hairstreak

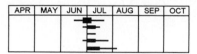

Acadian Hairstreak

APR	MAY	JUN	JUL	AUG	SEP	OCT

Edwards' Hairstreak

APR	MAY	JUN	JUL	AUG	SEP	OCT

Banded Hairstreak

APR	MAY	JUN	JUL	AUG	SEP	OCT

Hickory Hairstreak

APR	MAY	JUN	JUL	AUG	SEP	OCT

Striped Hairstreak

APR	MAY	JUN	JUL	AUG	SEP	OCT

Southern Hairstreak

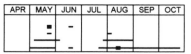

Red-banded Hairstreak

APR	MAY	JUN	JUL	AUG	SEP	OCT

Olive Hairstreak

APR	MAY	JUN	JUL	AUG	SEP	OCT

Brown Elfin

APR	MAY	JUN	JUL	AUG	SEP	OCT

Appalachian Azure

APR	MAY	JUN	JUL	AUG	SEP	OCT

Frosted Elfin

APR	MAY	JUN	JUL	AUG	SEP	OCT

Northern Metalmark

APR	MAY	JUN	JUL	AUG	SEP	OCT

Henry's Elfin

APR	MAY	JUN	JUL	AUG	SEP	OCT

American Snout

APR	MAY	JUN	JUL	AUG	SEP	OCT

Eastern Pine Elfin

APR	MAY	JUN	JUL	AUG	SEP	OCT

Variegated Fritillary

APR	MAY	JUN	JUL	AUG	SEP	OCT

White M Hairstreak

APR	MAY	JUN	JUL	AUG	SEP	OCT

Great Spangled Fritillary

APR	MAY	JUN	JUL	AUG	SEP	OCT

Gray Hairstreak

APR	MAY	JUN	JUL	AUG	SEP	OCT

Aphrodite Fritillary

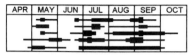

Eastern Tailed Blue

APR	MAY	JUN	JUL	AUG	SEP	OCT

Silver-bordered Fritillary

APR	MAY	JUN	JUL	AUG	SEP	OCT

Spring Azure

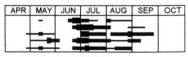

Meadow Fritillary

APR	MAY	JUN	JUL	AUG	SEP	OCT

Silvery Checkerspot

APR	MAY	JUN	JUL	AUG	SEP	OCT

American Lady

APR	MAY	JUN	JUL	AUG	SEP	OCT

Harris' Checkerspot

APR	MAY	JUN	JUL	AUG	SEP	OCT

Painted Lady

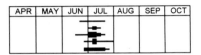

APR	MAY	JUN	JUL	AUG	SEP	OCT

Pearl Crescent

APR	MAY	JUN	JUL	AUG	SEP	OCT

Red Admiral

APR	MAY	JUN	JUL	AUG	SEP	OCT

Baltimore

APR	MAY	JUN	JUL	AUG	SEP	OCT

Common Buckeye

APR	MAY	JUN	JUL	AUG	SEP	OCT

Question Mark

APR	MAY	JUN	JUL	AUG	SEP	OCT

Red-spotted Purple

APR	MAY	JUN	JUL	AUG	SEP	OCT

Eastern Comma

APR	MAY	JUN	JUL	AUG	SEP	OCT

Viceroy

APR	MAY	JUN	JUL	AUG	SEP	OCT

Compton Tortoiseshell

APR	MAY	JUN	JUL	AUG	SEP	OCT

Hackberry Emperor

APR	MAY	JUN	JUL	AUG	SEP	OCT

Mourning Cloak

APR	MAY	JUN	JUL	AUG	SEP	OCT

Tawny Emperor

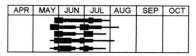

Northern Pearly Eye

Eyed Brown

Appalachian Brown

Southern Cloudywing

Northern Cloudywing

Dreamy Duskywing

Little Wood Satyr

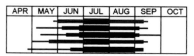

Sleepy Duskywing

Common Wood Nymph

Juvenal's Duskywing

Monarch

Horace's Duskywing

Silver-spotted Skipper

Wild Indigo Duskywing

Hoary Edge

Common Checkered Skipper

APR	MAY	JUN	JUL	AUG	SEP	OCT

Common Sootywing

APR	MAY	JUN	JUL	AUG	SEP	OCT

Tawny-edged Skipper

APR	MAY	JUN	JUL	AUG	SEP	OCT

Swarthy Skipper

APR	MAY	JUN	JUL	AUG	SEP	OCT

Crossline Skipper

Least Skipper

APR	MAY	JUN	JUL	AUG	SEP	OCT

Long Dash

APR	MAY	JUN	JUL	AUG	SEP	OCT

European Skipper

APR	MAY	JUN	JUL	AUG	SEP	OCT

Northern Broken Dash

APR	MAY	JUN	JUL	AUG	SEP	OCT

Leonard's Skipper

APR	MAY	JUN	JUL	AUG	SEP	OCT

Little Glassywing

APR	MAY	JUN	JUL	AUG	SEP	OCT

Cobweb Skipper

APR	MAY	JUN	JUL	AUG	SEP	OCT

Delaware Skipper

APR	MAY	JUN	JUL	AUG	SEP	OCT

Indian Skipper

APR	MAY	JUN	JUL	AUG	SEP	OCT

Mulberry Wing

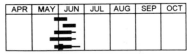

Peck's Skipper

APR	MAY	JUN	JUL	AUG	SEP	OCT

Hobomok Skipper

APR	MAY	JUN	JUL	AUG	SEP	OCT

Zabulon Skipper

APR	MAY	JUN	JUL	AUG	SEP	OCT

Dun Skipper

APR	MAY	JUN	JUL	AUG	SEP	OCT

Broad-winged Skipper

APR	MAY	JUN	JUL	AUG	SEP	OCT

Dusted Skipper

APR	MAY	JUN	JUL	AUG	SEP	OCT

Black Dash

APR	MAY	JUN	JUL	AUG	SEP	OCT

Salt Marsh Skipper

Checklist of Butterflies
of the Boston to Washington Area

_____ Swallowtail, Pipevine

_____ Zebra

_____ Black

_____ Giant

_____ Eastern Tiger

_____ Spicebush

_____ Palamedes

_____ White, Checkered

_____ West Virginia

_____ Cabbage

_____ Falcate Orangetip

_____ Sulphur, Clouded

_____ Orange

_____ Southern Dogface

_____ Cloudless Sulphur

_____ Yellow, Little

_____ Barred

_____ Sleepy Orange

_____ Harvester

_____ Copper, American

_____ Bronze

_____ Bog

_____ Hairstreak, Great Purple

_____ Coral

_____ Acadian

_____ Edwards'

_____ Banded

_____ Hickory

_____ Striped

_____ Southern

_____ Red-banded

_____ Olive

_____ Hessel's

_____ Elfin, Brown

_____ Hoary

_____ Frosted

_____ Henry's

_____ Eastern Pine

_____ Hairstreak, White M

_____ Gray

_____ Blue, Eastern Tailed

_____ Silvery

_____ Karner

_____ Azure, Spring

_____ Summer

_____ Appalachian

_____ Metalmark, Northern

_____ Little

_____ American Snout

_____ Fritillary, Gulf

_____ Variegated

_____ Great Spangled

_____ Aphrodite

_____ Regal

_____ Atlantis

_____ Silver-bordered

_____ Meadow

_____ Checkerspot, Silvery

_____ Harris'

_____ Crescent, Pearl

_____ Northern

_____ Tawny

_____ Baltimore

_____ Question Mark

_____ Comma, Eastern

_____ Green

_____ Gray

_____ Mourning Cloak

_____ Tortoiseshell, Compton

_____ Milbert's

_____ Small

_____ Lady, American

_____ Painted

_____ Red Admiral

_____ Common Buckeye

_____ White Peacock

_____ White Admiral

_____ Red-spotted Purple

_____ Viceroy

_____ Emperor, Hackberry

_____ Tawny

_____ Northern Pearly Eye

_____ Brown, Appalachian

_____ Eyed

_____ Satyr, Gemmed

_____ Carolina

_____ Georgia

_____ Mitchell's

_____ Little Wood I

_____ Little Wood II

_____ Common Ringlet

_____ Common Wood Nymph

_____ Monarch

_____ Queen

_____ Skipper, Silver-spotted

_____ Long-tailed

_____ Golden-banded

_____ Hoary Edge

_____ Cloudywing, Southern

_____ Northern

_____ Confused

_____ Hayhurst's Scallopwing

_____ Duskywing, Dreamy

_____ Sleepy

_____ Juvenal's

_____ Horace's

_____ Mottled

_____ Zarucco

_____ Columbine

_____ Wild Indigo

_____ Persius

_____ Grizzled Skipper

_____ Common Checkered Skipper   _____ Skipper, Arogos
_____ Common Sootywing   _____ Delaware
_____ Skipper, Arctic   _____ Rare
_____ Swarthy   _____ Mulberry Wing
_____ Clouded   _____ Skipper, Hobomok
_____ Least   _____ Zabulon
_____ European   _____ Aaron's
_____ Fiery   _____ Broad-winged
_____ Leonard's   _____ Dion
_____ Cobweb   _____ Black Dash
_____ Dotted   _____ Skipper, Two-spotted
_____ Indian   _____ Dun
_____ Peck's   _____ Dusted
_____ Tawny-edged   _____ Common Roadside Skipper
_____ Crossline   _____ Pepper and Salt Skipper
_____ Long Dash   _____ Skipper, Eufala
_____ Whirlabout   _____ Twin-spot
_____ Broken Dash, Southern   _____ Brazilian
_____ Northern   _____ Salt Marsh
_____ Little Glassywing   _____ Ocola
_____ Sachem

Butterfly Societies and Clubs

THE NORTH AMERICAN BUTTERFLY ASSOCIATION   is a recently formed group concerned with all aspects of butterflying, including field identification, photography, listing, gardening and conservation, and the facilitation of communication among butterfliers. NABA publishes *American Butterflies* and runs the annual 4th of July Butterfly Counts.

> NABA
> 4 Delaware Road
> Morristown, NJ 07960

THE XERCES SOCIETY   is an international nonprofit organization dedicated to the global protection of habitats for butterflies and other invertebrates. The Society publishes *Wings* and co-sponsors the annual 4th of July Butterfly Counts. Meetings are held annually.

> Xerces Society
> 10 SW Ash Street
> Portland, OR 97204
> (503) 222-2788

THE LEPIDOPTERISTS' SOCIETY   is a national organization devoted to the scientific study of all Lepidoptera. Membership is open to amateurs. The Society publishes the *Journal of the Lepidopterists' Society* as well as the *News of the Lepidopterists' Society*. There are annual meetings.

> Lepidopterists' Society
> William Winter, Secretary
> 257 Common Street
> Dedham, MA 02026

THE MASSACHUSETTS BUTTERFLY CLUB is a recently organized group of people interested in Massachusetts butterflies.

Massachusetts Butterfly Club
Brian Cassie
Box 211
Foxboro, MA 02035

THE NEW YORK CITY BUTTERFLY CLUB is dedicated to the field identification, study, and conservation of butterflies. The club publishes a field newsletter, *The Mulberry Wing* and usually meets on the first Monday of each month.

New York City Butterfly Club
Don Riepe, Secretary
29 West 9th Rd.
Broad Channel, NY 11693

THE CAPE MAY BIRD OBSERVATORY although originally focused on birds, now has active programs in all areas of natural history, including butterflies.

Cape May Bird Observatory
Pat Sutton
P. O. Box 3
Cape May Point, NJ 08212
(609) 884-2736

NABA–Xerces 4th of July Counts in the Region

Each year, the North American Butterfly Association (NABA) sponsors the 4th of July Butterfly Counts. The time in the field and the social occasion can be lots of fun, plus the data generated may prove useful in tracking the fate of many of our species of butterflies. Included here are all the counts held in our region in 1991. Because the count compilers tend to be fairly stable, I have also included their names and addresses. Contact a compiler if you are interested in joining future counts; most compilers will welcome your participation regardless of your level of butterflying ability.

FORT BELVOIR, VA
Mark Etheridge, 9422 Fairleigh Ct., Burke, VA 22015.

WESTERN MONTGOMERY CO., MD
Mark Garland, 8940 Jones Mill Rd., Chevy Chase, MD 20815.

BRYN MAWR, PA
Jane Ruffin, 1013 Great Springs Road, Rosemount, PA 19010.

HENDRICKS, PA
David Light, 327 South 6th Street, North Wales, PA 19454.

WHITE CLAY CREEK, PA
Jane Ruffin, 1013 Great Springs Road, Rosemount, PA 19010.

CAPE MAY, NJ
Patricia Sutton, c/o Cape May Bird Observatory, P.O. Box 3, Cape May Point, NJ 08212.

BELLEPLAIN, NJ
Patricia Sutton, c/o Cape May Bird Observatory, P.O. Box 3, Cape May Point, NJ 08212.

CUMBERLAND CO. NJ
Clay Sutton, 129 Buck Avenue, Cape May Court House, NJ 08210.

GALLOWAY TOWNSHIP, NJ
William J. Cromartie, NAMS-Stockton State College, Pomona, NJ 08240.

RARITAN CANAL, NJ
Michael Gochfeld, 54 Hollywood Avenue, Somerset, NJ 08873.

GREENBROOK SANCTUARY, NJ
Nancy Slowik, P.O. Box 155, Alpine, NJ 07620.

WEST MILFORD, NJ
Earle M. Post, 22 Pine Lane, West Milford, NJ 07480.

STATEN ISLAND, NY
Peggy Smith, 97 Arlo Road, Staten Island, NY 10301.

BROOKLYN-QUEENS, NY
Don Riepe, 28 9th Road, Broad Channel, NY 11693.

BRONX-MANHATTAN, NY
Guy Tudor, 111-14 76th Avenue, Apt. 107, Forest Hills, NY 11375.

MUTTONTOWN, NY
Rich Kelly, 622 S. 8th Street, New Hyde Park, NY 11040.

WESTERN SUFFOLK, NY
Steve Walter, 69-21 Springfield Blvd., Bayside, NY 11364.

NORTHERN WESTCHESTER CO., NY
Jeff Glassberg, 39 Highland Avenue, Chappaqua, NY 10514.

FAIRFIELD CO., CT
Isabel Gordon, 58 South Turkey Hill Road, Greens Farms, CT 06436.

SOUTHERN NEW HAVEN CO., CT
Larry Gall, Entomology, Peabody Museum, Yale University, New Haven, CT 06511.

SHERMAN, CT
Joan DeWind, RR 2, Briggs Hill Rd, Sherman, CT 06784.

STORRS, CT
D. Wagner, 916 Pudding Hill Road, Hampton, CT 06247.

BRISTOL CO., MA
Mark Mello, Box 7037, S. Dartmouth, MA 02748.

CONCORD, MA
Richard Walton, 458 Ornac, Concord, MA 01742.

LOWER PIONEER VALLEY, MA
Roger Pease, 100 Whittier Street, Springfield, MA 01108.

Glossary

ANAL MARGIN.   The lower edge of the HW.

ANDROPOGON.   A genus of grasses, especially *Andropogon Scoparius* (Little Bluestem Grass), which provides important habitat and serves as larval food plants for a number of butterfly species. Usually found in sandy areas or on soil impoverished in some other way.

APEX.   The upper tip of the FW.

APICAL.   Referring to the area at the upper tip of the FW.

APICES.   Plural of apex.

BASAL.   Referring the to area near the base of the wing adjacent to the body.

CELL.   The central area of the wing, bounded on all sides by veins.

COSTA.   The upper (forward) edge of the wing.

DISK.   The central area of the wing including, but larger than, the cell.

DISTAL.   Away from the body.

DORSAL.   Toward the back. The dorsal wing surface is the upper surface.

FOREWINGS (FWs).   The leading pair of wings.

FRONS.   The area on the top of the head between the eyes.

GROUND COLOR.   The basic or background color of the wing.

HINDWINGS (HWs).   The rear pair of wings.

HYALINE.   Translucent.

MARGINAL.   Referring to the area near the outside edge of the wing.

MEDIAN.   About one-half of the way out the wing, passing the distal end of the cell.

POST-MEDIAN.   The region distal to the median region.

STIGMA.   A structure, usually black and visible, on the FWs of most male folded-wing skippers, formed by specialized scales.

SUBAPICAL.   Referring to the region just before the upper tip of the FW.

SUBMARGINAL.   Referring to the region just before the area at the outside edge of the wing.

VENTRAL.   Toward the belly. The ventral wing surface is the lower wing surface.

VEINS.   A series of visibly raised structural elements on the wings which serve as wing struts. The branching pattern of the veins is important in Lepidopteran systematics.

Bibliography

Ackery, P. R. and Vane-Wright, R. I. 1984. *Milkweed Butterflies*. British Museum.

Beutenmuller, W. 1902. The butterflies of the vicinity of New York City. *Am. Mus. Nat. Hist. J. Supp. to Vol.* II No. 5, pp. 1–52.

Boyle, W. J. 1986. *A Guide to Bird Finding in New Jersey*. Rutgers University Press.

Burns, J. M. 1964. Evolution in skipper butterflies of the genus *Erynnis. Univ. Cal. Publ. Ent.* 37: 1–216.

Clark, A. H. 1932. The butterflies of the District of Columbia and Vicinity. *U.S. Natl. Mus. Bull.* 157: 1–337.

Clark, A. H. and Clark, L. F. 1951. The Butterflies of Virginia. *Smithsonian Misc. Collection* 116: 1–239.

Comstock, W. P. 1940. Butterflies of New Jersey. *J. NY Ent. Soc.* 48: 47–84.

Dirig, R. and Cryan, J. F. 1992. The status of Silvery Blue subspecies (*Glaucopsyche lygdamus lygdamus* and *G. l. couperi:* Lycaenidae) in New York. 1992. *J. Lepid. Soc.* 45: 272–290.

Drennan, S. R. 1981. *Where to Find Birds in New York State. The Top 500 Sites*. Syracuse University Press.

Edwards, W. H. 1868–1897. *The Butterflies of North America*. 3 vols. Am. Ent. Soc. Boston: Houghton-Mifflin.

Fales, J. H. 1984. Status of Maryland's Less Common Butterflies. In *Threatened and Endangered Plants and Animals of Maryland*. Norden, A. W., Forester, D. C., and Fenwick, G. H., eds. Maryland Natural Heritage Program Special Publication 84-I, pp. 273–280.

Fales, J. H. 1987. The Butterflies of Rock Creek Park, Washington, D.C. *The Maryland Naturalist* 31: 5–24.

Forbes, W. T. M. 1960. *Lepidoptera of New York and Neighboring States*. Part IV. Cornell University Agricultural Experiment Station, New

York State College of Agriculture, Ithaca, NY. Memoir 371: 1–188.

Genoways, H. H. and Brenner, F. J., eds. 1985. *Species of Special Concern in Pennsylvania.* Carnegie Museum of Natural History Special Publication No. 11.

Glassberg, J. 1992. *Aglais urticae* (Nymphalidae): a nascent population of this butterfly in North America. *J. Lepid Soc.* In press.

Hagen, R. H., Lederhouse, R. C., Bossart, J. L. and Scriber, J. M. 1992. *Papilio canadensis* and *P. glaucus* (Papilionidae) are distinct species. *J. Lepid. Soc.* 45: 245–258.

Howe, W. H. 1975. *The Butterflies of North America.* Doubleday.

Klots, A. 1951. *Field Guide to the Butterflies of North America, East of the Great Plains.* Houghton-Mifflin.

Lawrence, S. 1984. *The Audubon Society Field Guide to the Natural Places of the Mid-Atlantic States: Coastal.* Pantheon Books.

Lawrence, S. and Gross, B. 1984. *The Audubon Society Field Guide to the Natural Places of the Mid-Atlantic States: Inland.* Pantheon Books.

Miliotis, P. S. 1985. *An Annotated Checklist of the Butterflies of Massachusetts.* Massachusetts Audubon Society.

Miller, J. Y. 1992. *The Common Names of North American Butterflies.* Smithsonian Institution Press.

Norton, B. G. 1987. *Why Preserve Natural Variety?* Princeton University Press.

Opler, P. A. 1983. *County Atlas of Eastern United States Butterflies* (1840–1982). Privately printed.

Opler, P. A. and Krizek, G. O. 1984. *Butterflies East of the Great Plains: An Illustrated Natural History.* Johns Hopkins University Press.

Opler, P. A. 1986. An Atlas of the Butterflies and Skippers of the Upper Dogue Creek Drainage, Fairfax County, Virginia, 1978–1982. *Atala* 14: 21–44.

Opler, P. A. 1992. *A Field Guide to Eastern Butterflies.* Houghton-Mifflin.

Pavulaan, H. 1985. Field survey of the true butterflies (Papilionoidea) of Rhode Island. *J. Lepid. Soc.* 39: 19–25.

Pettingill, O. S. 1977. *A Guide to Bird Finding East of the Mississippi.* Second edition. Oxford University Press.

Pyle, R. M. 1981. *The Audubon Society Field Guide to North American Butterflies.* Knopf.

Pyle, R. M. 1992. *Handbook for Butterfly Watchers.* Houghton-Mifflin.

Robbins, R. 1981. The "falsehead" hypothesis: predation and wing pattern variation of lycaenid butterflies. *Amer. Nat.* 118: 770–775.

Scott, J. A. 1986. *The Butterflies of North America.* Stanford University Press.

Shapiro, A. M. 1966. *Butterflies of the Delaware Valley.* Special Publication of the Am. Ent. Soc.

Shapiro, A. M. 1970. The Butterflies of the Tinicum Region. In *Two Studies of Tinicum Marsh, Delaware and Philadelphia Counties, Pennsylvania.* The Conservation Foundation. Washington, D.C.

Shapiro, A. M. 1974. Butterflies and skippers of New York State. *Search* 4: 1–60.

Shapiro, A. M. and Shapiro, A. R. 1973. The ecological associations of the butterflies of Staten Island. *J. of Res. on the Lepidoptera* 12: 65–128.

Tekulsky, M. 1985. *The Butterfly Garden.* The Harvard Common Press.

Williams, C. B. 1930. *The Migration of Butterflies.* Oliver and Boyd.

Wright, D. M. 1985. Checklist of butterflies of Cape May County, N.J. *Cape May Geographic Society Bulletin* 39: 1–5.

Xerces Society/Smithsonian Institution. 1990. *Butterfly Gardening.* Sierra Club Books.

Ziegler, J. B. 1960. Preliminary contribution to a redefinition of the genera of North American hairstreaks (Lycaenidae) north of Mexico. *J. Lepid. Soc.* 14: 19–23.

Photographic Credits

Except as noted below, all photographs were taken by the author. For the overwhelming majority of the author's photographs, I used a Minolta 7000i automatic-focusing camera with a 100-mm macro lens and a 1200AF ring flash. Film was kodachrome ASA 64. Other photo credits are the following.

Plate 1 Pipevine Swallowtail, above and below, Don Riepe; Zebra Swallowtail, above, H. Darrow.

Plate 2 Black Swallowtail, female above, H. Darrow.

Plate 3 Giant Swallowtail, below, H. Darrow.

Plate 4 West Virginia White, above, H. Darrow.

Plate 5 Checkered White, below, C. Adams

Plate 6 Sleepy Orange, orange form, H. Darrow.

Plate 7 Bronze Copper, below, Bronze Copper, male above, H. Darrow.

Plate 12 Regal Fritillary, above and below, H. Darrow.

Plate 15 Tawny Crescent, above and below, H. Darrow.

Plate 16 Question Mark, red form above, Question Mark, unicolored form, below, Eastern Comma, above, D. Riepe; Eastern Comma, red form above, C. Adams.

Plate 17 Eastern Comma, red form above, C. Adams; Eastern Comma, red form below, P. Post.

Plate 18 Milbert's Tortoiseshell, above and below, C. Adams; Compton Tortoiseshell, below, H. Darrow; Small Tortoiseshell, above, D. Riepe.

Index

Page numbers in **boldface** refer to color plates.

Plate Section

The more than 300 photographs on the plates that follow were all taken by the author except as indicated in the photographic credits on page 149. This is the first field guide to any group of organisms that uses photographs and still shows each species on a plate in the correct size relationship to other species on that plate. The number in the upper right corner of the facing page to the plate indicates the absolute size of the butterflies. For example, the swallowtails on plate 1 are shown at one-half life-size (X ½). Black and white lines that appear in some photographs point to field marks whose location is difficult to describe in words. Although many butterfly photographers capture butterflies, place them on ice, then position the cold and immobile butterflies on flowers, all of the author's photographs are of wild, unrestrained, unmanipulated butterflies, except that the photograph of the upperside of a Gray Comma on plate 17 is of a museum specimen. For abbreviations used on the facing pages, see page 21.

PLATE 1   Black Swallowtails 1

1. | **Pipevine Swallowtail** *(Battus philenor)*, above. See page 23.
Jamaica Bay Wildlife Refuge, NY.
Iridescent blue HW.   Very dark above.   No FW markings. See page 23.
    B R · **N** R-LC · **P** C · **W** C

2. | **Pipevine Swallowtail** *(Battus philenor)*, below. See page 23.
Jamaica Bay Wildlife Refuge, NY.
Single orange spot-band on iridescent blue HW.

3. | **Eastern Tiger Swallowtail** *(Papilio glaucus)*, black ♀ above.
See page 25.
8/2/89 Chappaqua, NY.
Large size.   Flies higher than other swallowtails.
    B R · **N** U · **P** C · **W** C

4. | **Eastern Tiger Swallowtail** *(Papilio glaucus)*, black ♀ below.
See page 25.
8/2/89 Chappaqua, NY.
No post-median orange spot-band.
Usually retains "shadow" of Tiger pattern.

5. | **Zebra Swallowtail** *(Eurytides marcellus)* (summer form), above.
See page 23.
Winter Springs, FL.
Black and white stripes.   Long tails.
    B X · **N** X · **P** LR · **W** LC

6. | **Zebra Swallowtail** *(Eurytides marcellus)* (summer form), below.
See page 23.
6/13/87 Ocala National Forest, FL.
Black and white and red stripes.   Long tails.

1

2

3

4

5

6

PLATE 2   Black Swallowtails 2

1. **Black Swallowtail** *(Papilio polyxenes)*, ♂ above. See page 24.
   7/27/89 Chappaqua, NY.
   Bright yellow median bands, FW & HW.
   > B   C   ·   N   C   ·   P   C   ·   W   C

2. **Black Swallowtail** *(Papilio polyxenes)*, ♀ above. See page 24.
   Armonk, NY.
   Blue on HW.   Yellow FW subapical spot.
   Often flies with low, non-directional flight.
   Open areas and gardens.

3. **Spicebush Swallowtail** *(Papilio troilus)*, ♂ above. See page 26.
   5/18/90 Pound Ridge Reservation, NY.
   Greenish-blue cast on the HW.
   Usually flies with rapid, directional flight.
   Woodlands and adjacent fields.
   > B   U-C   ·   N   U-C   ·   P   C   ·   W   C

4. **Spicebush Swallowtail** *(Papilio troilus)*, ♀ above. See page 26.
   7/27/89 Pound Ridge Reservation, NY.
   Blue on HW.   Lacks yellow FW subapical spot.

5. **Black Swallowtail** *(Papilio polyxenes)*, ♂ below. See page 24.
   8/9/90 Oakwood Cemetery, Mt. Kisco, NY.
   HW median and submarginal orange spot-bands.
   HW yellow/orange cell spot.

6. **Spicebush Swallowtail** *(Papilio troilus)*, ♂ below. See page 26.
   8/9/90 Chappaqua, NY.
   HW median and submarginal orange spot-bands.
   Lacks HW yellow/orange cell spot.

1

2

3

4

5

6

PLATE 3 Yellow Swallowtails

x ½

1. **Eastern Tiger Swallowtail** *(Papilio glaucus)*, above. See page 25.
   7/27/89 Pound Ridge Reservation, NY.
   Yellow with black stripes.   Common.
   Larger than Black Swallowtail.   Flies both spring and summer.
   > **B** C · **N** C · **P** C · **W** C

2. **Eastern Tiger Swallowtail** *(Papilio glaucus)*, below. See page 25.
   8/5/90 Gettysburg, PA.
   Yellow with black stripes.

3. **Giant Swallowtail** *(Papilio cresphontes)*, above. See page 25.
   8/25/91 Newnan's Lake, Gainesville, FL.
   Very dark brown.   Yellow spot-bands form x's near FW apices.
   Yellow spot within tail.
   > **B** X · **N** R · **P** LR · **W** U

4. **Giant Swallowtail** *(Papilio cresphontes)*, below. See page 25.
   Marathon, FL.
   Cream-colored wings and body.   HW blue median spot-band.

5. **Palamedes Swallowtail** *(Papilio palamedes)*, above. See page 26.
   8/25/91 Newnan's Lake, Gainesville, FL.
   Wide yellow HW post-median band.
   > **B** X · **N** X · **P** S · **W** S

6. **Palamedes Swallowtail** *(Papilio palamedes)*, below. See page 26.
   3/22/90 Everglades National Park, FL.
   Yellow stripe along the base of the wings.
   Inhabitant of southern swamps.

1

2

3

4

5

6

PLATE 4   Whites (mainly spring)

x 1

1. Cabbage White *(Pieris rapae)*, ♂ above. See page 28.
5/14/90 Pound Ridge Reservation, NY.
Usually has black spot on FW and gray at FW apex but these
marks are reduced or absent in spring.
    B   A   ·   **N**   A   ·   **P**   A   ·   **W**   A

2. Cabbage White *(Pieris rapae)*, below. See page 28.
4/17/89 North Salem, Westchester, NY.
HW with yellowish overscaling.

3. West Virginia White *(Pieris virginiensis)*, above. See page 28.
5/2/80 Steep Rock Reservation, Washington, CT.
Unmarked white.   See text.   April–May.
    B   X   ·   **N**   LR   ·   **P**   X   ·   **W**   LR

4. West Virginia White *(Pieris virginiensis)*, below. See page 28.
4/28/90 Steep Rock Reservation, Washington, CT.
White with veins edged in gray.
Rich woodlands with toothwort.   April–May.

5. Falcate Orangetip *(Anthocharis midea)*, ♂ above. See page 29.
4/19/90 Hook Mtn., Rockland Co., NY.
Orange wing-tips.   Local north to CT.   Small with blunt FWs.
    B   X   ·   **N**   LC   ·   **P**   LC   ·   **W**   LC

6. Falcate Orangetip *(Anthocharis midea)*, ♂ below. See page 29.
4/19/90 Hook Mtn., Rockland Co., NY.
Orange FW tips.   Heavily marbled HW.   Late March–May.

7. Falcate Orangetip *(Anthocharis midea)*, ♀ See page 29.
4/19/90 Hook Mtn., Rockland Co., NY.
Blunt FW apex.   Marbled HW below.

1

2

3

4

5

6

7

PLATE 5   Whites (mainly summer)

x 1

1. **Cabbage white** *(Pieris rapae)*, ♂ above. See page 28.
   6/14/91 Pound Ridge Reservation, NY.
   Black spot on FW.
   >   B   A · N   A · P   A · W   A

2. **Cabbage White** *(Pieris rapae)*, ♀ above. See page 28.
   6/24/90 Marsh Sanctuary, New Castle, Westchester Co., NY.
   Two black spots on FW.

3. **Cabbage White** *(Pieris rapae)*, below. See page 28.
   6/21/90 Campfire Rd. power cut, New Castle, NY.
   HW largely unmarked, usually with yellowish cast.

4. **Clouded/Orange Sulphur** *(Colias philodice/eurytheme)*,
   ♀ white form below.
   See page 29.
   6/20/91 Pound Ridge Reservation, NY.
   Silvered spot in center of HW.
   Black borders of FW above can be seen in flight and through the wing.
   >   B   C · N   C · P   C · W   C

5. **Checkered White** *(Pontia protodice)*, ♂ below. See page 27.
   Date & locality data unavailable
   Black patch mid FW costa.   Disturbed areas and beachfront.
   >   B   S · N   R-LC · P   LC · W   LU

6. **Checkered White** *(Pontia protodice)*, ♀ above. See page 27.
   6/5/89 Peebles, Adams Co., OH.
   Local and usually rare to uncommon.   Extensive black markings on FW.

7. **Checkered White** *(Pontia protodice)*, ♂ below. See page 27.
   11/11/89 Bentsen State Park, Mission, TX.

1

2

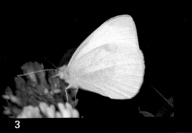

3

4

5

6

7

PLATE 6   Yellows

x 1

1. **Clouded Sulphur** *(Colias philodice)*, ♂ below. See page 29.
   6/28/90 Turkey Mtn. Yorktown, NY.
   Clear lemon-yellow above, shows no orange
   (best observed in flight).
   B   C • N   C-A • P   A • W   A

2. **Orange Sulphur** *(Colias eurytheme)*, ♂ below. See page 30.
   9/2/89 Pound Ridge Reservation, NY.
   Shows at least some orange on the FW.
   B   C • N   C-A • P   A • W   A

3. **Southern Dogface** *(Colias cesonia)* below. See page 30.
   11/11/89 Bentson State Park, Mission, TX.
   Bold yellow ''dog's head'' pattern on FW above, outlined
   in black and visible from below.   Pointed FWs.
   B   X • N   X • P   S • W   S

4. **Sleepy Orange** *(Eurema nicippe)*, reddish-suffused form below.
   See page 32.
   11/12/89 Roma, TX.
   Deep orange above.
   Characteristic diagonal brown markings on HW below.
   Antennae black and white (not pink).
   B   X • N   S • P   R • W   R-U

5. **Little Yellow** *(Eurema lisa)*, below. See page 31.
   11/12/89 Roma, TX.
   Small.   Bright yellow in flight.
   Usually has smudged spot at end of HW.
   Antennae black and white (not pink).
   B   R • N   R • P   R-C • W   C

6. **Sleepy Orange** *(Eurema nicippe)*, below. See page 32.
   5/79 Homestead, FL.

7. **Cloudless Sulphur** *(Phoebis sennae)*, ♂ below. See page 31.
   8/23/91 Gainesville, FL.
   Large.   Green-yellow below.   High sailing flight.
   Late summer immigrant.   Most common along coast.
   B   R • N   R • P   R-U • W   R-U

8. **Cloudless Sulphur** *(Phoebis sennae)*, ♀ below. See page 31.
   8/25/91 Gainesville, FL.
   Large.   Variable markings below.

1

2

3

4

5

6

7

8

PLATE 7   Coppers, Harvester, and Metalmark

x 1

1.   **American Copper** *(Lycaena phlaeas)*, above. See page 33.
5/20/90 Campfire Rd. power cut, New Castle, NY.
Bright orange FW, gray HW with orange band.
    B   A   ·   N   A   ·   P   C   ·   W   C

2.   **American Copper** *(Lycaena phlaeas)*, below. See page 33.
5/5/91 Mt. Pleasant, NY.
Orange FW disc.   Gray HW with narrow orange band.

3.   **Harvester** *(Feniseca tarquinius)*, below. See page 32.
5/30/88 Pound Ridge Reservation, NY.
Reddish-brown HW with white markings.   Local and erratic.
    B   LU   ·   N   LR   ·   P   R-U   ·   W   R-C

4.   **Bronze Copper** *(Lycaena hyllus)*, ♀ above. See page 33.
6/5/90 Middle Creek WMA, Lancaster, PA.
Wet habitats.   Much larger than American Copper.   Extra black
spots at FW base.   Paler yellow-orange than American Copper.
    B   LU   ·   N   LR   ·   P   LR   ·   W   LR

5.   **Bronze Copper** *(Lycaena hyllus)*, ♂ below. See page 33.
7/20/74 Salem, NJ.
Broad orange HW marginal band.   Wet habitats.

6.   **Harvester** *(Feniseca tarquinius)*, above. See page 32.
5/29/88 Pound Ridge Reservation, NY.
Orange FW and HW.   Bold black markings.   Local and erratic.

7.   **Bronze Copper** *(Lycaena hyllus)*, ♂ above. See page 33.
September, Salem, NJ.
Dull, iridescent purple.   Orange HW marginal band.

8.   **Bog Copper** *(Lycaena epixanthe)*, below. See page 34.
6/26/90 Lakehurst Bog, Lakehurst, NJ.
Very small and inconspicuous.   Very pale with black spots.
No orange.   Cranberry bogs.   June–July.
    B   LC   ·   N   LU   ·   P   LA   ·   W   X

9.   **Bog Copper** *(Lycaena epixanthe)*, ♂ above. See page 34.
6/26/90 Lakehurst Bog, Lakehurst, NJ.
Purplish (females gray).   Cranberry bogs.   June–July.

10.   **Northern Metalmark** *(Calephelis borealis)*, above. See page 47.
7/2/91 Fairfield Co., CT.
Orange-brown.   Metallic post-median lines.   July.
    B   X   ·   N   LR   ·   P   LR   ·   W   X

11.   **Northern Metalmark** *(Calephelis borealis)*, below. See page 47.
7/2/91 Fairfield Co., CT.
Bright yellow-orange.   Rows of black spots.
Row of gray-blue metallic spots.   July.

PLATE 8   Elfins and Red-banded Hairstreak

x 2½

1. **Frosted Elfin** *(Callophrys irus)*, below. See page 42.
   5/7/90 Manorville, NY.
   April through early June.   Large.   Frosted HW.
   Short, tail-like protuberance.   Black spot near tailed area.
   Found in barrens with lupine or *Baptisia*.
   B LU · **N** LU · **P** LR-LC · **W** LR

2. **Hoary Elfin** *(Callophrys polios)*, below. See page 41.
   5/1/90 Warren Grove, NJ.
   April–May.   Very dark, small.
   Frosting on both HW and FW margins.
   Low, sand barrens with Bearberry.
   B LU-LC · **N** LR? · **P** LC · **W** X

3. **Henry's Elfin** *(Callophrys henrici)*, below. See page 42.
   4/27/90 Sandy Hook, NJ.
   April–May.   Frosted HW margin.
   Bold white marks at ends of HW post-median line.
   B U · **N** LR · **P** LR · **W** LU

4. **Brown Elfin** *(Callophrys augustinus)*, below. See page 41.
   4/24/90 Mountain Lake Camp, Westchester Co., NY.
   April–May.   Commonest Elfin.
   Rich brown below, brighter reddish-brown along HW submargin.
   No frosting.   No white on post-median line.
   B C · **N** LC-LA · **P** LC-LA · **W** LU

5. **Eastern Pine Elfin** *(Callophrys niphon)*, below. See page 43.
   5/1/90 Chatsworth, NJ.
   April–June.   Stunningly banded.
   B C · **N** U-LC · **P** C · **W** LU

6. **Red-banded Hairstreak** *(Calycopis cecrops)*, below. See page 39.
   8/1/91 Sandy Hook, Monmouth Co., NJ.
   Bright red post-median line.   Bright blue flashes above.
   B X · **N** LU-LC · **P** LU-LC · **W** LU-LC

1

2

3

4

5

6

PLATE 9   Satyrium Hairstreaks

x 2½

1. Coral Hairstreak *(Satyrium titus)*, below. See page 35.
6/21/90 Dogue Creek power cut, Fairfax Co., VA.
June–July.   Marginal row of red-orange spots.
No blue marginal eye-spot.   No tail.   Widespread.
B C · **N** C · **P** R-C · **W** R-C

2. Acadian Hairstreak *(Satyrium acadica)*, below. See page 36.
6/27/89 Pound Ridge Reservation, NY.
June–July.   Pale gray ground color.
Post-median band of solid black spots.
Orange cap on blue spot.   Associated with shrubby willows.
B LU · **N** LC · **P** LU · **W** X

3. Edwards' Hairstreak *(Satyrium edwardsii)*, below. See page 36.
7/10/90 Pound Ridge Reservation, NY.
June–July.   Post-median band broken into spots surrounded by white.
Closely associated with scrub oaks.   See text.
B LC · **N** LC · **P** LC · **W** LC

4. Banded Hairstreak *(Satyrium calanus)*, below. See page 37.
6/19/89 Van Cortlandt Park, NY.
June–July.   Common and variable.
Usually browner and paler than illustrated.
See text for Edwards', Hickory, Banded discussion.
B C · **N** U-A · **P** C · **W** C

5. Hickory Hairstreak *(Satyrium caryaevorus)*, below. See page 37.
7/6/90 Bedford, NY.
June–July.   FW post-median band with white on both sides.
HW blue spot extends inward.
HW cell-end double bar aligned with bars above it.   See text.
B U · **N** U · **P** R? · **W** X

6. Striped Hairstreak *(Satyrium liparops)*, below. See page 38.
6/26/89 Lakehurst, NJ.
June–July.   Striped appearance.   Orange cap on HW blue spot.
B C · **N** U · **P** R-U · **W** R

PLATE 10   More Hairstreaks

x 1¾

1. **Southern Hairstreak** *(Satyrium favonius)*, below. See page 38.
6/19/89 Beaver Dam Sanctuary, Bedford, NY.
Rare. Lacks cell-end bars. June—July.
Brownish ground color. Post-median line composed of
simple white bars (Other *Satyrium* hairstreaks have post-median
lines composed of spots). Inwardly directed white chevron over largest
orange-red spot.
Gray Hairstreak has flat black line over orange-red spot.
B LR · **N** R · **P** R · **W** R

2. **White M Hairstreak** *(Parrhasius m-album)*, below. See page 43.
7/12/89 Pound Ridge Reservation, NY.
Large. Iridescent blue above.
Orange-red spot on HW doesn't reach margin.
Prominent white spot along HW upper margin.
B R · **N** R · **P** R-U · **W** U

3. **Gray Hairstreak** *(Strymon melinus)*, below. See page 44.
8/2/91 Glazier Arboretum, New Castle, NY.
True gray with prominent post-median line.
Has black line over orange eyespot.
B C · **N** U-C · **P** C · **W** C

4. **Gray Hairstreak** *(Strymon melinus)*, ♀ above. See page 44.
7/14/90 Gulf Shores, Alabama.
Orange eye spot on HW. Orange on head.

5. **Olive Hairstreak** *(Callophrys gryneus)*, below. See page 39.
5/18/89 Sandy Hook, NJ.
April—May. July—Aug. Olive-green below.
Found on red cedars. Bottom two HW post-median white
spots facing opposite directions and offset.
B LC · **N** LC-LA · **P** LC · **W** LC

6. **Great Purple Hairstreak** *(Atlides halesus)*, below. See page 35.
11/11/89 Bentsen State Park, Mission, TX.
Red spots at base of wings. Orange abdomen. Large.
B X · **N** X · **P** S · **W** LR

7. **Hessel's Hairstreak** *(Callophrys hesseli)*, below. See page 40.
5/1/90 Chatsworth, NJ.
April—May. July—Aug. Bright green below.
Found in, or near, white cedar swamps.
Bottom two HW post-median white spots both concave outwardly.
Brown patches outside postmedian line.
B LU · **N** LR · **P** LR-LC · **W** X

1

2

3

4

5

6

7

PLATE 11   Blues

x 1¾

1. **Spring Azure** *(Celastrina ladon)*, ♂ above. See page 45.
   4/9/90 Pound Ridge Reservation, NY.
   Shining blue.   Females have black borders.
   B   A   •   **N**   C-A   •   **P**   C   •   **W**   C

2. **Spring Azure** *(Celastrina ladon)* form marginata below. See page 45.
   4/11/90 Chappaqua Rd. power line, Mt. Pleasant, NY.
   Dull brownish HW marginal band.   April–May.

3. **Spring Azure** *(Celastrina ladon)* form lucia below. See page 45.
   4/18/89 Waccabuc, Westchester, NY.
   Dark smudge in center of HW; marginal band.   April–May.

4. **Spring Azure** *(Celastrina ladon)* form violacea below. See page 45.
   5/9/90 Blue Hills Reservation, MA.
   Small black spots on off-white ground.   May.

5. **Summer Azure** *(Celastrina ladon)* form neglecta below.
   See Spring Azure, page 45.
   7/1/90 Pound Ridge Reservation, NY.
   June–Sept.   Blue with much white overscaling above.
   Below, similar to form violacea.

6. **Appalachian Azure** *(Celastrina neglectamajor)*, below. See page 46.
   5/24/90 Pound Ridge Reservation, NY.
   Larger than Spring Azure.   May–June.
   Flies between Spring and Summer Azures.   See Text.
   B   X   •   **N**   LU   •   **P**   LC   •   **W**   LU

7. **Eastern Tailed Blue** *(Everes comyntas)*, spring ♀ above. See page 45.
   5/7/90 East Hampton, NY.
   Dull blue to gray.
   Tailed (but sometimes tails are worn as in this individual).
   B   C   •   **N**   C-A   •   **P**   A   •   **W**   A

8. **Eastern Tailed Blue** *(Everes comyntas)*, ♂ above. See page 45.
   5/5/91 Chappaqua, NY.
   Bright blue.   Tailed.   Flight usually low and weak.

9. **Eastern Tailed Blue** *(Everes comyntas)*, below. See page 45.
   7/30/90 Mt. Pleasant, NY.
   Pale below.   Tails.   Orange spot on HW margin.

10. **Eastern Tailed Blue** *(Everes comyntas)*, gray ♀ above. See page 45.
    7/30/90 Chappaqua, NY.
    No orange on head.

1

2

3

4

5

6

7

8

9

10

PLATE 12 **Some Striking Nymphalids**

x ¾

1. **Regal Fritillary** *(Speyeria idalia)*, below. See page 50.
   8/10/69 Cross River, NY.
   Large.   HW brownish-black with white spots.
   Brownish-black body.   Open, low grassland.
   Almost extinct.   July—Aug.

   > **B** LR · **N** LR · **P** LR · **W** ˙H

2. **Regal Fritillary** *(Speyeria idalia)*, above. See page 50.
   8/10/69 Cross River, NY.
   Large.   HW brownish-black with white spots.
   Open, low grassland.   Almost extinct.   July—Aug.

3. **Gulf Fritillary** *(Agraulis vanillae)*, below. See page 49.
   8/24/91 Ocala National Forest, FL.
   Long wings.   Heavily silvered spots.

   > **B** X · **N** X · **P** S · **W** X

4. **Gulf Fritillary** *(Agraulis vanillae)*, above. See page 49.
   3/21/90 Homestead, FL.
   Long wings.   Black-ringed white spots in FW cell.

5. **Baltimore** *(Euphydryas phaeton)*, below. See page 55.
   6/27/90 Cross River, NY.
   Orange, black and white spot bands.   June—July.

   > **B** LC-LA · **N** LC · **P** LC · **W** LR-LU

6. **Baltimore** *(Euphydryas phaeton)*, above. See page 55.
   6/27/89 Pound Ridge Reservation, NY.
   Mainly black.   Orange marginal band and white spots.
   June—July.

1

2

3

4

5

6

PLATE 13   Greater Fritillaries

x ¾

1. **Great Spangled Fritillary** *(Speyeria cybele)*, below. See page 49.
7/20/90 Pound Ridge Reservation, NY.
Silvered spots on orange-brown ground.   Wide cream-colored band
between post-median and marginal silvered spot-bands.   Widespread.
B C · **N** C-A · **P** C · **W** C

2. **Great Spangled Fritillary** *(Speyeria cybele)*, above. See page 49.
7/4/89 Bedford, NY.
Bright orange and warm orange-brown with black bands and spots.

3. **Aphrodite Fritillary** *(Speyeria aphrodite)*, below. See page 50.
7/30/88 Pound Ridge Reservation, NY.
Similar to Great Spangled Fritillary.   HW dark brown ground
color extends past the post-median spot band causing cream
colored band to be narrow.   Rosy FW disc.
B U · **N** R · **P** R · **W** R

4. **Aphrodite Fritillary** *(Speyeria aphrodite)*, above. See page 50.
7/30/88 Pound Ridge Reservation, NY.
Similar to Great Spangled Fritillary.   Black spot at the base of the FW.

5. **Atlantis Fritillary** *(Speyeria atlantis)*, below. See page 51.
7/25/91 Moose River Plains, Inlet, Hamilton Co., NY.
Very similar to Great Spangled but very small.   See text.
Possible stray to the northwest margins of our area.
B X · **N** X · **P** X · **W** X

6. **Atlantis Fritillary** *(Speyeria atlantis)*, above. See page 51.
7/25/91 Moose River Plains, Inlet, Hamilton Co., NY.
Small.   Bright orange with black borders.   See text.

1

2

3

4

5

6

PLATE 14 Lesser and Variegated Fritillaries

x 1

1. **Meadow Fritillary** *(Boloria bellona)*, above. See page 52.
6/28/90 Pound Ridge Reservation, NY.
Orange-brown ground color. Larger than Pearl Crescent.
Blunt FW apices. Flies with shallow wing-beats.
      B LU · **N** A · **P** LC-LA · **W** LU-LC

2. **Meadow Fritillary** *(Boloria bellona)*, below. See page 52.
6/25/90 Pound Ridge Reservation, NY.
Pattern indistinct.

3. **Silver-bordered Fritillary** *(Boloria selene)*, above. See page 52.
6/5/90 Middle Creek WMA, Lancaster, PA.
Orange-brown ground color. Larger than Pearl Crescent.
Black borders enclosing orange spots.
      B C · **N** LR · **P** LU · **W** H

4. **Silver-bordered Fritillary** *(Boloria selene)*, below. See page 52.
7/24/91 7 miles west of Inlet, Hamilton Co., NY.
Median and marginal bands of silvered white. Wet habitats.

5. **Variegated Fritillary** *(Euptoieta claudia)*, above. See page 49.
7/14/91 Kitchawan Center, New Castle, Westchester Co., NY.
Dull orange-brown. Chunky wings. Immigrant.
      B R · **N** R · **P** U · **W** U

6. **Variegated Fritillary** *(Euptoieta claudia)*, below. See page 49.
6/29/91 Pelham Bay Park, Bronx, NY.
Pale median HW band.

1

2

3

4

5

6

PLATE 15   Crescents and Checkerspots

x 1¼

1. Pearl Crescent *(Phyciodes tharos),* above. See page 54.
7/27/89 Chappaqua, NY.
Bright orange with black reticulation.
Small and common.   Flies low and glides.
B A · **N** A · **P** A · **W** A

2. Pearl Crescent *(Phyciodes tharos),* ♀ below. See page 54.
6/13/90 Chappaqua, NY.
Brown HW marginal "smudge."

3. Pearl Crescent *(Phyciodes tharos),* ♂ below. See page 54.
7/31/90 Chappaqua, NY.
Brown HW marginal "smudge."

4. Tawny Crescent *(Phyciodes batesii),* above. See page 54.
6/9/73 Jamesville, NY.
May no longer occur in our region.
More extensive black than Pearl Crescent.   Late June–early July.
B X · **N** X · **P** H · **W** X

5. Tawny Crescent *(Phyciodes batesii),* below. See page 54.
6/9/73 Jamesville, NY.
HW with reduced markings.

6. Silvery Checkerspot *(Chlosyne nycteis),* above. See page 53.
6/18/90 Van Cortlandt Park, Bronx, NY.
Larger than Pearl Crescent.   Wide black borders.   Palps very dark.
B LR · **N** LC · **P** LU · **W** LU

7. Silvery Checkerspot *(Chlosyne nycteis),* below. See page 53.
6/21/90 Pound Ridge Reservation, NY.
Broad white HW median band.

8. Harris' Checkerspot *(Chlosyne harrisii),* above. See page 53.
6/16/90 Pound Ridge Reservation, NY.
Larger than Pearl Crescent.   Orange-brown palps.
Found in wet meadows.   June–July.
B LU · **N** LU · **P** X · **W** X

9. Harris' Checkerspot *(Chlosyne harrisii),* below. See page 53.
6/16/90 Pound Ridge Reservation, NY.
HW has white basal, median, and submarginal bands.
Orange marginal band.   June–July.

1

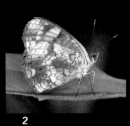

2

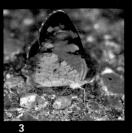

3

4

5

6

7

8

9

PLATE 16   Anglewings

x ³⁄₄

1. **Question Mark** *(Polygonia interrogationis),* orange form above.
See page 55.
September, Jamaica Bay, NY.
FW black horizontal subapical mark.   Violaceous HW margin.
       B   U   **·**   **N**   U   **·**   **P**   C   **·**   **W**   C

2. **Eastern Comma** *(Polygonia comma),* orange form above.
See page 56.
Smaller.   Lacks FW black horizontal subapical mark.

3. **Question Mark** *(Polygonia interrogationis),* black form above.
See page 55.
8/4/88 Chappaqua, NY.
Orange with outer halves of HWs black.   Short tails.
FW black horizontal subapical mark.
       B   U   **·**   **N**   U   **·**   **P**   C   **·**   **W**   C

4. **Eastern Comma** *(Polygonia comma),* black form above.
See page 56.
Smaller.   Lacks FW black horizontal subapical mark.
       B   U   **·**   **N**   R-U   **·**   **P**   U   **·**   **W**   U

5. **Question Mark** *(Polygonia interrogationis),* orange form below.
See page 55.
HW with silvered "question-mark."

6. **Question Mark** *(Polygonia interrogationis),* black form below.
See page 55.
5/24/90 Chappaqua, NY.
HW with silvered "question-mark."

7. **Eastern Comma** *(Polygonia comma),* below. See page 56.
6/25/89 Pound Ridge Reservation, NY.
HW with silvered "comma."   Brown ground color.

1

2

3

4

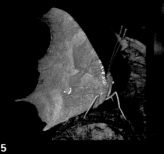

5

6

7

PLATE 17   Northern Anglewings

X ¾

1. **Eastern Comma** *(Polygonia comma)*, orange form above.
See page 56.

    B U · **N** R-U · **P** U · **W** U

2. **Eastern Comma** *(Polygonia comma)*, orange form below.
See page 56.

3. **Gray Comma** *(Polygonia progne)*, above. See page 57.
10/4/55 Am. Mus. Nat. Hist. specimen, Hunterdon Co., NJ.
See text.

    B X · **N** R · **P** LR · **W** X

4. **Gray Comma** *(Polygonia progne)*, below. See page 57.
7/26/91 Moose River Plains, Inlet, Hamilton Co., NY.
Less mottled than Eastern comma, more even gray-mauve-brown.
"Comma" thin and tapered at ends.   Often finely striated.

5. **Green Comma** *(Polygonia faunus)*, above. See page 56.
7/24/91 Moose River Plains, Inlet, Hamilton Co., NY.
Lacks FW black horizontal subapical mark.
Has extra spot adjoining dark spot at base of FW.
Black HW border with yellow spots.

    B X · **N** X · **P** R? · **W** X

6. **Green Comma** *(Polygonia faunus)*, below. See page 56.
7/24/91 Moose River Plains, Inlet, Hamilton Co., NY.
Very rare in our region.   Very jagged wings.
Gray ground color.   Bluish green submarginal band.
"Comma" thick & hooked at front end.

1

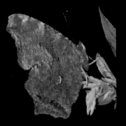

2

3

4

5

6

PLATE 18   Tortoiseshells

X ¾

1. **Milbert's Tortoiseshell** *(Nymphalis milberti)*, above. See page 58.
   Bright orange and yellow submarginal bands.   Dark ground color.
   B U · **N** X · **P** R · **W** X

2. **Milbert's Tortoiseshell** *(Nymphalis milberti)*, below. See page 58.
   Very dark ground color.   Striated.   Pale submarginal bands.

3. **Compton Tortoiseshell** *(Nymphalis vau-album)*, above. See page 57.
   7/4/89 Bedford, Westchester, NY.
   Large.   Orange, black, and brown.   White spot on HW.
   B U · **N** R-U · **P** R · **W** R

4. **Compton Tortoiseshell** *(Nymphalis vau-album)*, below. See page 57.
   7/3/79 Sussex Co., NJ.
   Large.   Very dark gray inward from the post-median line.
   Paler gray outside the postmedian line.   Heavily striated.

5. **Mourning Cloak** *(Nymphalis antiopa)*, above. See page 58.
   5/27/90 Chappaqua Rd., Mt. Pleasant, NY.
   Large.   Deep brown with cream-yellow borders.   Widespread.
   B C · **N** C · **P** U-C · **W** U-C

6. **Mourning Cloak** *(Nymphalis antiopa)*, below. See page 58.
   7/10/90 Route 21, Wingdale, Dutchess Co., NY.
   Very dark striated brown.   Cream-yellow borders.

7. **Small Tortoiseshell** *(Nymphalis urticae)*, above. See page 59.
   8/31/88 Jamaica Bay Wildlife Refuge, NY.
   Bright orange.   Black and yellow stripes along FW margin.
   European (see text).
   B X · **N** S? · **P** X · **W** X

1

2

3

4

5

6

7

PLATE 19   Ladies and Emperors

x ¾

1. **American Lady** *(Vanessa virginiensis)*, above. See page 59.
   7/25/90 Lakehurst, NJ.
   Dull orange.   Black FW apices with pale spots.
   FW with small white spot in orange ground.
   > **B** C · **N** C · **P** C · **W** C

2. **American Lady** *(Vanessa virginiensis)*, below. See page 59.
   8/26/90 Delmont, Cumberland Co., NJ.
   Pale HW with "cobwebbing."   Two large eye-spots on HW.

3. **Painted Lady** *(Vanessa cardui)*, above. See page 60.
   7/6/91 Chappaqua, NY.
   Deep orange often suffused with pink.
   Bold black median FW band.   No white spot in orange ground.
   Usually larger than American Lady.
   > **B** R · **N** R-U · **P** R-U · **W** R-C

4. **Painted Lady** *(Vanessa cardui)*, below. See page 60.
   6/24/91 Pound Ridge Reservation, NY.
   Pale HW with "cobwebbing."   Four smallish eye-spots on HW.

5. **Hackberry Emperor** *(Asterocampa celtis)*, above. See page 63.
   9/3/90 Tenafly, NJ.
   Dull brown ground.   FW eye-spot.   Flies around trees.
   NE to Springfield, MA.   Usually on or near Hackberries.
   > **B** X · **N** LU-LC · **P** LU · **W** LU-LC

6. **Hackberry Emperor** *(Asterocampa celtis)*, below. See page 63.
   6/28/80 Hook Mtn., Rockland Co., NY.
   Creamy gray-brown with FW eye-spots.

7. **Tawny Emperor** *(Asterocampa clyton)*, above. See page 63.
   6/22/91 Tottenville, Staten Island, NY.
   Rich orangish brown.   No FW eye-spots.   NE to Springfield, MA.
   > **B** X · **N** LR-LU · **P** LU · **W** LR

8. **Tawny Emperor** *(Asterocampa clyton)*, below. See page 63.
   7/4/90 Tenafly, NJ.
   Warm brown ground.   No FW eye-spots.

PLATE 20   Common Buckeye, Red Admiral, and American Snout

x 1

1. **Common Buckeye** *(Junonia coenia)*, above. See page 61.
   7/29/89 Oakwood Cemetery, Mt. Kisco, NY.
   Large eye-spots.   FW with cream band.
   Orange stripes in FW cell.
   B R-U · **N** R-C · **P** C · **W** C

2. **Common Buckeye** *(Junonia coenia)*, below. See page 61.
   8/26/90 Delmont, Cumberland Co., NJ.
   HW pale.   Eye-spots.   Orange stripes in FW cell.

3. **Red Admiral** *(Vanessa atalanta)*, above. See page 60.
   3/20/90 S. Miami, FL.
   Appears small and dark during its rapid flight.
   Bright orange-red stripes on FW, margins on HW.

4. **Red Admiral** *(Vanessa atalanta)*, below. See page 60.
   6/22/91 Oregon Rd., New Castle, Westchester Co., NY.
   Red, white, and blue on FW.   HW dark and mottled.
   B C · **N** C-A · **P** C-A · **W** C

5. **American Snout** *(Libytheana carinenta)*, above. See page 48.
   Orange stripes basally.
   Dark brown with large white spots distally.

6. **American Snout** *(Libytheana carinenta)*, below. See page 48.
   8/22/88 Vernon, Sussex Co., NJ.
   Very long palps.   Small with dull colors.
   B S · **N** LR · **P** LU · **W** LU

1

2

3

4

5

6

PLATE 21 *Limenitis* and Monarch

x ⅔

1. **Red-spotted Purple** *(Limenitis arthemis astyanax)*, above. See page 61.
7/11/89 Sea View, Staten Island, NY.
Iridescent blue HWs.   Red spots on FW.   No tails.
   B   U   ·   **N**   U   ·   **P**   U-C   ·   **W**   C

2. **Red-spotted Purple** *(Limenitis arthemis astyanax)*, below. See page 61.
5/21/91 Nottingham Park, Chester Co., PA.
Dark blue-black ground.   Red spots.

3. **White Admiral** *(Limenitis arthemis arthemis)*, above. See page 62.
6/9/90 Jamesville, Onadaga Co., NY.
Broad white bands on purplish-black ground.
   B   U   ·   **N**   X   ·   **P**   R   ·   **W**   X

4. **White Admiral** *(Limenitis arthemis arthemis)*, below. See page 62.
6/9/90 Jamesville, Onadaga Co., NY.
Broad white bands.   Red spots.

5. **Viceroy** *(Limenitis archippus)*, above. See page 62.
8/2/89 Pound Ridge Reservation, NY.
Deep orange.   Smaller than the Monarch.
Black HW post-median band.
Shallow wing-beats.   Glides on flat wings.
   B   C   ·   **N**   C   ·   **P**   C-A   ·   **W**   C

6. **Viceroy** *(Limenitis archippus)*, below. See page 62.
7/30/90 Kisco Swamp, Mt. Kisco, NY.
HW with black post-median band.

7. **Monarch** *(Danaus plexippus)*, ♂ above. See page 68.
7/27/89 Pound Ridge Reservation, NY.
Deep orange.   Larger than Viceroy.
Lacks black HW post-median band.
Deep powerful wing-beats.
Glides with wings held in a V.
   B   C   ·   **N**   U-A   ·   **P**   U-C   ·   **W**   U-C

8. **Monarch** *(Danaus plexippus)*, ♂ below. See page 68.
8/31/90 New Castle, NY.
HW without black post-median band.

PLATE 22 Large Satyrs

1. **Northern Pearly Eye** (*Enodia anthedon*), below. See page 64.
   July 1985 Adirondacks, NY.
   Dark brown ground.   Rocky woodlands.
   HW with eye-spots surrounded as a group by white line.
   B U · **N** U · **P** R · **W** R-U·

2. **Common Wood Nymph** (*Cercyonis pegala*), below. See page 68.
   6/27/90 Pound Ridge Reservation, NY.
   Dark brown striated ground.   Yellow/orange patch on FW.
   B C-A · **N** C-A · **P** C-A · **W** C

3. **Eyed Brown** (*Satyrodes eurydice*), below. See page 64.
   7/12/89 Pound Ridge Reservation, NY.
   HW basal line with inward "tooth."
   FW eye-spots surrounded as a group with white.
   See text.   Sedge-meadows and marshes.
   B LC · **N** LR · **P** LU · **W** X

4. **Eyed Brown** (*Satyrodes eurydice*), above. See page 64.
   7/8/72 Springdale, Sussex Co., NJ.
   FW median line without large dark area
   and not so angled as Appalachian Brown.

5. **Appalachian Brown** (*Satyrodes appalachia*), below. See page 65.
   6/8/91 Chappaqua Rd., Mt. Pleasant, NY.
   HW basal line without "tooth."
   FW eye-spots each surrounded by white.
   See text.   Wet woodlands.
   B U · **N** C · **P** LC · **W** LC

6. **Appalachian Brown** (*Satyrodes appalachia*), above. See page 65.
   6/24/91 Pound Ridge Reservation, NY.
   Eye-spots smaller than on N. Pearly Eye.
   FW median line with large dark area
   that forms a sharper angle than that of Eyed Brown.

PLATE 23   Smaller Satyrs

x1½

1. Little Wood Satyr *(Megisto cymela)*, below. See page 67.
6/22/91 Clay Pits Pond Park, Staten Island, NY.
Two eye-spots on FW.   Lacks HW cell-end bar.

2. Little Wood Satyr *(Megisto cymela)*, above. See page 67.
5/30/88 Oakwood Cemetery, Mt. Kisco, NY.
Brown ground.   Two eye-spots on FW.   Widespread.
B A · **N** A · **P** C · **W** C

3. Carolina Satyr *(Hermeuptychia hermes sosybius)*, below. See page 66.
8/25/91 Gainesville, FL.
Lacks lower FW eye-spot of Little Wood Satyr.   HW cell-end bar.
MD only.   See text.
B X · **N** X · **P** H · **W** LR

4. Carolina Satyr *(Hermeuptychia hermes sosybius)*, above. See page 66.
Same individual as in 3.
No eye-spots.

5. Georgia Satyr *(Neonympha areolatus)*, below. See page 66.
6/29/89 Lakehurst, NJ.
Orange line surrounding oval HW eye-spots.
Central and southern NJ bogs.   June–July.
B X · **N** X · **P** LC · **W** X

6. Mitchell's Satyr *(Neonympha mitchellii)*, below. See page 66.
7/5/79 Springdale, NJ.
HW usually with 6 eye-spots.   HW with eye-spots not as
elongate as Georgia Satyr.   Until 1988 in northern NJ fens,
now almost certainly extirpated.
B X · **N** H · **P** X · **W** X

7. Common Ringlet *(Coenonympha tullia)*. See page 67.
5/31/91 Chappaqua Rd., Mt. Pleasant, NY.
Smaller than Little Wood Satyr.   Reddish flush in flight.
HW grayish with white median line.   Expanding southward.
See text for range.   June & Aug.
B C-A · **N** C? · **P** X · **W** X

8. Gemmed Satyr *(Cyllopsis gemma)*, below. See page 65.
September 1990 Mission, TX.
HW with gray patch around eye-spots.   Small and inconspicuous.
Possible stray north to MD.
B X · **N** X · **P** X · **W** X

PLATE 24   Large Skippers

1. **Silver-spotted Skipper** *(Epargyreus clarus)*, above. See page 70.
8/4/90 Lititz, Lancaster Co., PA.
Large with angled wings.   Gold-brown median FW band.
   B C · **N** C-A · **P** C-A · **W** C-A

2. **Silver-spotted Skipper** *(Epargyreus clarus)*, below. See page 70.
6/12/90 Oakwood Cemetery, Mt. Kisco, NY.
Large silvery-white patch in center of HW.

3. **Hoary Edge** *(Achalarus lyciades)*, above. See page 71.
6/16/89 Redding, Fairfield Co., CT.
Gold-brown median FW band encloses small patch
of brown ground.
   B LU · **N** U-C · **P** LU-LC · **W** LU-LC

4. **Hoary Edge** *(Achalarus lyciades)*, below. See page 71.
6/13/90 Chappaqua Rd., Mt. Pleasant, NY.
Large white patch at HW margin.

5. **Long-tailed Skipper** *(Urbanus proteus)*, above. See page 70.
8/25/91 Gainesville, FL.
Long tails.   Bright green/blue on body and base of wings.
   B X · **N** X · **P** S · **W** S

6. **Golden-banded Skipper** *(Autochton cellus)*, above. See page 70.
8/15/89 Box Canyon, Santa Rita Mtns., AZ.
Wide, light yellow FW median band.
   B X · **N** X · **P** H · **W** LR

1

2

3

4

5

6

PLATE 25   Cloudywings

x 1¾

1. **Northern Cloudywing** *(Thorybes pylades)*, above. See page 72.
5/29/91 Pound Ridge Reservation, NY.
Brown ground with restricted white spots.   See text.
B C · N C · P C-A · W C

2. **Northern Cloudywing** *(Thorybes pylades)*, below. See page 72.
Same individual as in 1.
Brown or dark gray "face" (palps).

3. **Southern Cloudywing** *(Thorybes bathyllus)*, above. See page 71.
6/7/91 Oakwood Cemetery, Mt. Kisco, NY.
Extensive white spots.
Second spot from FW margin in shape of hourglass.
B LU · N LU · P C · W C

4. **Southern Cloudywing** *(Thorybes bathyllus)*, below. See page 71.
6/28/90 Oakwood Cemetery, Mt. Kisco, NY.
White or light gray "face."

5. **Confused Cloudywing** *(Thorybes confusis)*, above. See page 72.
8/23/91 Gainesville, FL.
Reduced markings.   Middle spot of lower group
of three spots a pale thin line (if present at all).   See text.
B X · N X · P R? · W R

6. **Confused Cloudywing** *(Thorybes confusis)*, below. See page 72.
Same individual as in 5.
White "face."   Some individuals with HW median band
extending across entire HW.   See text.

1

2

3

4

5

6

PLATE 26   Large Duskywings

x 1½

1. **Juvenal's Duskywing** *(Erynnis juvenalis)*, ♂ above. See page 74.
5/7/90 Easthampton, Suffolk Co., NY.
White spot below middle of FW costal margin.   Widespread.   April–June.

        B C · N C-A · P C · W C

2. **Juvenal's Duskywing** *(Erynnis juvenalis)*, ♀ below. See page 74.
5/28/89 Oakwood Cemetery, Mt. Kisco, NY.
Two pale subapical spots on HW.
Widespread.   April–June.

3. **Juvenal's Duskywing** *(Erynnis juvenalis)*, ♀ above. See page 74.
Upperside of individual in 2.
Much contrast.
White spot below middle of FW costal margin.
Widespread.   April–June.

4. **Horace's Duskywing** *(Erynnis horatius)*, below. See page 75.
7/11/91 Lakehurst, NJ.
Lacks HW subapical spots.   See text.
Mainly oak woodlands on poor soils.
April–May and July–Aug.

        B U · N U · P U · W C

5. **Horace's Duskywing** *(Erynnis horatius)*, ♀ above. See page 75.
6/13/87 Gainesville, FL.
Mainly oak woodlands on poor soils.
April–May and July–Aug.   See text.

6. **Horace's Duskywing** *(Erynnis horatius)*, ♂ above. See page 75.
7/25/90 Lakehurst, NJ.
Mainly oak woodlands on poor soils.
April–May and July–Aug.   See text.

1

2

3

6

5

4

PLATE 27   Smaller Duskywings

x 1½

1. **Wild Indigo Duskywing** *(Erynnis baptisiae)*, ♂ above. See page 76.
7/28/90 Chappaqua RR station, Chappaqua, NY.
Small, white FW subapical spots.   No spot in middle of FW.
Oily black on basal ⅓ of FW.
> B C · N C-LA · P C-LA · W C

2. **Wild Indigo Duskywing** *(Erynnis baptisiae)*, ♀ above. See page 76.
5/25/75 Oakridge, NJ.
Small, white FW subapical spots.   Rarely with spot in middle of FW.
Widespread.

3. **Mottled Duskywing** *(Erynnis martialis)*, ♂ above. See page 75.
7/19/89 Albany Pine Bush, Albany, NY.
HW with strong mottled pattern.
Narrow and sharp HW post-median dark band.   See text.
> B · H · N H · P LR · W H

4. **Zarucco Duskywing** *(Erynnis zarucco)*, above. See page 76.
8/24/91 Ocala National Forest, FL.
Very dark with narrow FW.
Lacks FW post-median "chain" of Wild Indigo.
Prominent light brown patch at FW "wrist."
Pale patch in middle of lower margin of FW not prominent.
> B X · N X · P S · W R-U

5. **Dreamy Duskywing** *(Erynnis icelus)*, ♂ above. See page 74.
5/17/91 Kisco Swamp, Mt. Kisco, NY.
No white spots on FW.   Small size.
FW with broad, chain-like post-median band.
Last segment of palps long.   Prominent silvery spot at FW "wrist."
> B C · N C · P C-A · W C

6. **Dreamy Duskywing** *(Erynnis icelus)*, ♀ above. See page 74.
5/23/90 Kisco Swamp, Mt. Kisco, NY.
See description in 5.

7. **Sleepy Duskywing** *(Erynnis brizo)*, ♂ above. See page 74.
No white spots on FW.   FW with broad, chain-like post-median band.
Usually larger than Dreamy Duskywing.
Last segment of palps short.   "Wrist" spot gray but usually not silvery.
Associated with small oaks and poor soil.
> B C · N R-U · P U · W R-U

8. **Sleepy Duskywing** *(Erynnis brizo)*, ♀ above. See page 74.
5/9/89 Easthampton, Suffolk Co., NY.
Similar to ♂ but "wrist" spot brown.   Found in areas with scrub oak.

1

2

3

4

5

6

7

8

PLATE 28   Some Small Skippers

x 1½

1. Common Sootywing *(Pholisora catullus)*, above. See page 78.
September 1985 Jamaica Bay Wildlife Refuge, NY.
Very dark brown-black with many tiny white spots.
Mainly in disturbed areas.
B C · **N** C · **P** C · **W** C

2. Hayhurst's Scallopwing *(Staphylus hayhurstii)*, above. See page 73.
8/23/91 Gainesville, FL.
Very dark brown-black.   Darker bands form concentric semicircles on HW.
Strewn with pale gray or gold flecks.   HW margins "scallopped."
B X · **N** X · **P** R · **W** R-U

3. Common Checkered Skipper *(Pyrgus communis)*, above. See page 78.
11/12/89 8 miles west of Roma, TX.
Extensive white markings.   Blue-tinged body hairs.
FW post-median band without offset spot.
B X · **N** R · **P** C · **W** C

4. Common Checkered Skipper *(Pyrgus communis)*, below. See page 78.
White and tan.

5. Grizzled Skipper *(Pyrgus centaureae wyandot)*, above. See page 77.
May 1980 Green Ridge State Forest, MD.
Restricted white markings compared to C. Checkered Skipper.
FW post-median band with second from bottom spot offset inward.
HW white median band reduced.   Northern barrens.   April–May.
B X · **N** H · **P** LR/H · **W** H

6. Least Skipper *(Ancyloxypha numitor)*, below. See page 80.
6/12/90 Pound Ridge Reservation, NY.
Bright orange.   Very small.   Rounded wings.
Flight weak and low through grass.
B C · **N** C-A · **P** A · **W** A

7. Least Skipper *(Ancyloxypha numitor)*, above. See page 80.
Very small with weak flight.   Rounded wings.

8. Arctic Skipper *(Carterocephalus palaemon)*, above. See page 79.
5/31/89 Rte. 110, Harvard, MA.
SE to northwestern CT and southwestern Boston area.   Small.
Checkered orange and brown.   June.
B LR · **N** X · **P** X · **W** X

9. Arctic Skipper *(Carterocephalus palaemon)*, below. See page 79.
SE to northwestern CT and southwestern Boston area.

1

2

3

4

5

6

7

8

9

PLATE 29   Fiery Skipper and Whirlabout

x 1½

1. **Fiery Skipper** *(Hylephila phyleus)*, ♂ below. See page 81.
   8/17/91 Somers, Westchester Co., NY.
   Bright yellow-orange with many small spots.
   Late summer immigrant.
   > **B** X · **N** R · **P** R-U · **W** R-C

2. **Whirlabout** *(Polites vibex)*, ♂ below. See page 85.
   8/25/91 Gainesville, FL.
   Bright yellow-orange with large brown/black blotches.
   Very rare late summer stray.
   > **B** X · **N** S · **P** S · **W** S

3. **Fiery Skipper** *(Hylephila phyleus)*, ♀ below. See page 81.
   9/2/91 Snug Harbor, Staten Island, NY.
   Similar to male but sometimes with greenish tinge.
   Spots usually faint.

4. **Whirlabout** *(Polites vibex)*, ♀ below. See page 85.
   8/23/91 Gainesville, FL.
   Green-gray with large dull brown blotches.

5. **Fiery Skipper** *(Hylephila phyleus)*, ♂ above. See page 81.
   9/13/91 Snug Harbor, Staten Island, NY.
   Jagged black border on FW and HW.

6. **Whirlabout** *(Polites vibex)*, ♂ above. See page 85.
   8/23/91 Gainesville, FL.
   Smooth black border on HW.

7. **Fiery Skipper** *(Hylephila phyleus)*, ♀ above. See page 81.
   8/25/91 Gainesville, FL.
   Five orange spots on a diagonal line on dark brown ground.
   Orange spot in cell.

8. **Whirlabout** *(Polites vibex)*, ♀ above. See page 85.
   8/25/91 Gainesville, FL.
   Brown with small pale spots.   No spot in cell.

1

2

3

4

5

6

7

8

PLATE 30 *Hesperia* Skippers

x 1½

1. **Leonard's Skipper** *(Hesperia leonardus)*, below. See page 81.
   8/27/88 Pound Ridge Reservation, NY.
   Aug.–Sept. in, or near, areas with *Andropogon*.
   Large. Bright reddish-brown with bright white spots.
     B U · **N** LU · **P** LU · **W** LU

2. **Leonard's Skipper** *(Hesperia leonardus)*, ♂ above. See page 81.
   9/3/90 Route 202, Somers, Westchester Co., NY.
   Aug.–Sept. in, or near, areas with *Andropogon*.

3. **Leonard's Skipper** *(Hesperia leonardus)*, ♀ above. See page 81.
   9/3/90 Route 202, Somers, Westchester Co., NY.
   Very dark with dull orange spots.   White HW fringe.

4. **Cobweb Skipper** *(Hesperia metea)*, below. See page 82.
   5/14/90 Pound Ridge Reservation, NY.
   Flies low in *Andropogon* fields in May.
   Dull brown with undulating white chevron.

5. **Cobweb Skipper** *(Hesperia metea)*, ♂ above. See page 82.
   5/14/89 Oakwood Cemetery, Mt. Kisco, NY.

6. **Cobweb Skipper** *(Hesperia metea)*, ♀ above. See page 82.
   5/24/90 Pound Ridge Reservation, NY.
   May.   Dull brown with pale spots.   FW costal margin white.
     B C · **N** C · **P** C · **W** U

7. **Indian Skipper** *(Hesperia sassacus)*, below. See page 83.
   5/29/91 Pound Ridge Reservation, NY.
   May–June.   HW pattern often indistinct.
   HW post-median band spots concave outwardly.
     B C · **N** C · **P** LU · **W** LR

8. **Indian Skipper** *(Hesperia sassacus)*, ♂ above. See page 83.
   6/13/90 Campfire Rd., New Castle, Westchester Co., NY.
   Orange FW with thin black stigma.
   No black in middle of orange HW.   See **Long Dash.**

9. **Indian Skipper** *(Hesperia sassacus)*, ♀ above. See page 83.
   6/22/90 Pound Ridge Reservation, NY.
   FW orange spots concave outwardly.

10. **Long Dash** *(Polites mystic)*, below. See page 85.
    6/13/90 Campfire Rd. power line, Chappaqua, NY.
    HW post-median band spots not concave outwardly.
      B C · **N** LC · **P** LU · **W** LR

11. **Dotted Skipper** *(Hesperia attalus slossonae)*, below. See page 82.
    7/25/90 Lakehurst Naval Air Station, Lakehurst, NJ.
    See Crossline Skipper.

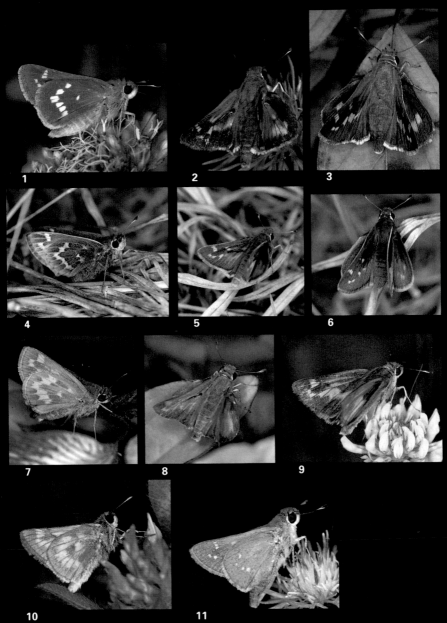

PLATE 31   Dotted, Crossline, Tawny-edged, and Swarthy Skippers

x 1½

1. **Dotted Skipper** *(Hesperia attalus slossonae)*, below. See page 82.
7/25/90 Lakehurst Naval Air Station, Lakehurst, NJ.   HW usually with
distinct bright white dots.   FW with two subapical spots.
Large.   Rare and local in sand barrens.   July.
B   S · **N**   S · **P** LU · **W**   S

2. **Dotted Skipper** *(Hesperia attalus slossonae)*, ♂ above. See page 82.
7/25/90 Lakehurst RR tracks, Lakehurst, NJ.   HW with post-median spot-band.

3. **Dotted Skipper** *(Hesperia attalus slossonae)*, ♀ above. See page 82.
8/26/91 Ocala National Forest, FL.   FW with two subapical white spots.
HW with post-median spot-band.
Similar to ♀ Cobweb & Crossline Skippers and ♀ Sachem.

4. **Crossline Skipper** *(Polites origenes)*, below. See page 84.
7/8/91 Route 202 Somers, Westchester, NY.   Brassy yellow-brown.
Contrast between HW color and color of FW costal margin is not as strong
as in Tawny-edged Skipper.   HW usually with post-median spot-band.
Larger than Tawny-edged but smaller than Dotted.
B   U · **N**   C · **P**   C · **W**   U-C

5. **Crossline Skipper** *(Polites origenes)*, ♂ above. See page 84.
7/6/89 Chappaqua Rd. power line, Mt. Pleasant, NY.   Stigma longer and narrower
than Tawny-edged Skipper.   Yellow spot distal to stigma.

6. **Crossline Skipper** *(Polites origenes)*, ♀ above. See page 84.
7/11/89 Chappaqua, NY.   HW with lighter, brighter central area.

7. **Tawny-edged Skipper** *(Polites themistocles)*, below. See page 84.
7/26/90 Arkville, Delaware County, NY.   HW dull olive-brown.
Often lacks HW spot-band.   Strong contrast
between HW color and brighter costal margin.   See text.
B   A · **N**   A · **P**   C · **W**   U

8. **Tawny-edged Skipper** *(Polites themistocles)*, ♂ above. See page 84.
5/24/90 Chappaqua Rd. power line, Mt. Pleasant, NY.   Intense black, short and
thick stigma.   FW lacks yellow spot distal to stigma that Crossline
Skipper has.

9. **Tawny-edged Skipper** *(Polites themistocles)*, ♀ above. See page 84.
5/24/90 North Salem, NY.   HW fairly unicolorous.

10. **Swarthy Skipper** *(Nastra lherminier)*, below. See page 79.
8/1/91 Sandy Hook, Monmouth Co., NJ.   Small.   Unmarked dull
yellow-gray-brown.   Slightly paler along veins.   Dark above.
B   X · **N** LC-LA · **P**   C · **W**   C

11. **Tawny-edged Skipper** *(Polites themistocles)*, below. See page 84.
5/31/91 Chappaqua Rd. power line, Mt. Pleasant, NY.
Variant showing pronounced post-median line.

12. **Crossline Skipper** *(Polites origenes)*, below. See page 84.
7/8/91 Route 202 Somers, Westchester Co., NY.
Variant showing much more distinct spot band than usual.

1

2

3

4

5

6

7

8

9

10

11

12

PLATE 32 Peck's Skipper, Long Dash, and Sachem

x 1½

1. **Peck's Skipper** *(Polites peckius)*, below. See page 83.
5/23/91 Oakwood Cemetery, Mt. Kisco, NY.   Two yellow patches on HW.
Middle spot of outer patch extends outward.
> B   A · N   A · P   A · W   A

2. **Peck's Skipper** *(Polites peckius)*, ♂ above. See page 83.
5/23/91 Oakwood Cemetery, Mt. Kisco, NY.
Stigma divides wing into orange and dark areas.   Elongate orange spot just past stigma.   HW central yellow spot extends outward.

3. **Peck's Skipper** *(Polites peckius)*, ♀ above. See page 83.
8/11/91 Bronx Botanical Gardens, Bronx, NY.
HW central yellow spot extends outward.

4. **Long Dash** *(Polites mystic)*, below. See page 85.
6/16/90 Pound Ridge Reservation, NY.   Broad yellow post-median band on HW.
Middle spot does not extend outward.
> B   C · N   LC · P   LU · W   LR

5. **Long Dash** *(Polites mystic)*, ♂ above. See page 85.
5/30/88 Pound Ridge Reservation, NY.
Black stigma and patch divide orange area in two.
Black lines divide orange of HW in two.   See **Indian Skipper.**

6. **Long Dash** *(Polites mystic)*, ♀ above. See page 85.
6/11/89 Oakwood Cemetery, Mt. Kisco, NY.
HW post-median band w/o large spot extending outward.

7. **Sachem** *(Atalopedes campestris)*, ♂ below. See page 87.
8/26/90 Delmont, Cumberland Co., NJ.
Mainly yellow-orange.   Dark patch in middle of lower margin of HW.
Southern immigrant.
> B   X · N   S · P   R-C · W   U-A

8. **Sachem** *(Atalopedes campestris)*, ♂ above. See page 87.
6/4/89 Wilderness Preserve, West Union, Adams Co., OH.
Large rectangular stigma.

9. **Sachem** *(Atalopedes campestris)*, ♀ above. See page 87.
11/10/89 Santa Ana NWR, Pharr, TX.
FW with hyaline white spots at end of darker area.

10. **Sachem** *(Atalopedes campestris)*, ♀ below. See page 87.
8/26/90 Delmont, Cumberland Co., NJ.
HW dull brown with prominent pale chevron as post-median band.

11. **Peck's Skipper** *(Polites peckius)*, below. See page 83.
7/28/91 Chappaqua, NY.   Variant with reduced central brown band.

12. **Peck's Skipper** *(Polites peckius)*, below. See page 83.
8/5/91 Yorktown, NY.   Variant with more prominent central brown band.

1

2

3

4

5

6

7

8

9

10

11

12

PLATE 33   The Witches

x 1½

1. **Southern Broken Dash** *(Wallengrenia otho)*, below. See page 85.
3/20/90 S. Miami, FL.
Reddish-brown ground color.
HW post-median band often in shape of a 3.   Broad gray FW fringe.
B X · **N** X · **P** X · **W** R-U

2. **Southern Broken Dash** *(Wallengrenia otho)*, ♂ above. See page 85.
3/20/90 S. Miami, FL.

3. **Southern Broken Dash** *(Wallengrenia otho)*, ♀ above. See page 85.
11/16/89 Bentsen State Park, Mission, TX.

4. **Northern Broken Dash** *(Wallengrenia egeremet)*, below. See page 86.
7/4/89 Pound Ridge Reservation, NY.
Yellow-brown ground color.   June–Aug.
Wide post-median band often in shape of a 3.
B C · **N** A · **P** C-A · **W** C

5. **Northern Broken Dash** *(Wallengrenia egeremet)*, ♂ above. See page 86.
7/2/91 Pound Ridge Reservation, NY.   Elongate orange spot at end of stigma.

6. **Northern Broken Dash** *(Wallengrenia egeremet)*, ♀ above. See page 86.
7/15/89 Pound Ridge Reservation, NY.   Elongate orange spot on FW.

7. **Little Glassywing** *(Pompeius verna)*, below. See page 86.
6/14/91 Pound Ridge Reservation, NY.
Dark brown ground color.   White patch just below antennal club.
HW usually has post-median line with discrete spots.
B C · **N** C · **P** C · **W** C

8. **Little Glassywing** *(Pompeius verna)*, ♂ above. See page 86.
6/27/90 Pound Ridge Reservation, NY.
White patch just below antennal club.
Large rectangular white spot in middle of FW.
White spot in FW cell.   June–Aug.

9. **Little Glassywing** *(Pompeius verna)*, ♀ above. See page 86.
7/7/91 Pound Ridge Reservation, NY.
White patch just below antennal club.
Large square white spot in middle of FW.   White spot in FW cell.

10. **Dun Skipper** *(Euphyes vestris)*, below. See page 92.
7/2/91 Pound Ridge Reservation, NY.
Faint, if any, HW post-median band.   Head (frons) of males often golden.
B C · **N** C-A · **P** C · **W** C

11. **Dun Skipper** *(Euphyes vestris)*, ♂ above. See page 92.
7/12/89 Pound Ridge Reservation, NY.   Completely dark with black stigma.

12. **Dun Skipper** *(Euphyes vestris)*, ♀ above. See page 92.
7/18/89 Pound Ridge Reservation, NY.   FW with two small white spots.

1

2

3

4

5

6

7

8

9

10

11

12

PLATE 34 **The Witches Below**

x 1½

1. **Little Glassywing** *(Pompeius verna)*. See page 86.
   6/14/91 Pound Ridge Reservation, NY.
   Dark brown.   White patch before antennal club.
   > B   C · N   C · P   C · W   C

2. **Little Glassywing** *(Pompeius verna)*. See page 86.
   7/2/91 Pound Ridge Reservation, NY).
   Variant.

3. **Little Glassywing** *(Pompeius verna)*. See page 86.
   7/12/89 Pound Ridge Reservation, NY.
   Variant.

4. **Little Glassywing** *(Pompeius verna)*. See page 86.
   6/25/90 Pound Ridge Reservation, NY.
   June–Aug.   Variant.

5. **Northern Broken Dash** *(Wallengrenia egeremet)*. See page 86.
   7/8/91 Rt. 202, Somers, Westchester Co., NY.
   Yellow-brown ground color.   No white patch below antennal club.
   > B   C · N   A · P   C-A · W   C

6. **Northern Broken Dash** *(Wallengrenia egeremet)*. See page 86.
   7/18/90 Pound Ridge Reservation, NY.
   Variant.

7. **Northern Broken Dash** *(Wallengrenia egeremet)*. See page 86.
   7/8/91 Rte. 202, Somers, Westchester Co., NY.
   June–Aug.   Variant.

8. **Dun Skipper** *(Euphyes vestris)*. See page 92.
   7/2/91 Pound Ridge Reservation, NY.
   Even coloration.   Faint, if any, HW post-median band.
   No white patch below antennal club.
   > B   C · N   C-A · P   C · W   C

9. **Dun Skipper** *(Euphyes vestris)*. See page 92.
   6/24/91 Pound Ridge Reservation, NY.
   Variant.

10. **Dun Skipper** *(Euphyes vestris)*. See page 92.
    7/2/91 Pound Ridge Reservation, NY.
    May–Sept.   Variant.

1

2

3

4

5

6

7

8

9

10

PLATE 35   Unmarked Orange Skippers

x 1½

1. **European Skipper** *(Thymelicus lineola)*, below. See page 80.
   6/19/90 Assunpink WMA, Monmouth Co., NJ.   Usually has variable amount of white dusting.   Fringes pale.   Short antennae.
      B A · N A · P C · W C

2. **European Skipper** *(Thymelicus lineola)*, above. See page 80.
   6/25/90 Pound Ridge Reservation, NY.
   Pale fringe.   Short reddish antennae with blunt ends.

3. **Least Skipper** *(Ancyloxypha numitor)*, below. See page 80.
   6/12/90 Pound Ridge Reservation, NY   Very small.   Rounded wings.   Weak flight.

4. **Delaware Skipper** *(Atrytone logan)*, below. See page 88.
   7/18/90 Pound Ridge Reservation, NY.
   Very bright unmarked orange (unless worn).   Fringe orange.   Widespread.
      B C · N C-A · P C · W U

5. **Delaware Skipper** *(Atrytone logan)*, ♂ above. See page 88.
   7/7/89 Turkey Mtn., Yorktown, Westchester, NY.
   Strong black border.   Orange fringe.   Abdomen orange.

6. **Delaware Skipper** *(Atrytone logan)*, ♀ above. See page 88.
   7/6/91 Pound Ridge Reservation, NY.   Black patch in FW cell.

7. **Rare Skipper** *(Problema bulenta)*, below. See page 88.
   7/11/91 southern NJ.
   Larger and not so bright as Delaware Skipper.   Rare and local in brackish marsh on the southern NJ coast.   July.   See text.
      B X · N X · P LC · W X

8. **Rare Skipper** *(Problema bulenta)*, ♂ above. See page 88.
   7/11/91 southern NJ.   Abdomen with white lines between segments.
   See text.   Rare and local on the southern NJ coast in July.
   See **Aaron's Skipper.**

9. **Rare Skipper** *(Problema bulenta)*, ♀ above. See page 88.
   7/11/91 southern NJ.   Abdomen with white lines between segments.   See text.

10. **Arogos Skipper** *(Atrytone arogos)*, below. See page 87.
    5/24/87 Bogue Chitta NWR, Tammany Parish, LA.
    Very similar to Delaware Skipper.   Fringe white in midwest populations but yellow-orange in ours.   Probably extirpated in our region.
      B X · N LR/H · P LR/H · W X

11. **Arogos Skipper** *(Atrytone arogos)*, ♂ above. See page 87.
    7/8/82 Hole-in-the-Mountain Preserve, Lincoln Co., MN.
    Usually wider brownish-black FW borders than Delaware Skipper.   Lacks the black veining of Delaware Skipper.   White fringes in the midwest, yellow-orange here.   July.   Probably extirpated in our region.

12. **Arogos Skipper** *(Atrytone arogos)*, ♀ above. See page 87.
    7/17/81 Hole-in-the-Mountain Preserve, Lincoln Co., MN.   See ♂ above.

1

2

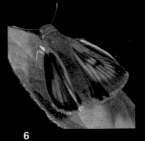

3

4

5

6

7

8

9

10

11

12

PLATE 36 Hobomok, Zabulon, and Clouded Skippers

x 1½

1. **Hobomok Skipper** *(Poanes hobomok)*, below. See page 89.
5/25/90 North Salem, Westchester Co., NY.
HW yellow with large brown patch at wing base.
Wide dark HW border.
    B C-A · **N** C · **P** C · **W** LU

2. **Hobomok Skipper** *(Poanes hobomok)*, ♂ above. See page 89.
5/20/90 Campfire Rd. power line, Chappaqua, NY.
Unlike Zabulon Skipper HW orange spot usually displaced outward.

3. **Hobomok Skipper** *(Poanes hobomok)*, ♀ above. See page 89.
·6/12/90 Pound Ridge Reservation, NY.
White spot in FW cell.

4. **Zabulon Skipper** *(Poanes zabulon)*, ♂ below. See page 90.
6/21/90 Sandy Point State Park, MD.
HW yellow with brown patch at wing base enclosing yellow.
Narrow indistinct HW border.
    B X · **N** C · **P** C · **W** C-A

5. **Zabulon Skipper** *(Poanes zabulon)*, ♂ above. See page 90.
8/9/90 Kisco Swamp, Mt. Kisco, NY.
HW orange spot not usually displaced outward.

6. **Zabulon Skipper** *(Poanes zabulon)*, ♀ above. See page 90.
6/7/91 Pound Ridge Reservation, NY.
No white spot in FW cell.   See Hobomok Skipper ♀ above.

7. **Hobomok Skipper** *(Poanes hobomok)*, ♀ (pocahontas) below.
See page 89.
Same individual as in 3.
No silvery white on upper margin of HW.

8. **Zabulon Skipper** *(Poanes zabulon)*, ♀ below. See page 90.
8/1/91 Garden State Arts Center, Monmouth Co., NJ.
Silvery white upper margin of HW.

9. **Clouded Skipper** *(Lerema accius)*, below. See page 79.
3/26/90 Miami, FL.
FW with gray patch and lacks 2 white submarginal spots
that Hobomok and Zabulon Skipper females have.
Immigrant from the south.
    B S · **N** S · **P** R-U · **W** U

10. **Clouded Skipper** *(Lerema accius)* ♂ above. See page 79.
3/26/90 Miami, FL.
FW subapical spots curve outward.

11. **Clouded Skipper** *(Lerema accius)*, ♀ above. See page 79.
8/25/91 Gainesville, FL.

1

2

3

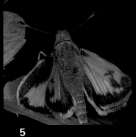

4

5

6

7

8

9

10

11

PLATE 37 Marsh Skippers (genus *Poanes*)

x 1½

1. **Mulberry Wing** *(Poanes massasoit)*, below. See page 89.
7/15/89 Pound Ridge Reservation, NY.
Distinctively shaped HW yellow patch on darker ground.
Local in wetlands.   July–Aug.
      B LU · **N** LC · **P** LC · **W** LU

2. **Mulberry Wing** *(Poanes massasoit)*, ♀ above. See page 89.
7/18/90 Pound Ridge Reservation, NY.
Brown-black with white spots.   Orange-brown at base of FW.

3. **Broad-winged Skipper** *(Poanes viator)*, below. See page 91.
8/9/90 Kisco Swamp, Mt. Kisco, NY.
Large.   HW with indistinct pattern with pale ray.
Usually lands with its body perpendicular to the ground.
      B LC · **N** A · **P** A · **W** LA

4. **Broad-winged Skipper** *(Poanes viator)*, ♀ above. See page 91.
8/9/90 Kisco Swamp, Mt. Kisco, NY.
Widespread near phragmites.

5. **Aaron's Skipper** *(Poanes aaroni)*, below. See page 90.
8/26/90 Delmont, Cumberland Co., NJ.
Dingy yellow-brown with a pale ray.
Lacks FW pale spots of Broad-winged Skipper.
Coastal salt marsh and adjacent areas.
Mainly June and August.
      B X · **N** X · **P** LC · **W** LU-LC

6. **Aaron's Skipper** *(Poanes aaroni)*, ♂ above. See page 90.
8/26/90 Delmont, Cumberland Co., NJ.
See **Delaware, Broad-winged,** and **Zabulon Skippers.**

7. **Aaron's Skipper** *(Poanes aaroni)*, ♀ above. See page 90.
8/26/90 Delmont, Cumberland Co., NJ.

8. **Mulberry Wing** *(Poanes massasoit)*, ♂ above. See page 89.
7/7/91 Pound Ridge Reservation, NY.
Black with orange-brown FW base.

1

2

3

4

5

6

7

8

PLATE 38   Marsh Skippers (genus *Euphyes*)

x 1¾

1. **Dion Skipper** *(Euphyes dion)*, below. See page 91.
   7/10/90 Wingdale, NY.
   Large.   Orange.   Pale ray through center of HW.
   > **B** X · **N** LR · **P** LU-LC · **W** LR

2. **Dion Skipper** *(Euphyes dion)*, ♂ above. See page 91.
   7/22/90 Lakehurst Bog, Lakehurst, NJ.
   Very local in wetlands.   See text.

3. **Black Dash** *(Euphyes conspicua)*, below. See page 92.
   7/7/89 Turkey Mtn., Yorktown, Westchester Co., NY.
   Reddish-yellow-brown.
   HW postmedian band with chunky middle.
   Open wetlands.   July–Aug.
   > **B** LU · **N** LC · **P** LU · **W** LR

4. **Black Dash** *(Euphyes conspicua)*, ♂ above. See page 92.
   7/2/91 Pound Ridge Reservation, NY.
   Prominent black stigma.

5. **Two-spotted Skipper** *(Euphyes bimacula)*, below. See page 92.
   6/29/89 Lakehurst Bog, Lakehurst, NJ.
   Orange with pale veining.
   Striking white line along HW lower margin.
   Bogs and acid marshes.   Mainly June.
   > **B** LR · **N** LR · **P** LU · **W** LR

6. **Two-spotted Skipper** *(Euphyes bimacula)*, ♂ above. See page 92.
   6/29/89 Lakehurst Bog, Lakehurst, NJ.
   Dark brown with dull orange patch surrounding stigma.

7. **Dion Skipper** *(Euphyes dion)*, ♀ above. See page 91.
   7/6/89 Chappaqua Rd. power line, Mt. Pleasant, NY.
   Large.

8. **Black Dash** *(Euphyes conspicua)*, ♀ above. See page 92.
   7/2/91 Pound Ridge Reservation, NY.

1

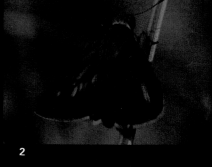

2

3

4

5

6

7

8

PLATE 39   Dusted Skipper, Roadside Skippers, and Panoquins

x 1¼

1. **Dusted Skipper** *(Atrytonopsis hianna)*, ♀ above. See page 93.
6/7/91 Pound Ridge Reservation, NY.
White eye-line.   *Andropogon* grasslands in May–June.
B C · **N** U · **P** LU-LC · **W** LU

2. **Dusted Skipper** *(Atrytonopsis hianna)*, below. See page 93.
6/1/89 Campfire Rd. power line, Chappaqua, NY.
"Masked" appearance.   Often has white dot at base of HW.

3. **Dusted Skipper** *(Atrytonopsis hianna)*, ♂ above. See page 93.
6/16/89 Redding, Fairfield Co., CT.
White eye-line.

4. **Common Roadside Skipper** *(Amblyscirtes vialis)*, below. See page 94.
5/21/91 Nottingham County Park, Chester Co., PA.
Very small and dark.   No white over eye.   Fringes checkered.
B LR · **N** LR · **P** LU · **W** U

5. **Common Roadside Skipper** *(Amblyscirtes vialis)*, above. See page 94.
6/4/89 Wilderness Preserve, West Union, Adams Co., OH.
Very small.   FWs held perpendicularly to plane of HWs.

6. **Pepper and Salt Skipper** *(Amblyscirtes hegon)*, above.
See page 93.
6/4/89 Adam's Lake State Park, W. Union, Adams Co., OH.
Rare in June along our northwest borders.

7. **Pepper and Salt Skipper** *(Amblyscirtes hegon)*, below.
See page 93.
6/4/89 Adam's Lake State Park, W. Union, Adams Co., OH.
Small.   Putty gray with pale post-median line.
Pale spot along HW upper margin.
B LR · **N** X · **P** LR · **W** X

8. **Ocola Skipper** *(Panoquina ocola)*, below. See page 95.
8/24/91 Ocala National Forest, FL.
Long and narrow wings.   Longitudinally striped abdomen.
Distal one-quarter of wings darker.   Southern immigrant.
B X · **N** S · **P** R · **W** R

9. **Salt Marsh Skipper** *(Panoquina panoquin)*, below. See page 95.
8/26/90 Delmont, Cumberland Co., NJ.
Yellow-brown with pale veins.   Elongate pale spot on HW.
Long and narrow wings.   Longitudinally striped abdomen.
Salt marshes and adjacent fields north to southern LI.
B X · **N** LR · **P** LU-LA · **W** LC

1

2

3

4

5

6

7

8

9

PLATE 40   Strays and Historically Occurring Species

x 1¼

1. **Pink-edged Sulphur** *(Colias interior).* See page 30.
   7/24/91 Moose River Plains, Inlet, Hamilton Co., NY.
   Recorded from Rockport, MA.   HW with a single central spot.

2. **White Peacock** *(Anartia jatrophae).* See page 61.
   3/21/90 Homestead, FL.
   Recorded from Port Norris, NJ.   Off-white with orange-brown borders.

3. **Queen** *(Danaus gilippus).* See page 69.   [×¾]
   11/10/89 Santa Ana NWR, Pharr, TX.
   Darker than the Monarch with white spots in the FW post-median area.

4. **Brazilian Skipper** *(Calpodes ethlius).* See page 95.
   Harlingen, TX.
   Large.   HW with three large white spots in an angled line.

5. **Barred Yellow** *(Eurema daira).* See page 31.
   3/21/90 S. Miami, FL.
   Recorded from Washington, D.C.   Small.   Variable below.
   Above ♂ with a black bar along the FW lower margin.
   Wings diaphanous.

6. **Silvery Blue** *(Glaucopsyche lygdamus).* See page 46.
   5/3/88 Los Altos Hills, Santa Clara Co., CA.
   Historically occurred in Philadelphia area.
   Post-median bands of large black spots.

7. **Karner Blue** *(Lycaeides melissa).* See page 47.
   7/19/89 Albany Pine Bush, Albany, NY.
   Historically recorded from New York area.   Submarginal orange band.

8. **Little Metalmark** *(Calephelis virginiensis).* See page 47.
   3/22/90 Everglades National Park, FL.
   Recorded from Fort Washington, Prince George Co., MD.
   Rich red-brown.   Vertical red-brown and black stripes on thorax.

9. **Eufala Skipper** *(Lerodea eufala).* See page 94.
   8/14/89 Patagonia, AZ.
   Recorded from Washington, D.C., area.
   Also recorded southern NJ in October 1991.   See text.

10. **Twin-spot Skipper** *(Oligora maculata).* See page 95.
    3/25/90 Dade Co., FL.
    Recorded from Montgomery Co., MD.   Three bold white spots on HW.